THE
COLLEGE
PRESS
NIV
COMMENTARY

EZRA-NEHEMIAH

THE
COLLEGE
PRESS
NIV
COMMENTARY

EZRA-NEHEMIAH

KEITH N. SCHOVILLE, PH.D.

Old Testament Series Co-Editors:

Terry Briley, Ph.D.
Lipscomb University

Paul Kissling, Ph.D.
Great Lakes Christian College

 COLLEGE PRESS
PUBLISHING COMPANY
Joplin, Missouri

Library of Congress Cataloging-in-Publication Data

Schoville, Keith N.
    Ezra-Nehemiah / Keith N. Schoville.
        p.   cm. — (The College Press NIV commentary. Old
    Testament series)
    Includes bibliographical references.
    ISBN 0-89900-884-4
    1. Bible. O.T. Ezra—Commentaries. 2. Bible. O.T.
Nehemiah—Commentaries.   I. Title. II. Series.
BS1355.53.S36 2001
222'.7077—dc21

                                                    2001047043

A WORD
FROM THE PUBLISHER

Years ago a movement was begun with the dream of uniting all Christians on the basis of a common purpose (world evangelism) under a common authority (the Word of God). The College Press NIV Commentary Series is a serious effort to join the scholarship of two branches of this unity movement so as to speak with one voice concerning the Word of God. Our desire is to provide a resource for your study of the Old Testament that will benefit you whether you are preparing a Bible School lesson, a sermon, a college course, or your own personal devotions. Today as we survey the wreckage of a broken world, we must turn again to the Lord and his Word, unite under his banner and communicate the life-giving message to those who are in desperate need. This is our purpose.

ABBREVIATIONS

ABD ..... *Anchor Bible Dictionary*
ANET .... *Ancient Near Eastern Texts Relating to the Old Testament*
Ant ...... *Antiquities (Flavius Josephus)*
BA ...... *Biblical Archaeologist*
BAR ..... *Biblical Archaeology Review*
BASOR ... *Bulletin of the American Schools of Oriental Research*
IDB ...... *Interpreter's Dictionary of the Bible*
ISBE ..... *International Standard Bible Encyclopedia*
JBL ...... *Journal of Biblical Literature*
JSOT ..... *Journal for the Study of the Old Testament*
KJV ...... *King James Version*
LXX ..... *Septuagint*
Macc ..... *Maccabees (Apocryphal Book)*
NBD ..... *New Bible Dictionary*
NEAEH .. *The New Encyclopedia of Archaeological Excavations in the Holy Land*
NEB ..... *New English Bible*
NRSV .... *New Revised Standard Version*
OEANE ... *The Oxford Encyclopedia of Archaeology in the Near East*
RSV ..... *Revised Standard Version*
ZAW ..... *Zeitschrift für die alttestamentliche Wissenschaft*

Simplified Guide to Hebrew Writing

Heb. letter	Translit.	Pronunciation guide
א	'	Has no sound of its own; like smooth breathing mark in Greek
ב	b	Pronounced like English B *or* V
ג	g	Pronounced like English G
ד	d	Pronounced like English D
ה	h	Pronounced like English H
ו	w	As a consonant, pronounced like English V or German W
וּ	û	Represents a vowel sound, pronounced like English long OO
וֹ	ô	Represents a vowel sound, pronounced like English long O
ז	z	Pronounced like English Z
ח	ḥ	Pronounced like German and Scottish CH and Greek χ (chi)
ט	ṭ	Pronounced like English T
י	y	Pronounced like English Y
כ/ך	k	Pronounced like English K
ל	l	Pronounced like English L
מ/ם	m	Pronounced like English M
נ/ן	n	Pronounced like English N
ס	s	Pronounced like English S
ע	'	Stop in breath deep in throat before pronouncing the vowel
פ/ף	p/ph	Pronounced like English P *or* F
צ/ץ	ṣ	Pronounced like English TS/TZ
ק	q	Pronounced very much like כ (k)
ר	r	Pronounced like English R
שׂ	ś	Pronounced like English S, much the same as ס
שׁ	š	Pronounced like English SH
ת	t/th	Pronounced like English T *or* TH

Note that different forms of some letters appear at the end of the word (written right to left), as in כָּפַף (*kāphaph*, "bend") and מֶלֶךְ (*melek*, "king").

Vowels in Hebrew (except where the ו is used to represent a vowel sound), are represented by "vowel points" added to the consonant. For example: הַ (*ha*, "the"). The letter *yod* (י, *y*) also becomes a *part of* certain vowel sounds, as in the conjunction כִּי (*kî*, "that"). Originally, Hebrew was written as "unpointed" text, with just the consonants. For convenience, the different vowel points are shown below on the letter Aleph (א).

אָ	ā	Pronounced not like long A in English, but like the broad A or AH sound
אַ	a	The Hebrew short A sound, but more closely resembles the broad A (pronounced for a shorter period of time) than the English short A
אֶ	e	Pronounced like English short E
אֵ	ē	Pronounced like English long A, or Greek η (eta)

אִ	i	Pronounced like English short I
אִ	î	The same vowel point is sometimes pronounced like אֵ (see below)
אָ	o	This vowel point sometimes represents the short O sound
אֹ	ō	Pronounced like English long O
אֻ	u	The vowel point ֻ sometimes represents a shorter U sound and
אֻ	ū	is sometimes pronounced like the וּ (û, see above)
אֵי	ê	Pronounced much the same as אֵ
אֵי	ê	Pronounced much the same as אֵ
אִי	î	Pronounced like long I in many languages, or English long E
אְ	ə	An unstressed vowel sound, like the first E in the word "severe"
אֳ, אֲ, אֱ	ŏ, ă, ĕ	Shortened, unstressed forms of the vowels אָ, אַ, and אֶ, pronounced very similarly to אְ

PREFACE

A biblical writer once noted that "Of making many books there is no end, and much study wearies the body" (Eccl 12:12). He expressed that opinion long before the invention of the printing press and our age of computerized word processing, in those ancient days when composition was laboriously done by the hand of scribes. This commentary is another book. It is a book about another ancient product of the pen, the biblical book of Ezra–Nehemiah. The process of producing it has been a labor of love as I have engaged the words, thoughts, and times of two exemplary servants of the Lord our God. Ezra was himself a writer, and Nehemiah was an able, literate person who had attained a position of exceptional responsibility in the highest levels of the Persian government. Both of them left their marks on Jerusalem and its renewed community in the aftermath of the exile. Their personal accounts were augmented by other available sources in the hands of the unidentified author of the work that bears their names. My desire is that you will come to understand and appreciate that final product.

The process of writing this commentary has been long and arduous. But I have had the benefit of others who have studied Ezra–Nehemiah before. Every page bears the sometimes-veiled influence of commentators whom I have read, drawn on, and admired for their contributions. The study of Scripture is a never-ending process in which each generation of scholars attempts to explain and enlighten his or her present generation. We owe much to those who have gone before.

Writing a work is one thing; publishing it is quite another. I want to express my deep appreciation for the contribution the College Press editors and staff have made to the final result of my efforts. We may count ourselves blessed to be able to benefit from such dedicated and capable practitioners of the art of publishing. May our joint efforts find favor in the sight of our Lord and value to our readers.

Keith N. Schoville
Professor Emeritus
Hebrew and Semitic Studies
University of Wisconsin–Madison

INTRODUCTION

THE PLACE OF EZRA–NEHEMIAH IN THE BIBLE

When we open the Bible to the books of Ezra and Nehemiah, we find them tucked in between Chronicles and Esther. They are among the books we call "historical." That seems appropriate because Chronicles, Ezra, Nehemiah, and Esther provide us with information and insights into the circumstances of God's people in the aftermath of the exile in Babylon. The history of Israel and Judah before the exile is contained primarily in the other historical books, from Joshua through the end of 2 Kings. Yet the present location of Ezra and Nehemiah was not always where we find them today. They are in their present location because that is where they were placed in the first translation of the Hebrew Scriptures into another language — Greek. That translation, the Septuagint (LXX), was begun by approximately 250 B.C. The order of the biblical books in the Septuagint was carried over into Latin translations, setting the pattern for subsequent European translations, including our English Bibles. But in Jewish Bibles Ezra and Nehemiah are joined as a single book and located in the last section of the Hebrew Bible.

The Jewish canon has three major sections. The first and most esteemed is the Torah: Genesis, Exodus, Leviticus, Numbers, and Deuteronomy. The Torah is also known as the Law of Moses; another name for it is the Pentateuch, "the (book of) five books."[1]

The second section of the Hebrew canon is the Prophets, further divided between the Former and the Latter prophets. The Former Prophets include Joshua, Judges, Samuel (1 & 2), and Kings (1 & 2). These are considered four books; the division of Samuel and Kings

---

[1]Pentateuch is derived from Gk. *pente,* "five" + *teuchos,* "a book."

(as well as Chronicles) into two books each occurred with the translation of the LXX. This was necessary because Hebrew is written without vowels, while vowel-letters are essential to Greek. Books written in Hebrew that could be contained within a single scroll required more space when translated into Greek, thus resulting in the division indicated. The Latter Prophets consist of four books: Isaiah, Jeremiah, Ezekiel, and the Twelve. The Twelve are Hosea, Joel, Amos, Obadiah, Jonah, Micah, Nahum, Habakkuk, Zephaniah, Haggai, Zechariah, and Malachi. This arrangement of the Twelve is based generally on historical progression, with Haggai, Zechariah, and Malachi coming from the Persian period, the same period in which Ezra and Nehemiah were active.

The Writings comprise the third part of the Hebrew canon: Psalms, Proverbs, Job, the Song of Songs, Ruth, Ecclesiastes, Lamentations, Esther, Daniel, Ezra–Nehemiah, and Chronicles (1 & 2). This section is also known as the Hagiographa, a name derived from Greek meaning "Holy Writings."

The division of the Hebrew Bible into three sections is quite ancient. It is referred to in the first section of the book of Ecclesiasticus, which is also known as the Wisdom of Jesus (Joshua) Son of Sirach. Ecclesiasticus was written by a wise Jewish teacher sometime before 180 B.C.[2] He refers to "the law and the prophets and the others that followed them." Similarly, in Luke 24:44 Jesus referred to "everything . . . written about me in the Law of Moses, the Prophets, and the Psalms." The psalms formed the opening and the longest section of the third division of the Hebrew canon. Ezra–Nehemiah and Chronicles close this section because they were written at least two centuries later than the history of the Former Prophets. That

---

[2]Ecclesiasticus was held in high respect by Jews and was translated into Greek and became a part of the LXX. Ecclesiasticus and other books written in the intertestamental period were a part of the LXX. The honored but noncanonical books became known as the Apocrypha and were interspersed among the canonical books in Catholic Bibles. During the Protestant Reformation, the Apocrypha was rejected as having any doctrinal value by the reformers. In response, the Council of Trent (1545-1563) declared the Apocrypha Deuterocanonical, "the Second Canon." It may be found in some Protestant Bibles, bound in a separate section between the Old and the New Testaments.

history ends with the Davidic king, Jehoiachin, living out his life in the palace of the Babylonian ruler (2 Kgs 25:27-30).

THE HISTORICAL SETTING OF EZRA–NEHEMIAH

The downward spiral to destruction of the kingdoms of Israel and Judah are clearly described in the books of Samuel and Kings.[3] The northern kingdom, Israel, ended with the Assyrian conquest and destruction of its capital, Samaria, in 722 B.C. The southern kingdom, Judah, survived approximately another century and a half, until rebellion against its Babylonian overlords brought it to a devastating end in 586 B.C. We must note in passing that a few years prior to the Babylonian conquest of Judah, during the reign of Josiah, the "Book of the Law"[4] was discovered in the temple while the sanctuary was undergoing renovation (2 Kgs 22).

The predicted destruction came in the time of the prophets Jeremiah and Ezekiel. As a result, many were killed. Of those who survived, some were deported and some were allowed to remain. The combined population of Jerusalem and the Judean hill country in the time of King Josiah is estimated to have been about 32,250.[5] The total number taken to Babylonia is unknown, but it must have consisted of several thousand; 10,000 were taken into captivity in 597 (2 Kgs 24:14), apparently including Ezekiel. Gedaliah was put in

---

[3]The Babylonians acquired the Assyrian Empire through conquest. Nabopolassar destroyed its capital Nineveh in 612 B.C. with the help of the Medes. The fall of the great city was prophesied by Nahum. Nabopolassar's son and successor, Nebuchadnezzar II, conquered Jerusalem in 597 B.C. and took into captivity to Babylon King Jehoiachin and the ruling elite of Jerusalem (2 Kgs 24:8-17). Ten years later (587), when Zedekiah rebelled against Babylonian rule, Nebuchadnezzar returned to Jerusalem. He besieged and destroyed it in 586 B.C., carrying away into captivity the bulk of the populace. The temple was destroyed and everything of value, including the gold and silver utensils (Dan 5:2), was transported to Babylon.

[4]This scroll was either a copy of Deuteronomy or contained it. See *Zondervan Handbook to the Bible* (Grand Rapids: Zondervan, 1999), p. 303.

[5]Carol L. Meyers and Eric M. Meyers, "Demography and Diatribes: Yehud's Population and the Prophecy of Second Zechariah," *Scripture and Other Artifacts,* ed. by M.D. Coogan, J.C. Exum, and L.E. Stager (Louisville: Westminster John Knox Press, 1994), p. 282.

authority over those who remained in Judah. In 581 he was assassinated. Many not taken to Babylon fled to Egypt, fearing retribution from the Babylonians. This resulted in a further depopulation of the region. Those who left for Egypt forced the prophet Jeremiah to go with them (Jer 41:17–43:7).

The period of the First Temple (Solomonic) thus ended tragically, and the period of the Second Temple (postexilic) would not begin until the temple was reconstructed (520–516 B.C.). This left a gap of seventy years predicted by Jeremiah (25:11-12; 29) and noted by the writer of Chronicles (2 Chr 36:21). Little is known about the life of the deportees during those two generations except what can be gleaned from the Book of Ezekiel. His ministry took place between 593 and 571 B.C. During the period between Nebuchadnezzar's conquest of Jerusalem and the city's later destruction, communication seems to have continued between the exiled community and the remnant still in Jerusalem, at least through the time of Zedekiah. So some of Ezekiel's visions have to do with Jerusalem. His other oracles speak to the community in exile. Along with condemnation for past sins, they implant a word of hope and restoration.

Both the prophetic work of Jeremiah and of Ezekiel were a part of the broader search for religious meaning which the destruction of the temple and the loss of the homeland produced. None of the few remaining in Judah possessed the intellectual energy nor the opportunity for deep contemplation of the national tragedy. They were largely peasants working their plots of land, struggling to survive. Jeremiah characterized them as "poor figs" (Jer 29:17). Any hope for restoration was in the exiled community in Babylonia. Jeremiah, in a letter sent to those in exile in Babylon, gave them the word of the Lord to "build houses and settle down; plant gardens and eat what they produce. Marry and have sons and daughters; find wives for your sons and give your daughters in marriage, so that they too may have sons and daughters. Increase in number there; do not decrease" (29:4-7). The promise of a return to Jerusalem after seventy years follows (29:10-14). Their experience in exile was to lead to a transformation of religious perceptions and practices.

First, the provincial view of Yahweh as God of the Promised Land[6]

---

[6]The idea that a deity was associated with a territory was widespread in the ancient Near East. King Mesha of Moab states that "Omri, king of Israel,

was modified. Within two generations that view was transformed into a profound conviction that he was Lord of the entire cosmos.[7] Even Nebuchadnezzar the powerful king of Babylon was his servant (Jer 25:9; 27:9; 43:10; Ezek 29:19-20; Ezra 5:12). By contrast, the Judeans who called the God of Israel "Lord," had rebelled against true service to the Almighty. Second, the Judeans had thought that Jerusalem was indestructible because it was the Lord's city and in it was the temple of the Lord.[8] That idea was obliterated with the destruction of both city and temple. Third, those in exile came to understand that they could worship Yahweh even in the sophisticated center of Babylonian idolatry. In Babylon the Judeans, who had themselves worshiped idols in their homeland, gave them up once and for all.[9] Separation from the surrounding Babylonian culture in terms of religious and social practices was the primary means of retaining an identity as the people of Yahweh.[10] This included the prohibition on intermarriage with those outside the exilic community, which we can infer from the similar prohibitions imposed by

---

oppressed Moab for many days because Kemosh (chief Moabite deity) was angry with his country" (Moabite Inscription, lines 4-5). First Kgs 20:23 indicates that the Arameans who were defeated by Israel thought that the defeat was because "their gods are gods of the hills." Even David, in his last encounter with Saul (1 Sam 26:19-20) reflects this general idea: "They have now driven me from my share in the Lord's inheritance and have said, 'Go serve other gods.'" The thought was that the Lord could be properly worshiped only in the land of Israel.

[7]The visions of Ezekiel at Tel Aviv near the Kebar River and the prophetic word that followed were clear testimony of Yahweh's presence in the land of exile (Ezek 3:12-15).

[8]Note the refrain of the Jerusalemites, "This is the temple of the LORD, the temple of the LORD, the temple of the LORD!" (Jer 7:4).

[9]Ephraim Stern, internationally recognized Israeli archaeologist and expert on the Persian period, has stated ". . . in the areas of the country occupied by Jews [after the return from exile], not a single cultic figurine has been found!" In "Religion in Palestine in the Assyrian and Persian Periods," in *The Crisis of Israelite Religion: Transformation of Religious Tradition in Exilic and Post-Exilic Times*, ed. by B. Becking & M.C.A. Korpel, Outestamentische Studiën, 42, (Leiden and Boston: Brill, 1999), pp. 245-255. See also E. Stern, "What Happened to the Cult Figurines? Israelite Religion Purified after the Exile," *BAR* 15:4 (1982): 22-29, 53-54.

[10]J. Andrew Dearman, *Religion & Culture in Ancient Israel* (Peabody, MA: Hendrickson, 1992), p. 105.

Ezra on the Jerusalem community in his reforms (Ezra 9–10). Fourth, prayer and the study of the word of the Lord became a substitute for animal sacrifice and a means of worship. This would prove to be a temporary development in terms of those who did return to Jerusalem. There the focus of worship returned to the temple and the altar of the Lord, while in Babylon the temporary development became permanent.

The descendants of those who were taken into exile did not all choose to return to the Promised Land. They and others who voluntarily settled throughout the world came to be known as the Diaspora. Male Jews of the Diaspora were expected to make pilgrimages to the temple in Jerusalem after it was rebuilt, thus retaining a connection with worship in the temple. Pilgrimages were especially made in connection with the religious festivals, such as the Feast of Pentecost. The multitudes gathered in Jerusalem, as reported in Acts 2:5, gives evidence that a religious practice begun some six hundred years earlier had continued generation after generation.

In Babylon the foundations of group meetings were laid that would ultimately result in the development of the synagogue, not as a substitute for a temple but as a place of prayer and study. The beginning of such meetings was evidently the assembling of those in exile to hear the word of the Lord from Ezekiel (Ezek 33:30-33).

From Jerusalem a faithful remnant had brought with them to Babylon the most precious items they could carry. These included scrolls like the one found in the temple in Josiah's time. Other historical records, prophetic sayings, songs used in worship, legal and wisdom materials were carried to Babylon and assembled into many of the books of the Hebrew Bible in the form we now have them in our Old Testament.

In this environment, the role of the sage and the scribe grew in importance. Ezra, who assembled and taught the people in Jerusalem, was known as a סֹפֵר מָהִיר (sōphēr māhîr), a ready, or able, scribe in the Law of Moses (Ezra 7:6). (This is translated in the NIV as "a teacher well versed in the Law of Moses.") Of course he was also a priest, one of the elite of biblical society who were literate, in contrast to the bulk of society who were illiterate. We assume he continued in Jerusalem what was common practice in Babylon.

In Babylon Israelite religion was transformed into an early form of Judaism. A modern Jewish rabbi has observed:

> . . . that which scholars call 'late Judaism,' or 'Rabbinic Judaism,' has its origins and evolution in the period of Israel's monarchy and even earlier. Proto-Judaism/Judaism never ceased evolving and changing. The quintessential theological doctrines, ethical principles, and rituals were present from the dim beginnings of Israel's odyssey. . . .
>
> In the fifth to fourth centuries B.C.E.,[11] Ezra and Nehemiah brought about a religious revival. Prior to this renewal, the biblical faith cannot be said to have had a name which can be verified in primary sources. Only after postexilic Judah became the successor state to the old northern kingdom of Israel and the southern kingdom of Judah, and after it laid sole claim to preserving the older Yahwistic religion and Mosaic tradition, is it proper to refer to this religion as 'Judaism.'"[12]

Other significant changes developed within the exilic community in Babylon. One change was the adoption of the Babylonian calendar. The calendrical system in use prior to the exile is unclear. Four month-names are known: Abib, Ziv, Ethanim, and Bul.[13] The first two have not been identified in Canaanite or Phoenician sources, but the latter two are Canaanite names. That the Israelites would use Canaanite names for the months is understandable since the Hebrew language is a form of Canaanite (Isa 19:18). However, the months in pre-exilic biblical texts are normally referred to by ordinal numbers, for example, "the first month" (Deut 16:1). This practice continued in use long after the Babylonian month names were adopted. The Hebrew form of the Babylonian months are: Nisan, Iyyar, Sivan, Tammuz, Av, Elul, Tishri, Marcheshvan, Kislev, Tevet, Shevat, and Adar. Nehemiah 2:1 refers to Nisan; 6:15 mentions Elul, while Kislev occurs in 1:1. Adar is found in Ezra 6:15.

In Babylon the people from Judah switched from speaking

---

[11]The abbreviation B.C.E., standing for "Before the Common Era," is used by many as a substitution for B.C., "Before Christ."

[12]Phillip Sigal, *Judaism: The Evolution of a Faith* (Grand Rapids: Eerdmans, 1988), p. 31.

[13]*ABD*, I:814.

Hebrew to Aramaic. The use of Hebrew as a literary and religious language was not lost, but Aramaic became the predominant tongue because it had already gained widespread use as an international language.[14] Aramaic then played a role similar to that of English now. Thus we find formal communications back and forth between officials in the provinces and the capital written in Aramaic, as recorded in Ezra 4:11-22, 5:7-17, 6:3-12, and 7:11-26. Further, when the Law was read in Jerusalem before the assembled people, it was read in Hebrew. The Levites then translated the Hebrew into Aramaic and taught the meaning of the Hebrew texts that were read (Neh 8:1-8).

Life in captivity not only brought a change of language but also a concurrent change in the script used to write Hebrew. The pre-exilic Hebrew alphabet was linear in form, similar to the related script of the Phoenicians. These Old Hebrew letters were never forgotten, but the more rounded Aramaic script, which is called Hebrew today, largely displaced their usage. The Aramaic script is mentioned twice in Ezra 4:7.

THE PERSIAN CONQUEST OF THE BABYLONIAN EMPIRE

THE BABYLONIANS

Nebuchadnezzar II was the predominant figure in the dynasty that ruled Babylon from 626–539 B.C. His father, Nabopolassar, wrested control of southern Mesopotamia from the Assyrians. In this venture he had the help of allies to the east — the Medes and their king, Cyaxeres,[15] We will note the rise of Cyaxeres and the Medes below but observe here that frequently in history political allies may in time become foes. In 612 B.C. Babylonians, Scythians, and Medes joined forces to destroy the capital city, Nineveh, in the heart of the Assyrian Empire. The final end of Assyrian domination came in 605 with their defeat, along with their Egyptian allies led by Pharaoh

---

[14]Note 2 Kgs 18:26, where in 701 B.C. the Judean leaders asked the chief officer of the Assyrians to speak to them in Aramaic, which the general populace did not understand, rather than in Hebrew, the language of the man in the street.

[15]*ABD*, IV:978.

Necho, at the Battle of Carchemish on the Euphrates River. In that same year Nabopolassar died and his son, Nebuchadnezzar, commander of his armies, took the throne. Providentially, in that year Nebuchadnezzar also took control of Jerusalem and Judah, along with much of the ancient Near East (Jer 25:8-14; 46:1-12). Thereafter Judean kings served at the pleasure of the Babylonian monarch. Therefore, when Jehoiakim, followed by his son, Jehoiachin, rebelled, the Babylonian response followed. Jerusalem was conquered in the spring of 597. Nebuchadnezzar placed Zedekiah in control of Judah. A decade later he rebelled. The Babylonian army responded by destroying Jerusalem and the temple of the Lord (2 Kgs 24:1-25:21). Many Judeans were swept away into captivity.

Those in exile lived in Babylon and the surrounding region. Nebuchadnezzar was in the process of rebuilding and beautifying Babylon, and no doubt the skilled artisans of Judah were involved in the project. The mighty monarch filled the city with magnificent temples and palaces, broad streets and beautifully decorated gates, as well as wonders of the ancient world — the hanging gardens and a bridge across the Euphrates River. The city was dedicated to its patron deity, Marduk. Daniel 4:30 reflects the grandeur that was Babylon. A dim echo of that past glory was recovered in the German excavations of the site from A.D. 1899-1917.[16]

Nebuchadnezzar died in 562 B.C. and was succeeded by his son, Amel-Marduk, who is referred to in Jeremiah 52:31 as Evil-Merodach, derived from Babylonian *amel marduk*, "Man of Marduk." He released the captive King Jehoiachin from prison and maintained him in the palace complex (2 Kgs 25:27; Jer 52:31).[17] Evil-Merodach ruled but two years before his brother-in-law, Neriglissar, assassinated him. This is the same Nergal-sharezer noted in Jeremiah 39:3, when he was an officer in Nebuchadnezzar's army. His rule was also short (560-556 B.C.). His son, Labashi-marduk, succeeded him and ruled less than a year before a palace rebellion replaced him with a military leader named Nabonidus.

---

[16]Many of the artifacts uncovered by the director of excavations, Robert Koldewey, are in a museum in Berlin. The Iraqi government has reconstructed some of the ruins to enhance the understanding of tourist visitors.

[17]Administrative documents recovered from Babylon refer to rations provided to Jehoiachin, king of Judah (*ANET*, p. 308).

Nabonidus ruled from 555–539 B.C., but his interests were more centered on religious matters than affairs of state, perhaps because his remarkable mother, Adad-guppi (who lived for 104 years!), was high priestess of the temple of Sin, the moon-goddess, in Harran in northern Syria.[18] He rebuilt that temple and focused his attention on the other centers of moon worship at Ur in Babylon and at the desert oasis of Tema in Arabia. For whatever reasons, he chose to spend the last several years of his reign living in Tema, five hundred miles across the Arabian desert from Babylon, leaving the government in control of his son, Belshazzar.[19] Some of the Jewish troops accompanying Nabonidus were likely the nucleus of colonies he established at oases in western Arabia.[20] Centuries later when Islam began, five of the oases were already occupied by Jews.

Nabonidus had neglected the religious duties of a Babylonian ruler. This angered the priests of Marduk because he failed to appear for the annual New Year's rituals in which the king had unique responsibilities. This was taken as a betrayal of the city's protective god, Marduk. Belshazzar was a poor choice for regent. Something of his character is reflected in the infamous feast in which he had the vessels of the temple of Yahweh brought out of storage so that his nobles, wives, and concubines could drink from them (Daniel 5). Supported by the Marduk priesthood, the people of Babylon turned against Belshazzar and openly welcomed the Persian conqueror, Cyrus. He took the city in a bloodless conquest on the very night Belshazzar was engaged in his infamous party.

THE PERSIANS

The Medes and the Persians were descendants of tribal groups who migrated south out of the Russian steppes several centuries before they became a power in the ancient world. They came to occupy and dominate what we call Iran today. The first historical

---

[18]W.W. Hallo & W.K. Simpson, *The Ancient Near East: A History* (New York: Harcourt Brace Jovanovich, 1971), pp. 147-149.

[19]Ibid., p. 149.

[20]H.W.F. Saggs, "Babylon," in *Archaeology and Old Testament Study,* ed. by D.W. Thomas (Oxford: Clarendon Press, 1967), p. 47.

mention of the Medes is in Assyrian texts of the ninth century B.C. They were initially the most powerful tribal group in the region.

The Assyrians campaigned against "the mighty Medes," and Sargon II, whom we know as the conqueror of Samaria and exiler of a Median leader, Deioces, to Syria in 715 B.C. Deioces had united the Medes and had established his capital at Ecbatana (modern Hamadan). Subsequent Assyrian rulers negotiated treaties with Median rulers in which the latter ruled as vassals under their Assyrian overlords.

The major figure in the development of Median power was Cyaxares, whom we noted above as an ally of Nabopolassar in the rebellion against the Assyrians. The Greek historian Herodotus recorded that Cyaxares (625–585 B.C.) reorganized the Median army and defeated the Scythians who had dominated Media for twenty-eight years. (The Scythians were fierce horse-nomads from the Russian steppes to the north.) Under his leadership the Medes conquered the ancient city of Asshur, the titular Assyrian center. Then he and Nabopolassar established an alliance, sealed by the marriage of a Median princess to Nebuchadnezzar. (It was for this wife that Nebuchadnezzar built the Hanging Gardens of Babylon.)[21] As noted earlier, the allies then attacked and destroyed Nineveh. Toward the end of his reign, Cyaxares campaigned against the Lydian kingdom in Asia Minor. A peace between the two opponents was ultimately arranged with the Halys River as the border; the political arrangement was sealed with a marriage between a Lydian princess and Astyages, the son of Cyaxares.

Astyages succeeded his father and ruled from 585–550 B.C. His daughter married a Persian and gave birth to Cyrus the Great. The Persian kingdom, located to the south of Media, had developed in the shadow of the Medes and was subservient to them. Unfortunately for Astyages, his grandson Cyrus led a successful revolt of the Persians against the Medes and in 550 B.C. established control over all the territory of the Medes and Persians. This event ushered in the Persian period, which is also known as the Achaemenid era, named after Achaemenes, an illustrious ancestor of the family line. Persia was destined to expand and control much of the eastern Mediter-

---

[21]Edwin M. Yamauchi, *Persia and the Bible* (Grand Rapids: Baker, 1990), pp. 53-54.

ranean world, including Egypt, as well as Mesopotamia and Asia all
the way to India. The Persian Empire lasted over two centuries compared to the relatively short-lived (Neo)Babylonian domination of
less than a century. Its demise came in 330 B.C. with the conquest
of Alexander the Great.

Cyrus set out to expand the kingdom of the Medes and Persians
by marching westward, across Upper Mesopotamia, Armenia, Cap-
padocia, and Cilicia before confronting Croesus, king of Lydia.
Croesus is remembered for his treasures of gold, and tradition has
it that a predecessor, the Lydian king Gyges, was the first to invent
coinage.[22] This conquest has been dated to 547–546 B.C. Having
established his dominance in the west, Cyrus apparently spent the
years 546–540 consolidating his control over the eastern region
of his empire. Then he turned his attention to the conquest of
Babylon.

As early as 543, Nabonidus had returned to Babylon after his
long absence in Tema, apparently having been informed of the
unsettled conditions in the capital city. Disgruntled priests and people were losing patience with Nabonidus and Belshazzar. Already
some Babylonians had defected to the Persian side, the most significant of whom was Gubaru, governor of Gutium to the north of
Babylon on the Zagros River. Cyrus, with the cooperation of Gubaru
and his forces, won a battle with the Babylonian army at Opis on the
Tigris River. He was then in position to threaten Babylon. On
October 12, 539, Babylon was taken for Cyrus by Gubaru and his
troops.[23] The Nabonidus Chronicle indicates that entrance to the
city was "without a battle," a victory in part due to the tactic
employed of diverting the Euphrates River to allow entrance into
the city along its waterbed.[24] Cyrus did not enter the city himself
until October 29, whereupon he was welcomed as a liberating hero.
The Cyrus Cylinder, discovered in Babylon in 1879, provides the
conqueror's view of the events:

---

[22]Ibid., p. 82, n. 82.

[23]Ibid., p. 86.

[24]A.K. Grayson, *Assyrian and Babylonian Chronicles* (Locust Valley: J.J.
Augustin, 1975), p. 110. The Greek historian Herodotus noted the diversion of the river (1.191); the biblical account of events on that fateful night
is recorded in Daniel 5. Nabonidus was taken prisoner; Belshazzar was
killed.

When I, well-disposed, entered Babylon, I set up the seat of dominion in the royal palace amidst jubilation and rejoicing. Marduk the great god caused the big-hearted inhabitants of Babylon to . . . me. I sought daily to worship him. My numerous troops moved about undisturbed in the midst of Babylon. I did not allow any to terrorize the land of [Sumer] and Akkad (southern Mesopotamia). I kept in view the needs of Babylon and all its sanctuaries to promote their well-being.[25]

Cyrus rewarded Gubaru for his faithful service by making him satrap over the Babylonian province.[26] A satrap ruled a region called a satrapy on behalf of the Persian monarch. He raised taxes needed for his administration and troops for the king's needs. Imperial troops under royal officers stationed within a satrapy as well as royal inspectors made certain that satraps acted responsibly toward the king. The entire Persian Empire was efficiently organized into satrapies, including Syria-Palestine to which the descendants of those in exile would return.

The conquests of Cyrus brought the exiled Jews under Persian control. Compared to the rule of the Babylonian Empire, the Persian rulers adopted a reasonably benevolent approach to their subject peoples. Cyrus allowed captive peoples to return to their homelands and rebuilt their temples. The Cyrus Cylinder says:

From . . . to the cities of Ashur and Susa, Agade, Eshnunna, the cities of Zamban, Meturnu, Der, as far as the region of the land of Gutium, the holy cities beyond the Tigris whose sanctuaries had been in ruins over a long period, the gods whose abode is in the midst of them, I returned to their places and housed them in lasting abodes. I gathered together all their inhabitants and restored (to them) their dwellings. The gods of Sumer and Akkad whom Nabonidus had, to the anger of the lord of the gods, brought into Babylon, I at the bidding of Marduk, the great lord, made to dwell in peace in their habitations, delightful abodes. May all the gods whom I have placed within their sanctuaries address a daily prayer in my

---

[25]D. Winton Thomas, ed., *Documents from Old Testament Times* (New York: Harper & Row, 1961), p. 93.

[26]Gubaru is noted as Cyrus' district-governor in the *Nabonidus Chronicle*; see ibid., p. 82.

favor before Bel and Nabu, that my days be long, and may they say to Marduk my lord, 'May Cyrus the king who reveres thee, and Cambyses his son . . . .'[27]

It was in the spirit of this policy that the Jews were encouraged to return to Jerusalem (2 Chr 36:23; Ezra 1:2-4).

The events in Ezra–Nehemiah occurred between 538 B.C. (the first return) and ca. 408 B.C. The latter date is derived from the Elephantine papyrus letter addressed to Bagohi, governor of Judah, and to Johanan the High Priest and his priest colleagues.[28] Although Nehemiah was no longer governor, the High Priest Johanan is identified with the Johanan of Nehemiah 12:22.[29] What the author of Ezra–Nehemiah considered significant for his work is drawn from a period of approximately 130 years and compressed into the form of the book that has come down to us.

The last high priest mentioned in Nehemiah 12:22 is Jaddua.[30] His name in the list may be a later addition since we know nothing of him except what Josephus reports (*Ant* XI.viii). He held office in the last days of the Persian Empire before Alexander the Great overthrew Darius III Codomannus in 332 B.C.

THE GREEKS

Greeks and Greek influences were evident in much of the Persian Empire, and particularly in the East Mediterranean, long before Alexander's conquest. But that conquest brought Greek culture into immediate and continuing contact with the inhabitants of Jerusalem and the province of Yehud as well as the large Jewish Diaspora that developed in Egypt under the Ptolemies. The Greek cultural influ-

---

[27]Thomas, *Documents,* pp. 93-94.

[28]Ibid., pp. 260-269. Cf. *ABD,* II:445-455. The Elephantine papyri were discovered in Egypt beginning in 1893 and consisted of the archive of a Jewish colony of mercenary soldiers and their families from ca. 650-400 B.C.

[29]These papyri also indicate that Samaria was then governed by Delaiah and Shelemaiah, sons of Sanballat, Nehemiah's adversary.

[30]Hugh G.M. Williamson (*Ezra, Nehemiah,* Word Biblical Commentary, vol. 16 [Waco: Word, 1985], p. 365) believes the reference is a later gloss and refers to Darius I.

COLLEGE PRESS NIV COMMENTARY

ences have been named Hellenism, resulting in the descriptive term "Hellenistic" for the period from Alexander to the appearance of Roman power in Palestine in 63 B.C.[31]

A powerful wave of influence followed in the wake of the Macedonian's armies. The power of a foreign, technologically superior culture began to weaken the traditional disciplines of oriental life, replacing them with Greek modes of thought and activity. The tendency to assimilate Greek ways was particularly strong in Jerusalem among the upper-class citizens, the commercial and political aristocracy.

Following the death of Alexander in 323 B.C., his empire disintegrated into major segments under the control of several of his generals. Ptolemy I acquired the rule of Egypt and also controlled Palestine. The Ptolemies established a benign policy toward the Palestinian territory. Judea was permitted to maintain self-government under the high priest, who combined religious and political authority. The major mark of Egyptian domination was the heavy tribute that was exacted, not greatly different from the previous Persian practices. The Ptolemies initiated a tax-farming program whereby local appointees collected the taxes and forwarded them to the Egyptian authorities, with the local agent receiving a commission in return for his services. In this manner local aristocrats, including members of the high priestly family, came to have a vested interest in the Ptolemaic regime. They also developed a tendency to assimilate to the Greek way of life, and a hellenizing party thus arose among the ranks of the wealthy and priestly aristocracy of Jerusalem. In time a reaction against Hellenism was to develop, leading finally to the Maccabean revolt.

It is in the early years of these influences we believe the author of Ezra–Nehemiah compiled the book as a reminder of their recent history and as countervailing instruction against the hellenizing tendencies that were beginning to become apparent.

---

[31]Cf. Martin Hengel, *Judaism and Hellenism,* one vol. ed. (Philadelphia: Fortess Press, 1981).

THE COMPOSITION OF EZRA–NEHEMIAH

DATE

Ezra traveled to Jerusalem in 458 B.C. Nehemiah's last recorded activities were late in the reign of Artaxerxes I, who reigned until 425 B.C. The first-person materials relating to their ministries would have been combined ca. 400 B.C. The position taken in this commentary is that the book as we have it was likely compiled for the benefit of the Jewish community in Jerusalem and Judah by the editor within a quarter century after Alexander's conquest, ca. 300 B.C.

SOURCES

The first-person materials in Ezra–Nehemiah are generally identified as the Ezra Memoirs and the Nehemiah Memoirs. The original forms of these probably comprised written reports given to the Persian monarch after the completion of their respective assignments. Copies of these would have been retained in the temple archives in Jerusalem. Other related materials in the form of genealogical lists, names of priests and Levites, etc., were also kept in the archives and were available to the editor. The variety of materials evident in the work indicates that the compiler drew on varied sources in producing the final book.

AUTHORSHIP

Jewish tradition holds that Ezra 'wrote' his book. That does not mean, however, that the work was originally his in its entirety. It is obvious that he incorporated other documents that were available, in particular the decree of Cyrus and the letter of Artaxerxes I. In this view it is also acknowledged that other records may have been included, such as documents preserved in the temple treasury as well as correspondence between Persian officials in Jerusalem and their king in his capital. Ezra might also have had available preserved lists of clans, families, officials, and accounts of building operations. It is understood that he incorporated the records of Nehemiah into the one work.

Another view held by many scholars is that Ezra–Nehemiah was produced by the author of Chronicles as a supplement to that work. Another somewhat related explanation is that the original ending of Chronicles was what is now known as 1 Esdras.[32]

A review of compositional theories and arguments may be found in articles in Bible encyclopedias and in the introductions to critical commentaries. In our study we have chosen to follow generally the carefully reasoned suggestions of H.G.M. Williamson.[33] The first-person materials of Ezra and those of Nehemiah have been combined along with other records by an editor or compiler sometime after the events took place.

The final author of Ezra–Nehemiah was aware of the general chronology of events in the restoration of God's people to Jerusalem and the surrounding region, but strict chronology was not his driving concern. His design was to emphasize two important accomplishments of Ezra and Nehemiah: the return and reconstruction (Part One, Ezra 1:1–Neh 7:3) and renewal and reform (Part Two, Neh 7:4–13:31). Strong, significant undercurrents were inherent in these overarching emphases. The community of the returnees was experiencing a second exodus and occupation of the land in the face of opposition. The renewed community was directly connected to and derived from pre-exilic Israel. The Law of God was to be the basis for life and worship. God's people must remain ethnically pure and the rebuilt temple ritually clean. And permeating the whole was

---

[32]First Esdras was but one of several ancient books that bear the name of Ezra, pointing to stories about him that arose after his time and expanded on his reputation. It survived as one of the books of the Apocrypha in its Greek form as a part of the LXX. The theory proposes that Ezra and Nehemiah were created from 1 Esdras material with substantial revision and elaboration. The Apocrypha also contains 2 Esdras, an apocalypse, in which Ezra receives seven revelations. Ezra is called to rewrite all the sacred books of Israel which have been destroyed. He was to make public twenty-four of these (the Hebrew canon) and to hide the other seventy. While outside the canon, they were to be given to the wise among his people. For further information on these books, the Apocrypha, and the somewhat related Pseudepigrapha, see D.S. Russell, *Between the Testaments* (Philadelphia: Fortress Press, 1965).

[33]H.G.M. Williamson, *Ezra and Nehemiah*, Old Testament Guides (Sheffield: Sheffield Academic Press, 1996).

an appreciation for the veiled hand of God at work to accomplish his will in all of these events.

THE IMPORTANCE OF EZRA–NEHEMIAH

The recollection of the return from Babylon and the reestablishment of Jewish life in Jerusalem and its environs under a foreign power was an example for the writer's era. The change of ruling power from Persian to Greek brought new challenges to the Jewish community in the old homeland as well as the Diaspora. The enticements to intermarriage and the attraction of Hellenistic culture began to threaten the erosion of religious patterns established by Ezra and Nehemiah. And the establishment of a rival Samaritan temple to the north on Mount Gerizim competed with the authority of the Jerusalem sanctuary.[34] Ezra–Nehemiah was a call to remember the struggles of the past that had made the Jewish community viable, a summons to walk in the old ways rather than be enticed away from God by the appeal of Hellenism. Ultimately their work paved the way for the survival of Judaism until "the fulness of time had come" (Gal 4:4).

---

[34]The schism between Samaritans and Jews was rooted in the events recorded in Ezra–Nehemiah but reached fruition on the eve of Alexander's conquest. Sanballat III, grandson of Nehemiah's adversary, built the Samaritan temple on Mt. Gerizim about 332 B.C. and established his son-in-law as high priest. That son-in-law was from the high priestly family in Jerusalem who had been expelled for marrying Sanballat's daughter. (Cf. Josephus, *Ant* XI.302-325.)

OUTLINE

C. Identified by Place — 7:26-38

D. Identified as Priests — 7:39-42

E. Identified as Levites, Singers, and Gatekeepers — 7:43-45

F. Identified as Temple Servants — 7:46-56

G. Identified as Servants of Solomon — 7:57-60

H. Those Unable to Prove Israelite Identification — 7:61-65

I. Totals and Results — 7:66-73a

II. EZRA READS THE LAW — 7:73b–8:18

A. Public Reading of the Law — 7:73b–8:8

B. A Time for Celebration — 8:9-12

C. The Feast of Booths Kept — 8:13-18

III. THE ISRAELITES CONFESS THEIR SINS — 9:1-37

A. A Day of Fasting and Penitence — 9:1-5a

B. The Prayer of Praise to God — 9:5b-37
  1. For Creating Heaven and Earth — 9:5b-6
  2. For the Covenant with Abraham — 9:7-8
  3. For the Exodus — 9:9-11
  4. For the Law and the Desert Experience — 9:12-21
  5. For the Land of Canaan — 9:22-25
  6. For Grace and Mercy to Forefathers — 9:26-31
  7. Petition for Present Grace and Mercy — 9:32-37

IV. THE AGREEMENT OF THE PEOPLE — 9:38–10:39

A. The Intent to Make a Binding Agreement — 9:38

B. Signers of the Agreement — 10:1-27

C. Vocal Sealers of the Agreement — 10:28-29

D. Specifics of the Agreement — 10:30-39

V. THE NEW RESIDENTS OF JERUSALEM — 11:1-36

A. The Plan for Repopulation — 11:1-4a

B. Specific Inhabitants and Locales — 11:4b-20

C. Individuals Bearing Official Responsibilities — 11:21-24

D. The Villages of Judah and Benjamin — 11:25-36

BIBLIOGRAPHY

Berquist, Jon L. *Judaism in Persia's Shadow: A Social and Historical Approach*. Minneapolis: Fortress Press, 1995.

Blenkinsopp, Joseph. *Ezra and Nehemiah*. Old Testament Library. London: SCM, 1988.

Breneman, Mervin. *Ezra, Nehemiah, Esther*. The New American Commentary. Vol. 10. Nashville: Broadman & Holman, 1993.

Brown, Raymond. *The Message of Nehemiah: God's Servant in a Time of Change*. The Bible Speaks Today. Old Testament Series. Edited by J.A. Motyer. Downers Grove, IL: InterVarsity, 1998.

Clines, David J.A. *Ezra, Nehemiah, Esther*. New Century Bible. Grand Rapids: Eerdmans, 1984.

Cowley, A.E. *Aramaic Papyri of the Fifth Century BC*. Oxford: Oxford University Press, 1923.

Cundall, A.E. *Ezra and Nehemiah*. The Eerdmans Bible Commentary. Third edition. Grand Rapids: Eerdmans, 1987.

Fensham, F. Charles. *The Books of Ezra and Nehemiah*. The New International Commentary on the Old Testament. Grand Rapids: Eerdmans, 1982.

Fritsch, Charles T. "The Book of Ezra" and "The Book of Nehemiah." In *The Interpreter's One-Volume Commentary on the Bible*. Edited by Charles M. Laymon. Nashville: Abingdon, 1980.

Frye, R.N. *The Heritage of Persia*. London: Weidenfeld and Nicolson, 1962.

Kidner, Derek. *Ezra & Nehemiah: An Introduction and Commentary*. Tyndale Old Testament Commentaries. Vol. 11. General editor, D.J. Wiseman. Downers Grove, IL: InterVarsity, 1979.

Klein, Ralph W. "Nehemiah." In *Harper's Bible Commentary*. Edited by James L. Mays. San Francisco: Harper, 1988.

Mare, W. Harold. *The Archaeology of the Jerusalem Area*. Grand Rapids: Baker, 1987.

McConville, James G. *Ezra, Nehemiah, and Esther*. Philadelphia: Westminster, 1985.

Myers, Jacob M. *Ezra–Nehemiah*. The Anchor Bible. Vol. 14. Garden City, NJ: Doubleday, 1965.

Olmstead, A. T. *History of the Persian Empire*. Chicago: Chicago University Press, 1948.

Porten, Bezalel. *Archives from Elephantine: The Life of an Ancient Jewish Military Colony*. Berkeley: University of California Press, 1968.

Slotki, Judah J. *Daniel –Ezra–Nehemiah*. London: The Soncino Press, 1966.

Stern, Ephraim. *Material Culture of the Land of the Bible in the Persian Period, 538–332 BC*. Warminster: Aris & Phillips, 1982.

Talmon, S. "Ezra and Nehemiah." In *The Interpreter's Dictionary of the Bible*. Supplementary Volume. Nashville: Abingdon, 1976.

Williamson, Hugh G.M. *Ezra, Nehemiah*. Word Biblical Commentary. Vol. 16. Waco: Word, 1985.

_____. *Ezra and Nehemiah*. Old Testament Guides. General editor, R.N. Whybray. Sheffield: Sheffield Academic Press, 1996.

Wilson, Robert R. "Ezekiel." In *Harper's Bible Commentary*. Gen. ed. James L. May. San Francisco: Harper & Row, 1988.

Yamauchi, Edwin M. *Persia and the Bible*. Grand Rapids: Baker, 1990.

EZRA 1:1–NEHEMIAH 7:3 — PART ONE

RETURN AND RECONSTRUCTION

The author/editor of Ezra–Nehemiah has a story to tell, a story not for the generation of those who experienced the return from Babylon and reestablished a Jewish presence in the ancient Promised Land, but for succeeding generations. No doubt he wrote with his own generation and their spiritual needs in mind. We have suggested in the introduction that he penned his story early in the period after Greek domination of the former Persian empire was established by the conquests of Alexander the Great. Of course the author drew on sources he had at hand in order not so much to recount history in a chronological sequence as to focus the attention of his readers on the hand of God at work in the affairs of men to accomplish his eternal purposes. The example of how the LORD (Yahweh) fulfilled his promises and restored a remnant of his people to the Holy Land, even in the midst of persistent opposition, was certain to be a story that would strengthen the faith of those who were being tested in the crucible of a world now controlled by new masters. The very existence of the restored Jewish community, in which those who first read this story participated, was due to the faith and dedication of the first returnees from Babylon and particularly that of their leaders, Zerubbabel, Ezra, and Nehemiah. God was with those who rose up to return to Jerusalem to begin the reconstruction just as his Spirit motivated the author to tell their story for the benefit of those who would follow after them.

I. CYRUS HELPS THE EXILES TO RETURN (EZRA 1:1-11)

A. THE DECREE OF CYRUS (1:1-4)

¹In the first year of Cyrus king of Persia, in order to fulfill the word of the LORD spoken by Jeremiah, the LORD moved the heart

of Cyrus king of Persia to make a proclamation throughout his
realm and to put it in writing:

²"This is what Cyrus king of Persia says:

"'The LORD, the God of heaven, has given me all the kingdoms of the earth and he has appointed me to build a temple for him at Jerusalem in Judah. ³Anyone of his people
among you—may his God be with him, and let him go up to
Jerusalem in Judah and build the temple of the LORD, the
God of Israel, the God who is in Jerusalem. ⁴And the people
of any place where survivors may now be living are to provide him with silver and gold, with goods and livestock, and
with freewill offerings for the temple of God in Jerusalem.'"

Cyrus applied the same benevolent policy towards the Jews in
Babylonia as he did toward other people groups whom Nebuchadnezzar had carried into exile during his conquests of the Assyrian
Empire. Just as the Lord had used the Chaldean conqueror to punish his wayward people, now he "moved the heart" of Cyrus to begin
the restoration. (The name Cyrus derives from Greek Κύρος [*Kyros*],
but the Persian form of the name was *Kūrush*.¹ The form in the
Hebrew text is כּוֹרֶשׁ [*kôreš*].)

Cyrus is mentioned several other places in the Bible. His name
appears twice in the second part of Isaiah (44:28; 45:1), where Cyrus
is identified as the one who will rebuild Jerusalem and the temple.
He is noted also as the anointed servant of the Lord, and all that the
Lord does for Cyrus is ultimately for the sake of the Lord's people.
Other passages in Isaiah that apparently allude to Cyrus are 41:2-
3,25-26; 45:13, and 46:11. He is referred to in Daniel 1:21; 6:28; and
10:1. The decree of Cyrus is also given in 2 Chronicles 36:22-23 and
Ezra 6:3-5.

1:1 In the first year of Cyrus king of Persia,

The date marks the beginning of his rule over the Babylonian
empire; he liberated the city of Babylon in October, 539 B.C. He
had already ruled the Medes and the Persians since approximately
559 B.C.

---

¹Yamauchi, *Persia and the Bible*, p. 72.

in order to fulfill the word of the Lord spoken by Jeremiah . . .

This is a reference to Jeremiah 29:10, "When seventy years are completed for Babylon, I will come to you and fulfill my gracious promise to bring you back to this place." The period of seventy years is mentioned again in Jeremiah 25:11. An almost identical passage referring to Jeremiah occurs in 2 Chronicles 36:22-23. Reference to the prophetic promise of restoration not only connects the reader with God's activity in the past but immediately sets the tone for the book of Ezra–Nehemiah. This is not secular history; it is the story of God at work in the politics of the day to accomplish what he had promised two generations earlier. Here the seventy years should not be pressed into a rigid mold. One seventy-year period would reach from 586, when the temple was destroyed, to 516, when it was rebuilt. Another possibility would be from approximately 606, the first Babylonian incursion into Judah, to 538, the first year of the return under Sheshbazzar.

to make a proclamation throughout his realm and to put it in writing:

Two methods of communication were used: one or more heralds were sent out to orally proclaim Cyrus's decree (since many people were illiterate), and it was put in writing, likely in Aramaic which had become the international language of that era. The written documents could be posted, and one or more copies were placed in the state archives for future reference, if needed (see 6:2).

1:2 . . . The LORD,

Yahweh, the name of God. That Cyrus was familiar with the name of the deity worshiped by the Jews was likely due to Jewish advisers among his royal entourage[2] and references to him in Isaiah, noted above. However, he is not here acknowledging Yahweh as the one and only God. According to inscriptions that survive, he spoke to the Babylonians of fulfilling the commands of Marduk, patron god of Babylon, and it is probable that he practiced the religion of Zoroaster and honored their *good* god Ahura Mazda.

---

[2]Cf. Daniel's role in both the Babylonian and Persian administrations. The Cyrus Proclamation was likely drafted by Jews and reflects their terminology which the king incorporated into the final form.

the God of heaven, . . .

While the concept in this title appears earlier in the Bible, as in Solomon's prayer of dedication of the first temple (1 Kgs 8:22-30), this is the first occurrence of this specific expression. The designation does appear frequently in the Elephantine Papyri, Jewish documents recovered in Egypt from the Persian period. Its use in the Bible is largely restricted to official interactions between Jews and Persians, so it may have been an acceptable and expected administrative term. The title does not limit God's sovereignty, for his earthly place of residence is to be in Jerusalem. Cyrus has been appointed to build a temple (בַּיִת, *bayith*, "house") for the Lord. To do this he gives the orders; others carry them out.

1:3 Anyone of his people . . .

While particularly applicable to the Judean exiles, the invitation could also apply to any descendants of the northern kingdom, Israel, that were carried into captivity by the Assyrians a century and a half earlier. The religion of the exiles from the northern kingdom had already been weakened before the Assyrian conquest. Likely the forces of assimilation in their new surroundings in exile had destroyed for many any allegiance to the religion of Yahweh, so few could be expected to respond. That there was a remnant of faithful northerners is indicated, however, by the story of Tobit in the Apocrypha.

let him go up to Jerusalem . . .

The proclamation did not require compliance; it was an invitation to whosoever was moved by **his God** who was with him. The call of God is an invitation to whosoever will. Babylon was set in a broad river valley, while Jerusalem's ruins lay on the mountains of Judah.

the God of Israel, . . .

Even though the people who respond are from the tribes of Benjamin and Judah (v. 5), this remnant of all the tribes of Israel are understood to represent the entire nation.

1:4 . . . provide him . . . .

that is, the person who is moved by God to go up. Those who chose not to return were to assist those who did with money, goods, and livestock. The livestock would have included pack animals for carrying the goods on the journey. They were also expected to provide freewill offerings for the temple that was to be reconstructed. The entire Jewish community in Babylonia was to participate in the movement to restore the temple and worship of the Lord God in Jerusalem. The expression **the people of any place** may also have included contributions by non-Jews.

B. THE JEWISH RESPONSE (1:5-11)

⁵Then the family heads of Judah and Benjamin, and the priests and Levites—everyone whose heart God had moved—prepared to go up and build the house of the LORD in Jerusalem. ⁶All their neighbors assisted them with articles of silver and gold, with goods and livestock, and with valuable gifts, in addition to all the freewill offerings. ⁷Moreover, King Cyrus brought out the articles belonging to the temple of the LORD, which Nebuchadnezzar had carried away from Jerusalem and had placed in the temple of his god.ᵃ ⁸Cyrus king of Persia had them brought by Mithredath the treasurer, who counted them out to Sheshbazzar the prince of Judah.

⁹This was the inventory:

gold dishes	30
silver dishes	1,000
silver pansᵇ	29
¹⁰gold bowls	30
matching silver bowls	410
other articles	1,000

¹¹In all, there were 5,400 articles of gold and of silver. Sheshbazzar brought all these along when the exiles came up from Babylon to Jerusalem.

ᵃ7 Or *gods*   ᵇ9 The meaning of the Hebrew for this word is uncertain.

1:5 . . . Judah and Benjamin, . . .

Most of the exiled Judeans were members of these two tribes; however, 1 Chronicles 9:3 also lists people from the tribes of Ephraim and Manasseh among the returnees living in Jerusalem. These could have been descendants of the northern tribes who found refuge in Jerusalem in the days of Hezekiah when the Assyrians were devastating the northern kingdom. Archaeological evidence has shown the dramatic expansion of the city in the late eighth century B.C.[3] The author, by including the four groups — Judah, Benjamin, priests, and Levites — establishes a direct connection and continuity between the pre-exilic Jerusalem community and those who will form the restored population of the Holy City.

Then the family heads . . . , and the priests and Levites

The expression "family heads" speaks of an extended family, groups less than a tribe but larger than a single household.

—everyone whose heart God had moved—

Here, as with Cyrus, God is at work to motivate the response to the proclamation. We can speculate that those who responded to God at work within them were previously prepared through the influence of the pre-exilic prophets, the exilic prophets, and particularly the words of Jeremiah.

1:6 All their neighbors . . . .

The use of the Hebrew expression וְכָל־סְבִיבֹתֵיהֶם (w⁰kol s⁰bîbōthêhem, literally "and all those who were round about them") could include non-Jewish as well as Jewish neighbors. This expression, plus the list of contributions, echoes the original exodus from Egypt (Exod 3:21-22; 11:2; 12:35-36; cf. Ps 105:37). The author intends his readers to understand that the return from Babylonian exile is comparable in some respects to the departure of Israel from Egypt. It marks a new beginning for God's people orchestrated by God himself. Here as always, God moves people to provide for his work and the fulfillment of his plans.

1:7 Moreover, King Cyrus brought out the articles belonging to the temple of the LORD . . . .

This was a princely act exemplifying his noble character. All that had been Nebuchadnezzar's fell to Cyrus as a result of his conquest of Babylon. Nebuchadnezzar had carried the temple treasures away as trophies of war in 587 B.C. (2 Kgs 24:13; 25:13-16; 2 Chr 36:10,18; Jer 52:17-19; Dan 1:2). He had deposited them in the treasury of his gods in Babylon, for in his pagan mind they represented the victory

---

[3]Amnon Ben-Tor, ed., *The Archaeology of Ancient Israel* (New Haven: Yale University Press, 1992), p. 367.

of his gods over the God of the Judeans. In contrast, Cyrus, sensitive and responsive to the leading of Yahweh to rebuild the temple, also recognized that as beautiful and costly as the objects were, they belonged in the house of the true owner, Yahweh. For the renewed worship in Jerusalem to be effective according to time-honored custom, the temple vessels were needed.

1:8 . . . Mithredath the treasurer, . . .

Both the name and the title are Persian rather than Hebrew, confirming the origin of this information in the Persian period. The name is derived from "Mithras," the Persian sun god, and *da*, "to give, or dedicate"; Persian names as well as Hebrew names often were religious expressions.

Sheshbazzar the prince of Judah

This is a Babylonian name. Similarly, Daniel bore the Babylonian name Belteshazzar (Dan 1:7). The identification of Sheshbazzar as the prince of Judah has been taken as evidence that he was a descendant of King David. It is clear that the title "prince of Judah" indicates a leader, but it does not require a connection to the royal lineage. "Prince" is used in 1 Chronicles 2:10 to designate a tribal leader,[4] and similar usage occurs in 2 Chronicles 1:2 and elsewhere.

Sheshbazzar has been identified with Shenazzar (1 Chr 3:18) by some scholars, but this identification is no longer viable. Sheshbazzar has no lineal connection to David, while Shenazzar does. And the two names are distinct. Sheshbazzar is derived from Babylonian *šaššu-aba-uṣur*, "may *šamaš/šaššu* protect the father," while the Babylonian for Shenazzar is *šin-ab-uṣur*, "may [the god] Sin protect the son."[5] It has also been argued that Sheshbazzar is identical with Zerubbabel, partially due to the similar roles both played in the restoration. Scholars have attempted to reconcile this similarity. Sheshbazzar is noted here and in verse 11 as having received the temple vessels. In 5:14 and 16 it is noted that Cyrus appointed him governor and that he laid the foundations of the temple. Zerubbabel, according to Ezra 2:2, was among a group of returnees, and

---

[4]The NIV translates נָשִׂיא (*nasî'*) as "leader"; NRSV translates "prince."

[5]Derek Kidner, *Ezra & Nehemiah: An Introduction and Commentary*, Tyndale Old Testament Commentaries, vol 11, ed. D.J. Wiseman (Downers Grove, IL: InterVarsity, 1979), p. 142, n. 3.

is also called "governor" in Haggai 1:1. Further, Ezra 3 places him among the group involved in rebuilding the altar. The similarities are striking but not compelling. The two are distinguished from one another in Ezra 5, however, for Zerubbabel is present on the occasion when the opponents of the renewed rebuilding of the temple attempted to stop the construction (v. 2), while Sheshbazzar is referred to as someone unknown to the opponents and not present. Archaeology has now made clear that Sheshbazzar, Zerubbabel, and Nehemiah were not the only governors of Persian Yehud; the evidence is in the form of stamped jar handles and seals.[6] A reasonable explanation for the scarcity of information in Ezra–Nehemiah about Sheshbazzar is that no firsthand account of the initial return survived and was available to the author/compiler. He worked with the information that survived and wrote the history of the return based on the documents at hand, which is not to imply that what he included was inaccurate, only that he did not have *all* the details.

1:9-11 . . . the inventory . . .

Two thousand four hundred ninety-nine items are listed, but the total given is 5,400. Although scholars have proposed several possible explanations, none is convincing. A Jewish commentator simply notes that both large and small vessels were included in the total but that only the larger ones are specified in the list.[7] Or the author may have provided only an example list plus the grand total. His main point seems to be to establish continuity between the Solomonic and the Second Temple. Even though the Second Temple would be a completely new construction, the same sacred vessels were used in both.

The NIV footnote to the word **pans** in verse 9b only hints at the textual problems in translating the list, since the exact meanings of several words are uncertain, and some of these are likely loan-words from the Persian original. Such difficulties of vocabulary suggest that the Hebrew text was based on an authentic list.

While we know little about Sheshbazzar, the author testifies that he faithfully discharged his duties. In the history of biblical religion and of the church, the fulfillment of responsibility by a great host of unnamed faithful has been God's means of extending his kingdom

---

[6]*ABD*, V:1209.

[7]Judah J. Slotki, *Daniel–Ezra–Nehemiah* (London: Soncino Press, 1966), p. 125.

to reach even to those of us alive today. May such faithfulness mark
our own generation.

II. THE LIST OF THE EXILES WHO RETURNED (2:1-70)

Modern readers should keep in mind that the author of
Ezra–Nehemiah, the person who assembled the historical materials
in the book and arranged them according to the purposes of the
Lord under the guidance of divine inspiration, was not writing a
minutely detailed history. He was sketching the way God was at work
to bring about the restoration of the remnant community in
Jerusalem and its environs. He was making connections between the
community that had been eradicated and the reestablished group.
He was stirring up memories of the more ancient exodus from
Egypt and suggesting that those who came out of Babylon were
involved in a similar exodus. A rebuilt temple in a largely depopu-
lated land, even with the sacred vessels that had been used in the former destroyed house of God, would be meaningless. His interests
naturally turned to the people who would serve in that temple and
those who would worship there as well as live in the region round
about. That is the focus of this chapter.

One should also keep in mind that in the original text there were
no chapter and verse divisions. His story flowed naturally. That is, it
flowed as naturally as he could arrange it while incorporating the
historical materials at hand. It is interesting, as well, that the materials he uses in Nehemiah 7:6-72[73] largely parallel this list in Ezra
This raises the question of which of the lists came first, that in Ezra
or that in Nehemiah. Neither time nor space allows the intricate
investigation of such questions; they have been presented in some
detail and are available in the work, for example, of Hugh Williamson.[8] It seems clear that the list in Ezra 2 depends on Nehemiah 7,
although it is likely that the information in the list has been assembled from earlier sources; it is a composite list. It seems reasonable
to hold that "it reflects a number of . . . modest journeys of return
at various times throughout the reigns of Cyrus and Cambyses."[9]

---

[8]Williamson, *Ezra, Nehemiah*, pp. 28-32.
[9]Ibid., p. 31.

The list apparently has no direct connection to chapter one; Shesh-bazzar is not mentioned, nor are the temple vessels included in the list of gifts given in 2:68-69.

When Nehemiah notes that he had found the records of those who had been the first to return, since some of them are listed according to the towns in which they were dwelling in the region round about Jerusalem, he refers to those who must have immigrated in a series from Babylon during the first decades after Cyrus issued the decree.

A. THE LEADERS (2:1-2)

¹Now these are the people of the province who came up from the captivity of the exiles, whom Nebuchadnezzar king of Babylon had taken captive to Babylon (they returned to Jerusalem and Judah, each to his own town, ²in company with Zerubbabel, Jeshua, Nehemiah, Seraiah, Reelaiah, Mordecai, Bilshan, Mispar, Bigvai, Rehum and Baanah):

The list of the men of the people of Israel:

2:1 . . . people of the province . . .

Likely Yehud (Judea) is meant. Yehud was the name of the Jewish region, known from coins and seal impressions stamped with YHD that date to about 538–331 B.C. It was a small district apparently carved out of surrounding territories in the large satrapy west of the Euphrates River known as "Beyond the River," translated as "Trans-Euphrates" in Ezra 5:3. If so, the loss of some territory previously controlled by surrounding rulers might have contributed to the hostility from them that surfaces later in Ezra–Nehemiah.

. . . each to his own town,

This suggests a process of resettlement over a period of time. Inherent in the expression, too, is an emphasis on continuity between those who returned and their ancestors who once inherited the land in the time of Joshua son of Nun (Josh 13–21). At that time the land of promise was allocated to specific families as a perpetual inheritance.

2:2a in company with

Eleven names of leaders are listed, but not Sheshbazzar. In the parallel list in Nehemiah 7 a twelfth name appears, that of Nahamani (7:7). The name may have dropped out of this verse as the result of a scribal error. The total of twelve names was another conscious connection with the past, representative of and recalling the twelve tribes that constituted ancient Israel.

Zerubbabel, Jeshua, [etc.]

Zerubbabel is a Babylonian name meaning "seed of (born in) Babylon," a fairly common name in Mesopotamia in that time. He was a grandson of king Jehoiachin and a direct descendant of King David. This was spiritually significant for the reconstituted community, but politically insignificant. The restoration was of the worshiping community, not the reestablishment of a kingdom with a Davidic ruler.

Jeshua was the High Priest (Zech 3:1). In Haggai (1:1) and Zechariah (3:1) his name is written Joshua. The slight modification of the spelling appears in Greek as "Jesu," that is, Jesus. Jeshua is identified as the son of Jehozadak in Haggai 1:1; 2:2,4; and Zechariah 6:11. His grandfather, Seraiah, was executed by Nebuchadnezzar at Riblah (2 Kgs 25:18ff).

The Nehemiah in this list is not Nehemiah son of Hacaliah, the major figure in the last part of Ezra–Nehemiah. That this Nehemiah appears third in the list suggests that he was a major leader in the early phases of the return. The name Nehemiah was fairly popular; it means "Yahweh comforts," a reality that those in exile had learned the hard way.

Seraiah was the name of Ezra's father (7:1). It is possible, but not likely, that he may have been intended here. The name means "Yahweh persists." That sentiment no doubt made it a popular name as well.

The name Mordecai brings to mind Queen Esther's uncle (Esth 2:5), but of course this is a different individual bearing the same name. The name may derive from the chief deity of Babylon, Marduk. Another name foreign to Hebrew is Bigvai, but the derivation is uncertain. German scholar Martin Noth maintained that it was of Persian origin. Others of the Bigvai family returned with Ezra

(8:14). The Elephantine Papyri from Egypt mention a governor of Judah with a similar name, Bagohi (410–407 B.C.).

The name Rehum identifies several different people in Ezra–Nehemiah.[10] This leader is named also in Nehemiah 7:7, but spelled Nehum, likely a scribal error. The name signifies, "compassion, gentleness." Others so named are a Persian official (4:8), a Levite (Neh 3:17), and a "leader of the people" (Neh 10:25).

Baanah occurs here and in Nehemiah 3:4 (with a spelling variant), 7:7, and 10:27. It is unclear if the same person is the referent in each of these cases. The name is known from pre-exilic references, for example, 2 Samuel 4:2.

2:2b . . . men of the people of Israel:

The first subheading identifies the following names as laity, in contrast to the priests and Levites later in the list. The author's use of the name Israel rather than Judah is intended to reconnect the identification of the returnees with God's people, Israel, who accepted the covenant at Sinai, rather than with the northern kingdom of Israel before Assyria conquered and exiled that people. The head of each clan named had likely died long before. Not all members of a clan necessarily came with the first returnees. Some remained in Babylon and returned with Ezra or earlier.

B. IDENTIFIED BY CLAN (2:3-19)

[3]the descendants of Parosh,	2,172
[4]of Shephatiah,	372
[5]of Arah,	775
[6]of Pahath-Moab (through the line of Jeshua and Joab),	2,812
[7]of Elam,	1,254
[8]of Zattu,	945
[9]of Zaccai,	760
[10]of Bani,	642
[11]of Bebai,	623
[12]of Azgad,	1,222

---

[10]*ABD*, V:664.

¹³of Adonikam,	666
¹⁴of Bigvai,	2,056
¹⁵of Adin,	454
¹⁶of Ater (through Hezekiah),	98
¹⁷of Bezai,	323
¹⁸of Jorah,	112
¹⁹of Hashum,	223

2:3 the descendants of Parosh   2,172

As a common noun, the word means "a flea." One wonders if the children of each generation suffered the taunts of their peers because of this name. Some of the family came up to Jerusalem with Ezra (8:3). One Paroshite helped repair the Jerusalem wall (Neh 3:25), but either he or another of the clan was guilty of ignoring the Law of God against intermarriage (Neh 10:14).

2:4 of Shephatiah   372

The name means "Yahweh has judged"; it occurs several times in the Bible, beginning with the fifth son of David (2 Sam 3:4//1 Chr 3:3). A Shephatiah was a contemporary of Jeremiah (38:1), though no friend of the prophet. It is possible he was carried into captivity after Zedekiah's rebellion and the subsequent destruction of Jerusalem and that some of his descendants were among the returnees.

2:5 of Arah   775

This family name derives from a word meaning "to wander, travel." First Chronicles 7:39 lists an Arah of the tribe of Asher, but there is no direct connection with the Arah listed here and in the parallel list in Nehemiah 7:10. Apparently the Arah in our text was among those returnees who were later actively involved with the opposition to Nehemiah's reforming efforts, for there was intermarriage between his house and that of Tobiah, Nehemiah's adversary (6:18).

2:6 of Pahath-Moab (through the line of Jeshua and Joab)   2,812

This clan name is literally, "governor of Moab"! A reasonable explanation for this peculiar family name is that an ancestor had been a ruler over part of Moab in pre-exilic times. Although marriage to Moabites was forbidden among the returnees, it did occur as early as the period of the Judges; David's ancestry was partially

Moabite. Further, two Judeans, Joash and Saraph, had married
Moabites, according to old traditions drawn on by the Chronicler
(1 Chr 4:22).

2:7 of Elam   1,254

While Elam was the name of a country and people, the Elamites,
this is a clan name. First Chronicles 8:24 lists an Elam from the tribe
of Benjamin, and one of the Levites, a temple gatekeeper, also bore
that name (1 Chr 26:3). Others of this clan later came to Jerusalem
with Ezra (8:7).

2:8 of Zattu   945

This name only occurs in Ezra–Nehemiah.

2:9 of Zaccai   760

This clan is noted only in Ezra–Nehemiah; however, it is known
from an archaeological discovery on a stamp seal.[11]

2:10 of Bani   642

The name occurs in Nehemiah 7:15 with a variant spelling as
Binnui and a total of 648. One of David's heroic followers was
named Bani (2 Sam 23:36).

2:11 of Bebai   623

This name occurs only in Ezra–Nehemiah. In Nehemiah 7:16 the
number is 628.

2:12 of Azgad   1,222

A name denoting "mighty is Gad" only occurs in the Bible in
Ezra–Nehemiah; however, the name appears in Aramaic documents
from Egypt.[12]

2:13 of Adonikam   666

This clan name, meaning "my lord has arisen," is found only in
Ezra–Nehemiah.

2:14 of Bigvai   2,056

Note the personal name, Bigvai in verse 2. Here it is a clan name.

---

[11]Sabatino Moscati, *L'epigrafia ebraica antica* (Rome: 1951), p. 75.

[12]A. Cowley, *The Aramaic Papyri of the Fifth Century B.C.* (Oxford: 1923),
pp. 37, 39.

2:15 of Adin   454

The name is based on the same root as the noun Eden, suggesting a meaning of "delight" or the like, but this family name only appears in Ezra–Nehemiah.

2:16 of Ater (through Hezekiah)   98

The name is related to "closing, binding," but the clan name occurs only in this list and the comparable one in Nehemiah. The Hezekiah branch of this family is not likely to be descendants of King Hezekiah, since this list through verse 35 consists of common people rather than descendants of the House of David.

2:17 of Bezai   323

This name is unknown outside Ezra 2:17 and Nehemiah 7:23. In the latter text, the number of people is given as 324.

2:18 of Jorah   112

The parallel family name in Nehemiah 7:24 is Hariph. The best explanation for the variant is word association: יוֹרֶה (jôreh) = "autumn rain" and חָרִיף (hārîf = "sharp, fresh") is related to "harvest time."[13]

2:19 of Hashum   223

Nehemiah 7:22 gives the number 328. Such variations were likely due to the difficulty of copying Hebrew numerical notations, which were not based on the later Arabic system that underlies our number symbols.[14]

C. IDENTIFIED BY PLACE (2:20-35)

[20]of Gibbar,	95
[21]the men of Bethlehem,	123
[22]of Netophah,	56
[23]of Anathoth,	128
[24]of Azmaveth,	42
[25]of Kiriath Jearim,[a] Kephirah and Beeroth,	743
[26]of Ramah and Geba,	621

[13]Williamson, *Ezra, Nehemiah*, p. 25, n. 18a.
[14]H.L. Allrick, "The Lists of Zerubbabel (Nehemiah 7 and Ezra 2) and the Hebrew Numerical Notation," *BASOR* 136 (1954): 21-27.

[27]of Micmash,	122
[28]of Bethel and Ai,	223
[29]of Nebo,	52
[30]of Magbish,	156
[31]of the other Elam,	1,254
[32]of Harim,	320
[33]of Lod, Hadid and Ono,	725
[34]of Jericho,	345
[35]of Senaah,	3,630

[a]*25* See Septuagint (see also Neh. 7:29); Hebrew *Kiriath Arim.*

2:20 of Gibbar   95

Although the NIV associates Gibbar with "the men of the people of Israel" (2:2), it is more likely a place name. In the parallel passage (Neh 7:25), the name given is Gibeon. Gibbar may be an alternate name for this place (now el-Jib) about five miles northwest of Jerusalem.

2:21 the men of Bethlehem   123

The place of Jesus' birth is about five miles south of Jerusalem.

2:22 of Netophah   56

First Chronicles 2:54 connects the Netophathites with Caleb, and this place produced Maharai and Heleb, two of the mighty men of David (2 Sam 23:28-29). The location was likely at modern Khirbet Bedd Falul, less than three and a half miles southeast of Bethlehem. Nehemiah 7:26 combines the men of Bethlehem and Netophah for a total of 188, a few more than the 179 total when combined here.

2:23 of Anathoth   128

This was Jeremiah's hometown (Jer 1:1), a priestly settlement in Benjamite territory. It is identified with Ras el-Kharrubeh near Anata, about three miles northeast of Jerusalem.

2:24 of Azmaveth   42

Nehemiah 12:29 employs this place name, but in 7:28 it is called Beth Azmaveth. It is identified with modern Hismeh near Geba and Anathoth.

2:25 of Kiriath Jearim, Kephirah and Beeroth   743

These three places first appear together in connection with the

Gibeonites in Joshua 9:17. Kiriath Jearim is identified with Tell el-Azhar, adjacent to modern Abu Ghosh,[15] about nine miles northwest of Jerusalem near the Tel Aviv-Jerusalem highway. Kephirah is identified with Khirbet el-Kefireh, about one and one-half miles north of Kiriath Jearim, five miles west southwest of Gibeon, in the territory of Benjamin. Beeroth is at Khirbet el-Burj three miles northwest of Jerusalem near Nebi Samwil.

2:26 of Ramah and Geba   621

Ramah, "the Height," was Samuel's home, usually identified with modern er-Ram, just over four miles north of Jerusalem. Geba was located five and a half miles northeast of Jerusalem at modern Jaba'. It was the northern limit of Yehud in the Persian period (Zech 14:10).

2:27 of Micmash   122

Located just to the north across a deep valley from Geba, modern Mukhmas. Before a decisive battle, Saul encamped at Geba and the Philistines at Micmash (1 Sam 13:5).

2:28 of Bethel and Ai   223

Bethel, now called Beitin, is about twelve miles north of Jerusalem, east of Ramallah. Ai is usually associated with et-Tell, one and a half miles east of Beitin. (In Neh 7:32 the number is 123.)

2:29 of Nebo   52

This place is not to be confused with Mt. Nebo in Transjordan, nor is its exact location known. A probable location is modern Nuba, about three miles northwest of Bethzur (north of Hebron).

2:30 of Magbish   156

Magbish does not appear in the parallel text of Nehemiah. Although its location is uncertain, Khirbet el-Makhbiyeh has been suggested.

2:31 of the other Elam   1,254

The "other" refers to the personal name Elam in verse 7. The location is likely Khirbet Beth 'Alam in the Judean hills east of Marisa.

---

[15]The ark was kept at Kiriath Jearim after the Philistines returned it to Judah and before David brought it into the city of Jerusalem (1 Sam 7:1-2; 1 Chr 13).

2:32 of Harim   320

This place was likely at Khirbet Horan at the base of the Judean hills about five miles northeast of Marisa (Beth Guvrin).

2:33 of Lod, Hadid and Ono   725

Lod (Lydda) is seven miles southeast of Joppa (Israel's international airport is nearby.). Hadid (al-Haditha) is three and a half miles east of Lod, and Ono (Kephar 'Ana) lies between Lod and Joppa.

2:34 of Jericho   345

The list of place names now switches from west to east, to the Jordan valley and Jericho, about eighteen miles east of Jerusalem. The eastern border of Yehud was the river.

2:35 of Senaah   3,630

Here, Senaah is a place-name, likely for later Magdalsenna (Khirbet 'Auja el-Foqa), eight miles northeast of Jericho. (Neh 7:38 gives the number 3,930.)

D. IDENTIFIED AS PRIESTS (2:36-39)

[36]The priests:

the descendants of Jedaiah	
(through the family of Jeshua)	973
[37]of Immer,	1,052
[38]of Pashhur,	1,247
[39]of Harim,	1,017

2:36 The priests: the descendants of Jedaiah (through the family of Jeshua)   973

Having identified the lay people among these initial returnees, the list-maker now turns to those responsible for the activities centered on the yet-unrestored temple, beginning with the priests. They total about ten percent of the returnees.

Twenty-four priestly family groups were organized by King David (1 Chr 24) to take turns of duty. Only four of these are listed here among the returnees. They are mentioned again in 10:18-22, several decades later. From these four families the twenty-four courses were reconstituted according to Jewish tradition, taking the names of the original families.[16] Thus Zechariah, father of John the Baptist, was a member of the reconstituted priestly division of Abijah (Luke 1:5).

Jedaiah is the general name of the clan (1 Chr 24:7), but the more immediate connection is to Jeshua. It is unclear to whom this name refers — to Jeshua son of Jehozadak, the high priest (so called in Hag 1:1; Zech 3:1; and referred to in Ezra 3:2, etc., but not as high priest) or the Jeshua mentioned above in 2:2. These two may be the same Jeshua. In any case, it is preferable to understand the reference in this verse to the Jeshua noted previously in 2:2.

2:37 of Immer   1,052

The priestly progenitor of this line was assigned the sixteenth order in 1 Chronicles 24:14.

2:38 of Pashhur   1,247

A priest by this name (interestingly called "son of Immer") had Jeremiah put in stocks (20:1-2). Jeremiah then told him that he and his family would be exiled to Babylon. Apparently that crisis resulted in a conversion experience for the priestly family so that they were among the earliest of those to return to Zion.

2:39 of Harim   1,017

(This family name should not be confused with the place name noted above in v. 32.) The priestly head of this family was chosen for the third order in 1 Chronicles 24:8.

E. IDENTIFIED AS LEVITES, SINGERS, AND GATEKEEPERS (2:40-42)

[40]The Levites:

the descendants of Jeshua and Kadmiel (through the line of Hodaviah)	**74**

[41]The singers:

the descendants of Asaph	**128**

[42]The gatekeepers of the temple:

the descendants of Shallum, Ater, Talmon, Akkub, Hatita and Shobai	**139**

---

[16]*Tosephta* 2.1.216.

2:40 The Levites:

This clan of Levites descended from Hodaviah through the families of Jeshua and Kadmiel. Hodaviah ["give praise to Yah(weh)] was a popular name. It appears three times in 1 Chronicles 3:24; 5:24; and 9:7, but not in reference to the Levites. No Hodaviah appears in the Levitical lists in 1 Chronicles, but this progenitor was in one of the pre-exilic levitical family lines.

These seventy-four Levites probably were direct assistants to the priests, while those numbered below in verses 41-42 fulfilled other responsibilities. All told, the Levites are a small number in comparison to the priests. This may have been due to the lower status of levitical service as compared to the priestly. Later, Ezra was only able to recruit thirty-eight Levites to return with him to Jerusalem (8:15-20). This is in contrast to pre-exilic times. As Derek Kidner has pointed out, "For now the Levites, whom the tithe law treats as greatly outnumbering the priests, had suddenly become a tiny minority with only a fraction of their former claim on the community's support. Yet the law gives them everything, 'every tithe in Israel,' and only requires them to hand on a tenth of this to the priests: 'a tithe of the tithe' (Nu. 18:21,26)."[17]

2:41 The singers:

First Chronicles 25:17ff records that David established a group of Levites into twenty-four orders of temple singers, similar to the twenty-four priestly orders. The name Asaph is associated with a number of the Psalms (50, 73–83). None of the other great guilds of singers (Jeduthun or Heman) seem to have returned, although they are listed as leaders along with Asaph in 1 Chronicles 15:17.[18] This suggests that the demand for singers in the Babylonian situation was quite limited and that many of them found other types of employment there, so that fewer were available or inclined to return. Here singers are listed separately from Levites; however, they are Levites with specialized responsibilities. (The number in Neh 7:44 is 148.)

---

[17]Kidner, *Ezra & Nehemiah*, p. 40. The fact that this older legislation was retained by the postexilic community testifies that it was not created by them, but faithfully transmitted as they had received the pre-exilic tradition.

[18]Ethan was subsequently succeeded by Jeduthun (1 Chr 16:41,42).

2:42 The gatekeepers of the temple:

The number is one less in Nehemiah 7:45. The gatekeepers were responsible for locking and unlocking the gates of the temple and to keep watch over the treasury, according to 1 Chronicles 9:17-29. Of these names, a descendant of Shallum is mentioned as a gatekeeper in the time of Jeremiah (35:4).

F. IDENTIFIED AS TEMPLE SERVANTS (2:43-54)

[43]The temple servants:

the descendants of
  Ziha, Hasupha, Tabbaoth,
[44]Keros, Siaha, Padon,
[45]Lebanah, Hagabah, Akkub,
[46]Hagab, Shalmai, Hanan,
[47]Giddel, Gahar, Reaiah,
[48]Rezin, Nekoda, Gazzam,
[49]Uzza, Paseah, Besai,
[50]Asnah, Meunim, Nephussim,
[51]Bakbuk, Hakupha, Harhur,
[52]Bazluth, Mehida, Harsha,
[53]Barkos, Sisera, Teman,
[54]Neziah and Hatipha

G. IDENTIFIED AS SERVANTS OF SOLOMON (2:55-58)

[55]The descendants of the servants of Solomon:

the descendants of
  Sotai, Hassophereth, Peruda,
[56]Jaala, Darkon, Giddel,
[57]Shephatiah, Hattil, Pokereth-Hazzebaim and Ami

[58]The temple servants and the descendants
  of the servants of Solomon   392

2:43-57 These two groups are apparently almost identical. The "temple servants" are the נְתִינִים (nĕthînîm), literally "the given/dedicated ones." The name is derived from Numbers 8:16, "They [the Levites] . . . are to be given wholly to me." They were to assist the Levites (Ezra 8:20). Several temple servant names are non-Israelite. Ziha occurs in the Elephantine Papyri, and Asnah is a well-known Egyptian name. Other questionably Israelite names are Rezin and Sisera. This is not unexpected. Some of them may have been descendants of Gibeonites, whom Joshua made "woodcutters and water carriers . . . for the altar of the LORD . . ." (Josh 9:27). First Chronicles 22:2 records that David brought in "the aliens living in Israel" to prepare them to work on the temple. Foreigners could be incorporated into Israel through Israelite conquest, through the use of mercenary soldiers (2 Sam 15:18-22), and through voluntary immigration. By accepting the covenant obligations they could be incorporated into Israel and receive the blessings of the covenant (Exod 12:48; Num 15:14f.). Numbers 31:25-47 implies that some of the individuals acquired through war could be allocated to temple service under the Levites.

2:58 Servants of Solomon is a puzzling category, and it is unclear what they were supposed to do. The returnees may have been descendants of non-Israelites drafted by Solomon as forced labor for building the temple (1 Kgs 5:13-18). The servants of Solomon are also mentioned in Nehemiah 10:28.

H. THOSE UNABLE TO PROVE ISRAELITE IDENTIFICATION (2:59-63)

[59]The following came up from the towns of Tel Melah, Tel Harsha, Kerub, Addon and Immer, but they could not show that their families were descended from Israel:
[60]The descendants of
Delaiah, Tobiah and Nekoda   652
[61]And from among the priests:
The descendants of
Hobaiah, Hakkoz and Barzillai (a man who had married a daughter of Barzillai the Gileadite and was called by that name).

[62]These searched for their family records, but they could not find them and so were excluded from the priesthood as unclean. [63]The governor ordered them not to eat any of the most sacred food until there was a priest ministering with the Urim and Thummim.

2:59-63 These families could not provide genealogical evidence of their lineage. One group who could not do so were lay people; the other group were priests. The inclusion of this list indicates the importance placed on racial and religious purity of the returnees. As Mervin Breneman has noted, "In addition to emphasizing the continuity of the people of God, Ezra–Nehemiah also stresses the physical as well as spiritual purity of the Jewish community, which was important at this point in history. Later this led to an attitude of spiritual pride (John 8; Rom 9:6). Therefore the New Testament condemns reliance on one's physical ancestry for acceptance with God (e.g., Phil 3:3-8). Often an emphasis that is important at one time may be wrongly emphasized and become a stumbling block at a later time."[19]

Genealogical records were kept in Israel, as referred to in 1 Chronicles 5:17 and Nehemiah 7:5, and these were apparently carried to Babylon by those going into exile. Those who considered themselves eligible to serve as priests (v. 61) were prevented from doing so in order to maintain the purity of the sacred area and the altar and, ultimately, the rebuilt temple. Neither group was excommunicated from the people of Israel, but the concern for authentic Israelite connections was an effort to prevent foreign elements from leading the renewed Israel into apostasy. The questionable priests might be enrolled when there was a (high) priest who could discern the will of God in the matter by means of Urim and Thummim. The sacred casting of lots involved the breastplate worn by the high priest (Exod 28:15-30; Lev 8:8, etc.). The reference here (and in the parallel passage in Neh 7:65) suggests that a high priest and sacred breastplate were lacking when the list was made. Since no further reference is made to Urim and Thummim in the Bible, we are left to wonder if or when these unrecognized priests ever had the opportunity to be proven legitimate.

---

[19]Mervin Breneman, *Ezra, Nehemiah, Esther,* Old Testament Library (London: SCM, 1988), p. 83.

תִּרְשָׁתָא (*tiršāthā'*), translated "the governor" in verse 63, is a
Persian word. It is used again in Nehemiah 7:65,70; 8:9; and 10:1.
No doubt it refers here to Sheshbazzar, as in 5:14 where, however,
the Hebrew word for governor, פֶּחָה (*peḥāh*), is used.

The places from which these people came up, mentioned at the
beginning of this section, were apparently places in Babylonia.
There is no other reference to them, either biblical or nonbiblical.

I. TOTALS (2:64-67)

**[64]The whole company numbered 42,360, [65]besides their
7,337 menservants and maidservants; and they also had 200
men and women singers. [66]They had 736 horses, 245 mules,
[67]435 camels and 6,720 donkeys.**

2:64-67 The total of 42,360 does not agree with the sum of the
separate figures, even though Nehemiah 7:66 and the apocryphal
1 Esdras 5:41 also provide the same total. These three lists, however,
provide three varied sums: Ezra, 29,818; Nehemiah, 31,089; 1 Esdras,
30,143. Various suggestions have been made to alleviate the discrepancy: those not listed but numbered in the total were (1) members of
the northern tribes, (2) children under twelve, (3) women. The latter
is the most likely. Keep in mind, also, the ease of copyist error and
the observation above of the difficulty of reproducing numerical lists.

The large number of singers is unrelated to the levitical temple
singers noted above. These professional singers could be hired to
perform at marriage feasts, funerals, etc. (Neh 7:67 gives the number as 245.)

The large number of servants indicates the relative wealth of
many of the returnees. Wealth is also suggested by the large number
of horses, used by the wealthy, compared to the commoners' use of
donkeys. The wealth of these initial returnees (note also the gifts
mentioned in vv. 68-69) apparently did not last. The prophet
Haggai, two decades later, notes the poverty of the community
(1:6,10-11), possibly due to a series of poor harvests.

J. FREEWILL OFFERINGS (2:68-69)

[68]**When they arrived at the house of the LORD in Jerusalem, some of the heads of the families gave freewill offerings toward the rebuilding of the house of God on its site. [69]According to their ability they gave to the treasury for this work 61,000 drachmas[a] of gold, 5,000 minas[b] of silver and 100 priestly garments.**

[a]*69* That is, about 1,100 pounds (about 500 kilograms)   [b]*69* That is, about 3 tons (about 2.9 metric tons)

2:68-69 Those returning from exile came to the ruins of the house of the LORD. The Persian motivation for the return was the rebuilding of the temple, as indicated in the edict of Cyrus. He encouraged Jews in Babylonia to provide freewill offerings for the project. We are not told how many of them responded or how much they gave. Here, some of the leaders of the returning families contributed freewill offerings for the beginning of the restoration. God has always depended upon the freely given gifts of his people to accomplish his will. (Compare 1 Cor 16:2; 2 Cor 8:3.) The return from exile was like a new exodus, and as those who came out of Egypt gave gladly for the construction of the tabernacle (Exod 25:2-9; 35:21-29), so these of the new exodus did likewise.

The totals in the parallel passage in Nehemiah differ (7:70-72). A.E. Cundall suggests that the differences can be explained: "The Ezra version is a condensed account in which the offerings of the governor, clan chiefs, and the people have been grouped together and a cash estimate of 20,000 gold darics added in lieu of the 50 basins (cf. Neh 7:70). The precise totals for the silver minas and priests' garments in the Nehemiah version are here represented by round figures. One textual emendation is assumed in the harmonization of the two accounts: it is that the unlikely figure of 530 priests' garments of Nehemiah 7:70 should read as 500 silver minas and 30 priests' garments."[20]

Gold drachmas were the equivalent of the Persian daric, 61,000 weighed approximately 1,100 pounds. The mina was of Babylonian

---

[20]A.E. Cundall, "Ezra and Nehemiah," in *The Eerdmans Bible Commentary*, 3rd ed., (Grand Rapids: Eerdmans, 1987), pp. 399-400.

origin, a silver coin. The NIV footnote indicates 5,000 minas was equal to about three tons of silver.

K. SETTLEMENT PATTERN (2:70)

[70]The priests, the Levites, the singers, the gatekeepers and the temple servants settled in their own towns, along with some of the other people, and the rest of the Israelites settled in their towns.

2:70 Clearly some of the religious personnel would have settled in Jerusalem, and in the LXX and in 1 Esdras 5:46 the name of the city appears. Others of the Levites settled in the levitical sites related to their ancestry. Along with them were some of the lay people. Others of the returnees returned to the towns from which their ancestors had been uprooted and carried into exile. This verse resonates with the account in Joshua 11:23 when, after the conquest, the land had rest.

Chapter 2 is long and tedious with its lists, names, and numbers, but it is preparatory for the major event it anticipates — the restoration of the worship of Yahweh and the rebuilding of the temple. As Breneman recognizes, "God had founded Israel as an ethnic as well as a spiritual entity. The renewal of God's plan of redemption depended on the reestablishment of that entity on the land God had given them. It was a great blessing for those who returned to be part of what God was doing. Their jubilation is expressed in Psalm 126:2–'Our mouths were filled with laughter, our tongues with songs of joy.'"[21]

III. REBUILDING THE ALTAR (3:1-6)

A. RESUMPTION OF SACRIFICES (3:1-3)

[1]When the seventh month came and the Israelites had settled in their towns, the people assembled as one man in Jerusalem. [2]Then Jeshua son of Jozadak and his fellow priests and Zerubbabel

---

[21]Breneman, *Ezra, Nehemiah, Esther*, p. 86.

son of Shealtiel and his associates began to build the altar of the God of Israel to sacrifice burnt offerings on it, in accordance with what is written in the Law of Moses the man of God. ³Despite their fear of the peoples around them, they built the altar on its foundation and sacrificed burnt offerings on it to the LORD, both the morning and evening sacrifices.

3:1 Notice that the people are identified as **the Israelites.** The majority were from the tribes of Benjamin and Judah, but in accordance with the perception that they were participating in a second exodus, the restoration was in spirit that of all Israel. With the matter of settlement on the land now accomplished, it was time to turn their attention to the primary, religious reason for their return. **The seventh month** (Tishri/September–October) was most appropriate for them to gather **in Jerusalem.** The Day of Atonement, the Jewish New Year, and the Feast of Tabernacles all occur in this period. Although the year of this assembly is not indicated, we should assume that it was in the first year of the return, likely 538 B.C. That they gathered **as one man** indicates that the same vision and desire for what needed to be done motivated all of them.

3:2 For **Jeshua son of Jozadak,** see above at 2:2a. **Zerubbabel** is also discussed above at 2:2a; however, it is puzzling that Zerubbabel is indicated and not Sheshbazzar, who is specifically mentioned in 1:8,11 as the leader designated by Cyrus. Several explanations have been offered to resolve this: (1) Sheshbazzar and Zerubbabel are the same person; (2) Zerubbabel was a subordinate to Sheshbazzar; (3) Sheshbazzar was the official, government-sponsored leader, and Zerubbabel was the unofficial, popular leader.[22] Another alternative is the possibility that Sheshbazzar died or was incapacitated to the point that he was unable to join the assembly gathered in Jerusalem. Later in Ezra (5:14-16), Sheshbazzar is mentioned again, but as if in the past rather than the present, although he is credited with coming and laying the foundations of the house of God in Jerusalem. Suffice it to say that there are problems with any of these explanations. Sheshbazzar and Zerubbabel may both have been involved in the events reported here, but Zerubbabel fit the purposes of the author because

---

[22]Kidner, *Ezra & Nehemiah*, pp. 139-142.

he was a direct descendant of the Davidic line: Jehoiachin, Shealtiel, Pedaiah, Zerubbabel (1 Chr 3:16-19). Further, although Sheshbazzar is noted for laying the foundations of the temple, the reconstruction was completed under the governorship of Zerubbabel, and he was ultimately the individual recognized for completing the work two decades later (Zech 4:8-9; Ezra 5:2).

The purpose for rebuilding the altar was **to sacrifice burnt offerings on it**. These were the daily offerings. A yearling male lamb, with the appropriate cereal and drink accompaniments, was offered each morning (Lev 6:8-13; Exod 29:38-42; Num 28:3-8). A similar offering was made in the evening. A whole burnt offering signified dedication and commitment, total consecration to God. It is possible that an altar already existed in the demolished temple area. This can be inferred from the incident recorded in Jeremiah 41:5. Even so, such an altar would have been considered defiled and unusable by the returnees, because those who had been using it would have been the people of the land (both the remnant not taken into captivity as well as others). And the assembled congregation were intent on building an altar according to what was written in the Law of Moses. They would have built the altar of field stones rather than stones shaped by human hands (Exod 20:25; Deut 27:6). Building the altar before construction of the temple was also in line with the previous example of David, who had constructed an altar on the threshing floor of Araunah after the king had purchased the hilltop (2 Sam 24:25). The place became the Temple Mount.

This focus on Scripture as authoritative and the only rule for religious practices is commendable and should be followed by every generation. The returnees recognized Moses as **the man of God**, that is, as a divinely inspired prophet. The expression appears numerous times in the Bible in reference to other prophets (Samuel in 1 Sam 9:6; Elijah in 1 Kgs 17:18, and Elisha in 2 Kgs 4:7).

3:3 The reconstructed altar was built by the assembled priests and people on the exact same spot as the altar of David and that of Solomon's temple, **on its foundation**. They were motivated by faith acting in the face of the opposition of **the peoples around them**. The opposition of those living in the region, who had perhaps sacrificed at the old altar, confronted them from the very beginning and continued. As Kidner observes, ". . . these settlers were moved as much by fear as by faith . . . ."[23] The fear would hinder the plans for the immediate construction of the temple, but the altar was built in the face of it so that they could benefit from the protection of Almighty God. His presence was promised in Exodus 29:43: "there also I will meet with the Israelites . . . ." While the continual sacrifices on the Jerusalem altar provided an indirect link between these Jews and the Lord, the atoning sacrifice of Jesus has opened the way for believers to have direct access to God through him (Heb 9:11–10:23).

B. RESUMPTION OF THE RELIGIOUS CALENDAR (3:4-6)

[4]Then in accordance with what is written, they celebrated the Feast of Tabernacles with the required number of burnt offerings prescribed for each day. [5]After that, they presented the regular burnt offerings, the New Moon sacrifices and the sacrifices for all the appointed sacred feasts of the LORD, as well as those brought as freewill offerings to the LORD. [6]On the first day of the seventh month they began to offer burnt offerings to the LORD, though the foundation of the LORD's temple had not yet been laid.

3:4 With the altar established, they proceeded to keep **the Feast of Tabernacles** (Succot) **in accordance with what is written**. The details are provided in Numbers 29:12-38. Tabernacles began on the fifteenth day of the seventh month and lasted seven days, with a closing assembly on the eighth day. Tabernacles recalled God's protection for his people in the wilderness wandering, after the exodus. Now, to those gathered here who had themselves participated in a second exodus (from Babylonia) and who were in special need of God's care, this holy festival must have been particularly meaningful. Some years later, during another Feast of Tabernacles, Ezra would read the Law to the people (Neh 8:14-18).

J.G. McConville has astutely observed: "It is far more difficult to hear the message of fragility of life and the fact of dependence upon God for each succeeding breath amid the settled affluence and long life-expectancy that so many in the modern western world enjoy. Yet

---

[23]Ibid., p. 45.

all our securities are ultimately illusory. Any attempt to peel them away, whether by temporary abstention from some of the good things of life, or whether by deliberate exposure to and sharing of the hard realities experienced by the poor and disadvantaged, can only be salutary."[24]

3:5 Once set into motion by the building of the altar and the keeping of the Feast of Tabernacles, the regular offerings and the appointed feasts were kept in strict adherence to "what is written." Special recognition of the **New Moon** is indicated in Numbers 28:11-15 and 1 Samuel 20:5. Besides the compulsory communal offerings specified in the Law of Moses, voluntary and individual **freewill offerings to the LORD** (וּלְכֹל מִתְנַדֵּב נְדָבָה לַיהוה, *ûlᵉkōl mithnaddēb nᵉdābāh laYHWH*) could be given on any occasion (Num 29:39; Deut 16:10). Something of the faith of an individual is evident in what is not required but is freely given. Tithes are required; only after the tithe is given can a worshiper give above and beyond that as a freewill offering. The individual who loves God and appreciates his blessings will not be miserly.

3:6 The worship of God on the Temple Mount had been reinstituted, even though no temple existed; not even the foundations for the second temple had been laid. Although their forefathers had placed their trust in the sanctuary rather than in the Lord of that sanctuary (Jeremiah 7), these, their descendants, had learned in their land of exile that God's presence and God's worship did not require a building.

IV. REBUILDING THE TEMPLE (3:7-13)

In this section the author seems to imply that the laying of the foundations of the temple of the Lord followed about seven months after the altar was built. However, this seems to conflict with the prophet Haggai's call to Zerubbabel son of Shealtiel and Joshua (Jeshua) son of Jehozadak, the high priest, to rebuild the temple. This occurred in the second year of King Darius, 520 B.C., almost a

---

[24]James G. McConville, *Ezra, Nehemiah, and Esther* (Philadelphia: Westminster, 1985), pp. 20-21.

quarter of a century later than indicated here. The simplest solution to the problem is to acknowledge an initial effort at beginning construction under Sheshbazzar (5:14-16) which was halted by the adversaries. The project then languished for two decades before the prophets Haggai and Zechariah (4:8) spurred renewed construction and completion. Our author may also have telescoped information relating to the construction in the time of Darius to this initial effort. At this point in his narrative, he is interested in communicating to his readers that the community was eager to fulfill the restoration of the worship and facilities of the Solomonic temple.

A. LAYING THE FOUNDATION (3:7-9)

⁷Then they gave money to the masons and carpenters, and gave food and drink and oil to the people of Sidon and Tyre, so that they would bring cedar logs by sea from Lebanon to Joppa, as authorized by Cyrus king of Persia.

⁸In the second month of the second year after their arrival at the house of God in Jerusalem, Zerubbabel son of Shealtiel, Jeshua son of Jozadak and the rest of their brothers (the priests and the Levites and all who had returned from the captivity to Jerusalem) began the work, appointing Levites twenty years of age and older to supervise the building of the house of the LORD. ⁹Jeshua and his sons and brothers and Kadmiel and his sons (descendants of Hodaviahª) and the sons of Henadad and their sons and brothers—all Levites—joined together in supervising those working on the house of God.

ª9 Hebrew *Yehudah*, probably a variant of *Hodaviah*

3:7 Then they gave money . . .

The desire of the devout led them to give money for the building of the sanctuary above and beyond the sacrifices and freewill offerings noted above.

Much here reminds us of the construction of the first temple. The masons were stoneworkers rather than bricklayers, shaping the quarried stones to fit. The carpenters shaped the cedar logs from Lebanon to fit into the alternating construction of three courses of hewn stone

and one course of cedar beams, as did Solomon's workmen (1 Kgs
6:36; 7:12). Solomon also paid the Phoenicians with food (1 Kgs 5:25;
2 Chr 2:9). The cedar logs came from Tyre and Sidon and were float-
ed down the Mediterranean coast to Joppa, to the same place logs for
Solomon were off-loaded (1 Kgs 5:23; 2 Chr 2:15).

as authorized by Cyrus king of Persia
is best understood not in reference to the edict (1:2-4) but to explain
that two different Persian provinces were involved in the acquisition
of the cedar logs, and it had to be approved by the satrap of
"Beyond the River" in the name of the king.[25]

3:8 In the second month . . .
continues the similarity to the construction of the first temple, for
that is when Solomon began building (2 Chr 3:2).

after their arrival at the house of God in Jerusalem,
This must mean the site in Jerusalem on which the destroyed
temple had stood.

Zerubbabel . . . Jeshua . . .
This is the normal order in which these two leaders are listed,
except for 3:2 above. The reversal there probably is due to the construction of the altar, particularly related to the religious leader of
the community.

. . . appointing Levites twenty years of age . . .
According to Mosaic regulation, the Levites could begin their
ministry when twenty-five years old (Num 8:24), but David reduced
that age to twenty, perhaps because the number of Levites available
had diminished (1 Chr 23:24,27). The oversight of Levites would
ensure proper construction as well as the maintenance of ritual purity on the site.

3:9 The leading priestly and levitical families were naturally in
charge of the work. Kadmiel and Hodaviah are listed above in 2:40.
Henadad appears in Nehemiah 10:9.

---

[25]R.N. Frye, *The Heritage of Persia* (London: Weidenfeld and Nicolson,
1962), p. 103.

B. COMMUNAL CELEBRATION (3:10-13)

[10]**When the builders laid the foundation of the temple of the LORD, the priests in their vestments and with trumpets, and the Levites (the sons of Asaph) with cymbals, took their places to praise the LORD, as prescribed by David king of Israel.** [11]**With praise and thanksgiving they sang to the LORD:**

> **"He is good;**
> **his love to Israel endures forever."**

And all the people gave a great shout of praise to the LORD, because the foundation of the house of the LORD was laid. [12]**But many of the older priests and Levites and family heads, who had seen the former temple, wept aloud when they saw the foundation of this temple being laid, while many others shouted for joy.** [13]**No one could distinguish the sound of the shouts of joy from the sound of weeping, because the people made so much noise. And the sound was heard far away.**

3:10-11a Much like the ceremonies of laying a cornerstone, when the [final stone of the] foundation was laid, it was marked with a holy celebration. There is "a time to be silent and a time to speak" (Eccl 3:7), and this was a time to praise the Lord. This they did, with the priests in full regalia, with trumpets sounding. The Levites kept time on the cymbals, and the singers all were orchestrated **as prescribed by David King of Israel**. (David's role in the music of the temple is noted in 1 Chr 16:5 and 25:1.) The NIV does not make clear that the singing was antiphonal; the choir was divided into two sections with one leading and the other responding, as in Psalm 136. Similar expressions of praise and thanksgiving appear at the beginning of Psalms 106 and 136. This praise is in exact fulfillment of the word of the Lord to Jeremiah, that in the streets of Jerusalem, though deserted (in the aftermath of the destruction), will be heard once more:

> "Give thanks to the LORD Almighty,
>   for the LORD is good;
>   his love endures forever" (33:10-11).

3:11b-13 No doubt what all the people shouted was "Hallelu-yah!" This Hebrew phrase is a plural imperative verb, "You (all) praise" followed by the name of the object to be praised, "Yah," an abbreviated form of the personal name of God, Yahweh. To praise is to tell of his goodness, his graciousness, his deeds. They shouted because before their eyes they saw the immediate evidence of his goodness, the foundation finished.

But many . . . wept aloud . . .

What a paradox — weeping in the midst of joyous shouting! Some of the older people had seen Solomon's temple before its destruction. They would have been but youths fifty years earlier. Some of the weeping might have been of joy at seeing the foundations of the temple once more laid. But some wept recalling the glory of that first temple which was gone, existing only in their memories. The noise of weeping and shouting was so intermixed that a listener standing nearby could not distinguish the one from the other. Weeping and joyful shouting are strong expressions of deep human emotions. There are occasions when we need to express our emotions openly, rather than bottling them up within, as we tend to do in our modern, western culture.

The combined voices were so loud that the sound could be heard far away, much like the roar of an excited crowd from a football game today. (We might recall, too, that in ancient Jerusalem there were no distracting sounds of traffic, lawn mowers, aircraft flying overhead and the like.)

V. INITIAL OPPOSITION TO THE REBUILDING (4:1-5)

[1]**When the enemies of Judah and Benjamin heard that the exiles were building a temple for the LORD, the God of Israel,** [2]**they came to Zerubbabel and to the heads of the families and said, "Let us help you build because, like you, we seek your God and have been sacrificing to him since the time of Esarhaddon king of Assyria, who brought us here."**

[3]**But Zerubbabel, Jeshua and the rest of the heads of the families of Israel answered, "You have no part with us in building a temple to our God. We alone will build it for the LORD, the God of Israel, as King Cyrus, the king of Persia, commanded us."**

[4]**Then the peoples around them set out to discourage the peo-**

ple of Judah and make them afraid to go on building.ᵃ ⁵They hired
counselors to work against them and frustrate their plans during
the entire reign of Cyrus king of Persia and down to the reign of
Darius king of Persia.

ᵃ4 Or *and troubled them as they built*

4:1 When the enemies of Judah and Benjamin heard that the exiles were building a temple for the LORD . . .

The author has added a nice literary touch. Remember that in the
original manuscript there was no division into chapters and verses.
What he has done has been to connect the noise of the assembled
congregation (3:13) which could be "heard" far away with the enemies who "heard" that the exiles were building a temple for the Lord.

Despite the fact that numerous commentators identify these unnamed enemies with the Samaritans, it is unlikely that they can be
so identified. Otherwise, our author would have named them. More
likely here the enemies were the "peoples around them," mentioned
above (3:2) in connection with the rebuilding of the altar.

4:2-3 Let us help you build . . .

How sincere was this offer? No one can say with certainty. But as
events unfold through the remainder of Ezra–Nehemiah, it is clear
that this group was intent on hindering the returnees from fulfilling
the edict of Cyrus as well as the plan of God to establish an exclusive community of faith that was committed to him alone. These
adversaries did not desire nor intend to become members of the
restored community. They would remain distinct, with their own
unorthodox religious practices, even though they **seek your God
and have been sacrificing to him**. There is a lesson here for the
church. Even though the gospel invitation is open to all who will
hear and respond in faith, there is no place in the church for those
who reject Jesus as the Messiah, the Son of the Living God, or who
try to combine Christianity with eastern religious ideas, etc.

These potential and then real enemies were mixed groups living
in the land when the first wave of returnees arrived. Some of them
were from the region of Samaria, which had formerly been the
northern kingdom of Israel. The first of these displaced peoples
were settled in that region by the Assyrians under Sargon II sometime after the conquest in 721 B.C. According to 2 Kings 17:24, they

were from Babylon, Cuthah, Avva, Hamath, and Sepharvaim. They became aware of Yahweh through the Israelite priest the Assyrians sent back from his captivity to teach the people "what the god of that country requires" (2 Kgs 17:26). We do not have a biblical record, other than here in Ezra, that Esarhaddon also sent deportees from elsewhere in his realm to Samaria. Historical records from Esarhaddon's reign (681–669 B.C.), however, indicate that he conquered Sidon in one campaign,[26] and a vassal treaty between Baal of Tyre and Esarhaddon that mentions the deportation of people exists.[27] Esarhaddon's Palestinian campaign (ca. 676 B.C.) in which the events in our text could have happened is well documented.[28]

[we] have been sacrificing to him . . . .

They could have been referring to the altar in Jerusalem (see above at 3:2), now replaced by the one rebuilt by the returnees, as the place where they had sacrificed. More likely, the offerings were made "in the shrines of the high places" (2 Kgs 17:32) scattered about the region.

On the Samaritans, recent scholarship has recognized that a difference must be made between the Samarians, inhabitants of Samaria, and the "ancient off-shoot of Judaism" that is the sect of the Samaritans.[29] The roots of Samaritanism are traceable to Ezra 4:1-5 in terms of the beginning of tensions between the north and the south. However, the real break between Jerusalem and Shechem developed in the Maccabean period due to the hostile policies of the Hasmonean house toward the northerners. The climax of those policies was the destruction of the Samaritan temple on Mt. Gerizim by John Hyrcanus in 128 B.C. It had apparently been built shortly after the conquest of the region by Alexander the Great and existed

---

[26]Donald J. Wiseman, "An Esarhaddon Cylinder from Nimrud," *Iraq* 14 (1952): 54-60.

[27]R. Borger, *Die Inschriften Asarhaddons, Königs von Assyrien* (1956), # 69; idem, *Zeitschrift für Assyriologie* 54 (1957): 183ff. Cf. F Charles Fensham, *The Books of Ezra and Nehemiah*, The New International Commentary on the Old Testament (Grand Rapids: Eerdmans, 1982), p. 67.

[28]*ANET*, pp. 290-291.

[29]Reinhard Pummer, "Samaritans," *The Oxford Encyclopedia of Archaeology in the Near East* (New York: Oxford University Press, 1997), 4:469 and bibliography.

for two centuries. In biblical and postbiblical history, political and religious issues were often intertwined. The details of the rift between Jerusalem Jews and Samaritans of Shechem are vague, but in terms of God's providence we can be thankful for the determination of the Jerusalem group of returnees to adhere strictly to the decree of Cyrus, that they and they alone were charged with rebuilding the temple. In the process, they were also responsible for rebuilding the community of the committed. It was this group, rather than the northerners, through whom we received the Hebrew Bible and who paved the way for the redemptive plan of God in Jesus, the Messiah.

4:4 . . . set out to discourage the people of Judah and make them afraid to go on building.

The same Hebrew phrase for "discourage" (יָד רִפָּה, rāphāh yād, lit. "weaken hand") is used of Jeremiah, who was telling all who would listen that Jerusalem would be captured by the king of Babylon (38:4). The peoples around them were continually discouraging their efforts. The nagging of naysayers can grind efforts to a halt. It is unclear what these discouragers did to make the builders afraid to continue, but a significant explanation is given in the following verse.

4:5 They hired counselors . . . .

These counselors were likely local or regional Persian officials of the province. Clearly they were open to bribes and accommodated those from whom they took money. What is unclear is how they worked against the rebuilders and frustrated their plans. Perhaps it was by sending false reports to the central government. These devious and detrimental activities continued during the reigns of Cyrus and Cambyses (ca. 539–522 B.C.). Darius succeeded Cambyses but his throne was secured against competitors and revolts only in 520. Apparently in the aftermath of Darius's rise to rule, the opposition to the rebuilding waned. But the work had languished for some sixteen years. Besides this organized and persistent opposition, "the excuse to postpone something as expensive and burdensome as building the house of God was rather tempting," as Kidner observes.[30] This is true especially if individuals focus on their own "paneled houses" (Hag 1:2-3).

---

[30]Kidner, *Ezra & Nehemiah*, p. 50.

VI. EXAMPLES OF LATER OPPOSITION (4:6-23)

This segment of Ezra is not in historical sequence with the flow of the narrative. It is an insertion between the mention of Darius in verse 5 and the continuation when Darius is named again in verse 24. The author's purpose is clear enough. It is to provide the reader with an example of the persistent opposition that began early (vv. 4-5) and continued long (this letter dates to the reign of Xerxes, 486 B.C.). It was still in process twenty years into Xerxes' reign, when Nehemiah came to Jerusalem.

A. UNDER XERXES (4:6)

⁶**At the beginning of the reign of Xerxes,ᵃ they lodged an accusation against the people of Judah and Jerusalem.**

ᵃ**6 Hebrew *Ahasuerus*, a variant of Xerxes' Persian name**

4:6 "Xerxes" is the Greek equivalent of the Hebrew, אֲחַשְׁוֵרוֹשׁ (*'ăhašw°rôš*). He was the son and successor of Darius, taking the throne in 486 B.C. His name occurs frequently in the Book of Esther. We know nothing of the impact of the complaint lodged against the people of Yehud in his time. What is significant is that the troublemakers were at work.

B. LETTERS TO ARTAXERXES (4:7-16)

⁷**And in the days of Artaxerxes king of Persia, Bishlam, Mithredath, Tabeel and the rest of his associates wrote a letter to Artaxerxes. The letter was written in Aramaic script and in the Aramaic language.ᵃ,ᵇ**

⁸**Rehum the commanding officer and Shimshai the secretary wrote a letter against Jerusalem to Artaxerxes the king as follows:**

⁹**Rehum the commanding officer and Shimshai the secretary, together with the rest of their associates—the judges and officials over the men from Tripolis, Persia,ᶜ Erech and Babylon, the Elamites of Susa, ¹⁰and the other people whom the great**

and honorable Ashurbanipal[d] deported and settled in the city of Samaria and elsewhere in Trans-Euphrates.

[11](This is a copy of the letter they sent him.)

To King Artaxerxes,

From your servants, the men of Trans-Euphrates:

[12]The king should know that the Jews who came up to us from you have gone to Jerusalem and are rebuilding that rebellious and wicked city. They are restoring the walls and repairing the foundations.

[13]Furthermore, the king should know that if this city is built and its walls are restored, no more taxes, tribute or duty will be paid, and the royal revenues will suffer. [14]Now since we are under obligation to the palace and it is not proper for us to see the king dishonored, we are sending this message to inform the king, [15]so that a search may be made in the archives of your predecessors. In these records you will find that this city is a rebellious city, troublesome to kings and provinces, a place of rebellion from ancient times. That is why this city was destroyed. [16]We inform the king that if this city is built and its walls are restored, you will be left with nothing in Trans-Euphrates.

[a]7 Or *written in Aramaic and translated*   [b]7 The text of Ezra 4:8–6:18 is in Aramaic.   [c]9 Or *officials, magistrates and governors over the men from*   [d]10 Aramaic *Osnappar*, a variant of *Ashurbanipal*

4:7 Artaxerxes, also known as Longimanus, succeeded Xerxes and ruled from 465–425 B.C. The agitators — **Bishlam, Mithredath, Tabeel**, etc. — lodged a complaint by means of a letter directly to the king. We do not have the content of the letter, but this is a second example of the persistent opposition of the adversaries. "Bishlam" is rendered "in peace" in the LXX. The Hebrew consonants allow that; however, it is more likely a personal name, as here in the NIV. A different Mithredath is mentioned in 1:8. The name is Persian, derived from "Mithras," the Persian sun god. He was likely a Persian official assigned to this locality. Tabeel, meaning, "God is good," is Aramaic. A different individual with that name is found in Isaiah 7:6.

written in the Aramaic script and in the Aramaic language

This was the diplomatic writing system and language in use in the Persian empire. Further, the author of Ezra–Nehemiah has been writing in the Hebrew language, probably written in the old, Phoenician-type alphabet. Now he alerts his readers to the change in language. The text of Ezra 4:8–6:18 is in Aramaic.

4:8 The author of Ezra–Nehemiah here notes that a subsequent letter was written to **Artaxerxes**; this time **Rehum** and **Shimshai** composed it. The author provides the full letter this time to his readers. Both Rehum and Shimshai are good Semitic names. Rehum was a government official, but not the governor. The Persian central administration was careful to keep an independent check on local leaders whom they had placed in positions of authority. They did this by appointing "watchdogs" who were directly responsible to the king. Rehum may have been such an appointee. Royal agents also annually inspected each satrapy.

The main point here is that the letter was **against Jerusalem**, thus a continuation of the pattern of accusations our author is bringing to the attention of his readers.

4:9-10 These two verses serve as an introductory docket to the actual letter, identifying the senders. It may well have been inscribed on the exterior of the papyrus or leather upon which the letter would have been written. We are informed that Rehum and Shimshai were writing on behalf of a contingent of leading citizens and officials. All of them came from families that had been longtime residents. (They were not newcomers like the inhabitants of Jerusalem!) They had been displaced from their countries of origin by Ashurbanipal (669–627 B.C.). The name in the text is **Osnappar**, the Aramaic form of Ashurbanipal, the last great king of Assyria. No extrabiblical records survive of this deportation to the Trans-Euphrates region, including Samaria.

4:11 The author of Ezra–Nehemiah here informs his readers that he has before him as he writes a copy of the letter which follows. The word for "letter" here and in verse 8, Aramaic אִגְּרָה (*'iggerah*), differs from the Hebrew נִשְׁתְּוָן (*ništ°wān*) used in verse 7. An *'iggerah* denotes an official communication.

4:12 . . . the Jews who came up . . .

These are not those who returned under Cyrus, although this group no doubt joined those earlier returnees. This group came during the reign of this same Artaxerxes, probably with Ezra. They are charged with rebuilding the city, not the temple.[31] Specifically, they were restoring the walls and repairing the foundations. This was a defensive measure for the security and protection of the inhabitants of Jerusalem against their adversaries. These same adversaries, however, depict the construction as aggressive, inclining toward rebellion. Since rebellions were a frequent problem in the Persian Empire in the fifth century, these canny politicians were exploiting the wariness of the king.

4:13 . . . no more taxes, tribute or duty will be paid . . .

Apart from outright rebellion, the next major concern of the empire was the potential for the loss of revenue. Three different forms of taxation are indicated here. Babylonian parallels of the terms used suggest that the first was a direct payment made by the provinces to the royal treasury. The second represented duty charged on merchandise, produce, etc., probably with payment in kind. This would have been a type of sales tax. The third was a tax on travelers and merchants, a type of toll.

4:14 since we are under obligation . . .

A more literal translation is, "since we eat the salt of the palace," that is, receive a salary from the royal treasury. Our word "salary" is derived from the Latin *salarium*, "salt money." The letter writers are touting their personal and political loyalty to Artaxerxes, in contrast to the implied disloyalty of the Jews.

4:15 . . . so that a search may be made . . .

They also suggest that their accusations about Jerusalem as a rebellious and wicked city be confirmed by a search of the historical records. The Persians saw themselves as rightful successors of the previous Assyrian and Chaldean empires. Their archives would have contained records of the rebellions encountered by their predecessors, including the destruction of Jerusalem by Nebuchadnezzar.

---

[31]The temple had been rebuilt a half a century earlier. The readers are brought back to the account of that reconstruction in chapters 5–6.

4:16 . . . you will be left with nothing in Trans-Euphrates.

This statement draws the worst-case scenario for the king, and it flies in the face of reality. The thought that the impoverished community of Jerusalem could, by rebuilding the city walls, start a revolutionary movement that would sweep the entire province of Trans-Euphrates from the king's control is an absurd exaggeration.

C. THE RESPONSE OF ARTAXERXES (4:17-23)

[17]The king sent this reply:

To Rehum the commanding officer, Shimshai the secretary and the rest of their associates living in Samaria and elsewhere in Trans-Euphrates:

Greetings.

[18]The letter you sent us has been read and translated in my presence. [19]I issued an order and a search was made, and it was found that this city has a long history of revolt against kings and has been a place of rebellion and sedition. [20]Jerusalem has had powerful kings ruling over the whole of Trans-Euphrates, and taxes, tribute and duty were paid to them. [21]Now issue an order to these men to stop work, so that this city will not be rebuilt until I so order. [22]Be careful not to neglect this matter. Why let this threat grow, to the detriment of the royal interests?

[23]As soon as the copy of the letter of King Artaxerxes was read to Rehum and Shimshai the secretary and their associates, they went immediately to the Jews in Jerusalem and compelled them by force to stop.

4:17 The king sent this reply

The author of Ezra–Nehemiah also had before him a copy of Artaxerxes' reply, as he here notes.

To Rehum . . .

This brief note was likely a docket written on the exterior of the letter, as discussed in verses 9-10.

Greetings

šᵊlām, "peace," the equivalent of Hebrew "Shalom."

4:18 . . . read and translated . . .

It was normal and more dignified for a document to be read to the king. Since the letter had been written in Aramaic, it was translated into Persian for the king's benefit and understanding.

4:19-20 . . . search was made, and it was found . . .

The archives produced information about the history of Jerusalem's rulers and rebellions against previous empires.

4:21-22 . . . issue an order . . .

The king allowed the provincial officials to issue a temporary stop-work order. There is no record that the rebuilding of the walls had previously received royal authorization, so he was no doubt suspicious. However, he left open the possibility of resumption of rebuilding in the future, upon his order. A further review of the situation was possible, and by the grace of God it was to come through Nehemiah (2:8-10).

4:23 As soon as the copy of the letter of King Artaxerxes was read . . .

The letter was possibly read to them by the messenger. We can assume that Rehum, and certainly the scribe Shimshai, could read.

compelled them by force to stop.

With royal authorization, the adversaries forced the Jews to stop construction. Apparently they brought along a squad of soldiers to enforce their commands. They may have done more than issue the order to cease construction. Nehemiah 1:3 can be interpreted to mean that this beginning construction had been destroyed.

VII. TEMPLE CONSTRUCTION COMPLETED (4:24–6:22)

A. AUTHOR'S TRANSITIONAL STATEMENT (4:24)

²⁴**Thus the work on the house of God in Jerusalem came to a standstill until the second year of the reign of Darius king of Persia.**

4:24 Thus the work on the house of God . . .

The parenthetical insertion ended with verse 23. As noted above, the author now returns to the subject of rebuilding the temple from which he had digressed after verse 5. He does this by mentioning again the reign of Darius king of Persia.

B. PROPHETIC PROVOCATION —
CONSTRUCTION RESUMED (5:1-2)

¹Now Haggai the prophet and Zechariah the prophet, a descendant of Iddo, prophesied to the Jews in Judah and Jerusalem in the name of the God of Israel, who was over them. ²Then Zerubbabel son of Shealtiel and Jeshua son of Jozadak set to work to rebuild the house of God in Jerusalem. And the prophets of God were with them, helping them.

5:1 Now Haggai the prophet and Zechariah the prophet . . . .

The word of the Lord came to Haggai "in the second year of King Darius, on the first day of the sixth month" (Hag 1:1). This was Darius Hystaspes. The year was 520 B.C. Haggai came to Zerubbabel and Jeshua on the first day of the month, sometime in our August.[32] His forceful preaching was so effective that the languishing work resumed three weeks later. The Lord was not content to simply stir the people to action by the prophet. Three months later words of encouragement came for both people and leaders (2:10-23). Zechariah was moved by the Lord to join the prophetic effort two months after the work was renewed.

We know nothing of Haggai apart from references to him here, in 6:14, and in the Book of Haggai. No lineage is given for him; he is simply identified as the prophet both here and in Haggai 1:1. Zechariah is identified as **a descendant of Iddo** here. In Zechariah 1:1 he is called "son of Berekiah, the son of Iddo." He may have been from a priestly family; a priest named Iddo is mentioned in Nehemiah 12:4 and 16. The Zechariah mentioned in Nehemiah 12:16 may have been a descendant of the prophet. Alternatively, his

---

[32]The Jews adopted the Babylonian month names in captivity; the sixth month was named Elul (cf. *ABD*, I:816).

lineage may reach back to the pre-exilic prophet Iddo, whose "annotations" are mentioned twice in 2 Chronicles 12:15 and 13:22.

5:2 Nothing of the content of the prophecies is given here in Ezra, but that they were effective is made clear. **Zerubbabel** and **Jeshua** initiated the rebuilding effort in response to the prophets and with their help. Likely the encouraging messages of the prophets are intended here, rather than actual construction labor. Jeshua is identified as the high priest in Zechariah 3:1 and Haggai 1:1.

The stimulus of the prophetic word and the energetic response of the leaders of the community are a powerful example of what God's people can accomplish when challenged. "Where there is no vision, the people perish . . ." (Prov 29:18, KJV). But clear divine guidance powerfully proclaimed will move God's people to action and accomplishment, to his honor and glory.

C. INVESTIGATION BY TATTENAI (5:3-4)

³**At that time Tattenai, governor of Trans-Euphrates, and Shethar-Bozenai and their associates went to them and asked, "Who authorized you to rebuild this temple and restore this structure?" ⁴They also asked, "What are the names of the men constructing this building?"**ᵃ

ᵃ*4 See Septuagint; Aramaic ⁴We told them the names of the men constructing this building.*

5:3-4 . . . Tattenai, governor of Trans-Euphrates . . .

The name is of unknown origin. It is known that Tattenai served as governor of the western part of a satrapy that included Babylon and Trans-Euphrates. He served under Ushtannu, who was responsible for the entire governmental unit. The word signifying governor, (חָהֶפ, *peḥāh*) has broad connotations. Zerubbabel is called the governor of Judah (Hag 1:1), a very small region. Tattenai probably governed from Damascus, a place more central to the large area he administered. With him on this trip to Jerusalem to investigate reports of major construction were Shethar-Bozenai (perhaps his scribe) and other unnamed associates.

[they] asked . . . .

This verb is in the plural, indicating that all the members of the party were involved in the inquiry. Unlike the antagonistic attitude of the adversaries noted earlier, these Persian officials were simply pursuing a normal legal inquiry. They sought the answer to two questions: Who authorized you (all) to build this temple? and What are the names of the men constructing it?[33] We can assume that both questions were answered to the best of their ability and to the satisfaction of the official inquirers. However, a copy of the Cyrus edict was apparently not available, and Tattenai knew nothing of it prior to this visit.

D. REFLECTION OF THE AUTHOR (5:5)

[5]But the eye of their God was watching over the elders of the Jews, and they were not stopped until a report could go to Darius and his written reply be received.

This is a theological reflection on the positive outcome of Tattenai's visit.

5:5 But the eye of their God . . . .

The expression occurs also in Deuteronomy 11:12 and Psalm 33:18. The watch-care of the Lord was at work in favor of the leaders of the construction. Tattenai and his associates allowed the work to continue while he contacted the Persian court before making a final decision on the matter. Estimates are that the process would take four or five months. During that time construction could continue.

The persistence of the builders is indicated here. It was possible that King Darius would rule against them. Then all of their work in the interim would be for naught. But they trusted in God to resolve the problem according to his will. No doubt the words of Haggai and Zechariah strengthened them.

---

[33]As the NIV footnote indicates, the translation is from the LXX. The Aramaic reads "We told them the names of the men constructing this building." Williamson suggests that this request may have (continued) occasioned the drawing up of the list of names in Ezra 2.

E. THE LETTER TO DARIUS (5:6-17)

⁶This is a copy of the letter that Tattenai, governor of Trans-Euphrates, and Shethar-Bozenai and their associates, the officials of Trans-Euphrates, sent to King Darius. ⁷The report they sent him read as follows:

To King Darius:

Cordial greetings.

⁸The king should know that we went to the district of Judah, to the temple of the great God. The people are building it with large stones and placing the timbers in the walls. The work is being carried on with diligence and is making rapid progress under their direction.

⁹We questioned the elders and asked them, "Who authorized you to rebuild this temple and restore this structure?" ¹⁰We also asked them their names, so that we could write down the names of their leaders for your information.

¹¹This is the answer they gave us:

"We are the servants of the God of heaven and earth, and we are rebuilding the temple that was built many years ago, one that a great king of Israel built and finished. ¹²But because our fathers angered the God of heaven, he handed them over to Nebuchadnezzar the Chaldean, king of Babylon, who destroyed this temple and deported the people to Babylon.

¹³"However, in the first year of Cyrus king of Babylon, King Cyrus issued a decree to rebuild this house of God. ¹⁴He even removed from the temple[a] of Babylon the gold and silver articles of the house of God, which Nebuchadnezzar had taken from the temple in Jerusalem and brought to the temple[a] in Babylon.

"Then King Cyrus gave them to a man named Sheshbazzar, whom he had appointed governor, ¹⁵and he told him, 'Take these articles and go and deposit them in the temple in Jerusalem. And rebuild the house of God on its site.' ¹⁶So this Sheshbazzar came and laid the foundations of the house of God in Jerusalem. From that day to the present it has been under construction but is not yet finished."

[17]Now if it pleases the king, let a search be made in the royal archives of Babylon to see if King Cyrus did in fact issue a decree to rebuild this house of God in Jerusalem. Then let the king send us his decision in this matter.

ᵃ*14* Or palace

5:6-7a The author here summarizes the docket that would have been the address of the letter. The word translated **associates** is left untranslated by the KJV (and ASV). "Apharsachites" (אֲפַרְסְכָיֵא, *'ăphars°kayē'*) is taken as an ethnic group by its translators.

5:8 . . . the temple of the great God. . . .
Some commentators question that this letter is genuine. They doubt that Persian officials would speak of the deity of the Jews in these terms. The expression "the great God," however, is attested in the nonbiblical Persian fortification tablets, as noted by Williamson.[34]

large stones and . . . timbers . . . .
The first temple was also built of three courses of stone and one of timbers (1 Kgs 6:36; 7:12). The excavators have identified similar construction at the high place at Tel Dan,[35] and comparable construction has been documented across the ancient Near East in most historical periods. Ancient engineers may have developed the technique to counter earthquake forces, since destructive earthquakes are common in that region.

The description of the stones as **large** does not do full credit to the original, גְּלָל (*g°lāl*). These were ashlars, shaped stones. Examples of huge ashlars from the rebuilding of the Second Temple by Herod the Great may still be seen in the western wall of the Temple Mount.

with diligence and is making rapid progress . . . .
This testimony from a disinterested observer is an affirmation of the energy and effort the Jewish community was investing in the project.

5:9 We questioned the elders . . .
Tattenai and Shethar-Bozenai were fulfilling their administrative

---

[34]Williamson, *Ezra, Nehemiah*, p. 78.
[35]Avraham Biran, *Biblical Dan* (Jerusalem: Israel Exploration Society, 1994), p. 184.

responsibilities by questioning the elders. A monumental building was undergoing reconstruction. This was the type of construction normally carried out by royal edict and with resources of a monarch, so the significant question was, **Who authorized you to rebuild . . . and restore . . . ?** The construction of a temple or palatial structure without royal permission could signal an action against the interests of the throne, so this was a serious matter. The courteous, straightforward answer follows in verses 11-16. Their response no doubt contributed to Tattenai's positive tone in his report to King Darius.

5:10 We also asked them their names, . . .

The names are not included in the report for reasons we can only surmise. No doubt they were on record in the governor's archives, if requested later by the royal court.

5:11 This is the answer they gave us:

The answer does not provide the names requested in the preceding verse. The list may have been provided on a separate document. Or our author may have abbreviated the letter, to avoid repetition of the names listed in chapter 2.

We are servants of the God of heaven and earth, . . .

The builders identified themselves in relation to the deity for whom they were constructing a temple. Ahuramazda, the Persian god, was also known as "god of the heaven" and "creator of heaven and earth."

But it is not likely this title was used by the Jews to curry favor with the Persians. The identification did, however, underline that their God was worthy of the temple they were rebuilding. A brief history of the flow of events requiring the reconstruction follows. The king who built the temple Nebuchadnezzar had destroyed is not named. The name Solomon would have meant nothing to the Persians.

5:12 But because our fathers angered the God of heaven, . . .

This is clear testimony to the effectiveness of the exile. The prophets and leaders of those in exile had been used by God to convict his people of sin, righteousness, and judgment (see John 16:8). They had also instilled hope in the restoration in which these builders were involved.

5:13-14a . . . King Cyrus issued a decree . . .

This is the answer to the question Tattenai and his associates had asked the elders: Who authorized you to rebuild this temple? Cyrus is identified as "king of Babylon." This was appropriate in recalling the decree issued from Babylon in his first year, and in an extrabiblical record Cyrus used the title of himself.[36] The copy of the decree in 1:2-4 uses the title, "Cyrus King of Persia." That copy was likely the one found in the Ecbatana archives in the search prompted by this letter.

5:14b-16 . . . Sheshbazzar . . .

Although no mention is made here of Zerubbabel, the current governor, Sheshbazzar is identified as the first governor, the one under whom the rebuilding of the temple began. His appointment by Cyrus and the charge given to him were important connections with the current effort. That the construction had been ongoing **from that day to the present**, however, is an exaggeration. The construction of the altar was a beginning, and the intent may always have lain there latent, but actual construction languished until Haggai and Zechariah spurred a renewed effort. Perhaps the Jewish leaders were making the point that the decree of Cyrus had not been simply ignored despite the passage of time.

5:17 Tattenai and his associates have now completed the report. Their request of King Darius here concludes the letter. The expression, **if it pleases the king**, is the normal protocol for letters of request in the Persian period. A number of examples are known in the Elephantine Papyri. He asks that a search be made for the edict of Cyrus **in the royal archives of Babylon**. That was the logical place to search for the document, since it was from Babylon that Cyrus' decree was issued. Whether it could be found or not, Tattenai would await the decision of Darius on the matter.

---

[36]See the Cyrus Cylinder, *ANET*, p. 316.

F. THE DECREE OF DARIUS (6:1-12)

1. Discovery of Cyrus' Decree (6:1-5)

¹**King Darius then issued an order, and they searched in the archives stored in the treasury at Babylon. ²A scroll was found in the citadel of Ecbatana in the province of Media, and this was written on it:**

Memorandum:

³**In the first year of King Cyrus, the king issued a decree concerning the temple of God in Jerusalem:**

Let the temple be rebuilt as a place to present sacrifices, and let its foundations be laid. It is to be ninety feet[a] high and ninety feet wide, ⁴with three courses of large stones and one of timbers. The costs are to be paid by the royal treasury. ⁵Also, the gold and silver articles of the house of God, which Nebuchadnezzar took from the temple in Jerusalem and brought to Babylon, are to be returned to their places in the temple in Jerusalem; they are to be deposited in the house of God.

ᵃ3 Aramaic *sixty cubits* (about 27 meters)

6:1 . . . archives stored in the treasury . . .

The stored cuneiform tablets and scrolls were literary treasures, historical records from the early days of the Persian Empire. At Persepolis, rooms related to the treasury were also used as archives.

6:2 . . . Ecbatana . . .

The rather abrupt literary shift to this Persian capital, far removed from Babylon, indicates that we have an abbreviated form of a longer document. It is now known that Cyrus spent the summer of 538 B.C. in Ecbatana (where the climate is more comfortable in that season).[37] The name was changed to Hamadan after the Muslim conquest.

6:3-5 This is not a word-for-word repetition of the decree; it is a memorandum about the edict. It may have been a longer document, but what was drawn from the memorandum bore directly on the

---

[37]E.J. Bickerman, "The Edict of Cyrus in Ezra 1," *JBL* 65 (1946), 251 (after Kidner, *Ezra & Nehemiah*, p. 56).

concerns expressed in Tattenai's letter. Yes, Cyrus had issued a decree permitting the rebuilding of the Jerusalem temple. The specifications of dimensions, materials to be used, purpose, and financing are defined.

Clearly a scribal error has occurred in verse 4 in terms of the height and the omission of the length. Following Williamson's reconstruction, read, "Its height shall be thirty cubits [45 feet], its length sixty cubits [90 feet] and its width twenty cubits [30 feet] . . . ."[38] Thus the dimensions and details of construction exactly replicate those of the first temple. This is in agreement with Tattenai's observation that they were **restoring** the structure (5:9).

Cyrus could only have known these specifics by conferring with Jews in Babylon. Not directly revealed in the copy of the decree in 1:2-4 is that the costs are to be paid by the royal treasury. However, it is implied within the statement, ". . . he has appointed me to build a temple for him . . . ." Textual and archaeological evidence indicate that the use of royal funds for repairs and restitution of temples was not unique to the reconstruction of the Jerusalem temple. By such benevolent works the Persian rulers sought the goodwill and blessings of the respective deities. The memorandum also notes that the temple vessels are to be returned to Jerusalem and replaced in the temple.

2. Reply of Darius to Tattenai (6:6-12)

[6]**Now then, Tattenai, governor of Trans-Euphrates, and Shethar-Bozenai and you, their fellow officials of that province, stay away from there. [7]Do not interfere with the work on this temple of God. Let the governor of the Jews and the Jewish elders rebuild this house of God on its site.**

[8]**Moreover, I hereby decree what you are to do for these elders of the Jews in the construction of this house of God:**

The expenses of these men are to be fully paid out of the royal treasury, from the revenues of Trans-Euphrates, so that the work will not stop. [9]Whatever is needed—young bulls, rams, male lambs for burnt offerings to the God of heaven,

---

[38]Williamson, *Ezra, Nehemiah*, p. 71. See also NIV 1 Kgs 6:2, fn.

and wheat, salt, wine and oil, as requested by the priests in Jerusalem—must be given them daily without fail, [10]so that they may offer sacrifices pleasing to the God of heaven and pray for the well-being of the king and his sons.

[11]Furthermore, I decree that if anyone changes this edict, a beam is to be pulled from his house and he is to be lifted up and impaled on it. And for this crime his house is to be made a pile of rubble. [12]May God, who has caused his Name to dwell there, overthrow any king or people who lifts a hand to change this decree or to destroy this temple in Jerusalem.

I Darius have decreed it. Let it be carried out with diligence.

6:6-7 . . . stay away from there

is an order not to interfere with those carrying on the rebuilding. Darius desires to fully implement the decree of Cyrus without interference. Nevertheless, some contact between Tattenai and the Jewish leaders would be expected and understandable, since the transfer of funds from the revenues of Trans-Euphrates to Jerusalem would be necessary. In fact, daily contact is ordered below. But the Persian officials were not to impede the work.

6:8-10 . . . I hereby decree what you are to do for these elders of the Jews . . .

Darius's orders are both negative and positive. His underlings are not to interfere with the work; to the contrary, they are to assist the project leaders. The assistance is **so that the work will not stop**. Besides the payment of expenses, whatever is needed for the cultic rituals must be provided day in and day out. The king's purposes are both to honor the God of heaven and to seek his favor and blessing on the royal house. To these ends, sacrifices and prayers were to be offered. That the king was aware of the specific requirements of the temple ritual suggests that he had knowledgeable Jewish counselors in his court advising him. The wheat, salt, wine, and oil are all specified in Leviticus 2:1,13,15 and 23:13.

6:11-12 Furthermore, . . .

Darius follows the normal pattern of royal decrees, stipulating the penalties that can befall anyone who modifies the content of the document so as to contravene the command of the king. The penalty for modifying the edict is severe. Impalement on a sharpened pole was an excruciatingly painful and deadly form of punishment. It was practiced by the Assyrians as portrayed in the reliefs depicting their conquest of Lachish in the time of King Hezekiah. These were recovered from Sennacherib's palace in Nineveh by Austen Henry Layard in the mid-1800s. This method of punishment was apparently taken over by the Persians.

The phrase . . . **God, who has caused his name to dwell there** recalls Deuteronomy 12:5 and is another hint that a Jewish scribe helped the king to draw up the decree.

A certain poetic justice is threatened by Darius. Anyone who will interfere in the rebuilding of God's house will have his own house destroyed.

G. COMPLETION AND DEDICATION OF THE TEMPLE
(6:13-18)

1. Work on the Temple Completed (6:13-15)

[13]**Then, because of the decree King Darius had sent, Tattenai, governor of Trans-Euphrates, and Shethar-Bozenai and their associates carried it out with diligence. [14]So the elders of the Jews continued to build and prosper under the preaching of Haggai the prophet and Zechariah, a descendant of Iddo. They finished building the temple according to the command of the God of Israel and the decrees of Cyrus, Darius and Artaxerxes, kings of Persia. [15]The temple was completed on the third day of the month Adar, in the sixth year of the reign of King Darius.**

6:13-15 Tattenai and his associates had asked Darius for his decision. Having received it, they did not hesitate to carry out the specific requirements of the decree. The combination of the ongoing work of the builders while awaiting the decision from Persia, the benefits of Darius's decree, and the continued encouragement of Haggai and Zechariah brought the project to completion on the third of Adar (March/April), 515 B.C.

Skeptics may argue that the prophecies of Haggai date to 519

B.C. and Zechariah's to no later than 518 B.C. How, then, could they have encouraged the completion of the work some four years later? Clearly, we do not have all that these prophets may have spoken. What was collected and recorded of their prophecies, however, is sufficient to inform us of their part in the plan of God for the reestablishment of the Jerusalem temple. All Scripture is sufficient — inspired and useful for teaching (2 Tim 3:16).

Mention of Artaxerxes is puzzling since his rule postdates the completion of the temple and is related to the repair of the city's walls. However, our author has mentioned him previously, as noted above (4:7-8). One explanation is that it is a later addition at the hands of a copyist. A better reason is that he was to be instrumental later in the reconstruction of the city walls, a part of which connected to the temple. Our author is using all three kings involved in the restoration as illustrations of how even mighty kings are tools to accomplish **the command of the God of Israel**.

2. The Second Temple Dedicated (6:16-18)

¹⁶**Then the people of Israel—the priests, the Levites and the rest of the exiles—celebrated the dedication of the house of God with joy. ¹⁷For the dedication of this house of God they offered a hundred bulls, two hundred rams, four hundred male lambs and, as a sin offering for all Israel, twelve male goats, one for each of the tribes of Israel. ¹⁸And they installed the priests in their divisions and the Levites in their groups for the service of God at Jerusalem, according to what is written in the Book of Moses.**

6:16 Then the people of Israel—

Although all of the priests and Levites and most of the rest of the participants in the dedication were Judeans, the event is seen as involving all Israel. The offerings are for all Israel, including the twelve goats for the twelve tribes. A similar number had been offered when the altar in the wilderness was dedicated (Num 7:87).

6:17 . . . dedication . . .

The Hebrew חֲנֻכָּה (ḥănukkah) is the same as the festival name, Hanukkah, instituted in 165 B.C., after the rededication of the temple following its cleansing after being profaned by Antiochus Epiphanes. That later festival is still celebrated by Jews. No annual observance of the dedication of the second temple was established, but the actual event was marked with joy. The project had been completed despite delays and opposition. What elation follows the attainment of a worthy goal after enduring the struggle to reach it!

6:18 It had been approximately seventy years since the Solomonic temple had been destroyed. With the rebuilt temple, the articles that belonged in it were now able to be used again, and with the priestly and levitical officiants reinstalled **according to what is written in the Book of Moses**, the daily ritual was reestablished.

H. THE FIRST PASSOVER CELEBRATED
IN THE SECOND TEMPLE (6:19-22)

[19]On the fourteenth day of the first month, the exiles celebrated the Passover. [20]The priests and Levites had purified themselves and were all ceremonially clean. The Levites slaughtered the Passover lamb for all the exiles, for their brothers the priests and for themselves. [21]So the Israelites who had returned from the exile ate it, together with all who had separated themselves from the unclean practices of their Gentile neighbors in order to seek the LORD, the God of Israel. [22]For seven days they celebrated with joy the Feast of Unleavened Bread, because the LORD had filled them with joy by changing the attitude of the king of Assyria, so that he assisted them in the work on the house of God, the God of Israel.

6:19-20 (The author changes from Aramaic back to the Hebrew language here.) Shortly after the dedication of the restored temple, the first Passover on its premises was celebrated. The date was that specified in Exodus 12:6, approximately April 21, 515 B.C. Rabbi Slotki has noted that "Whenever the celebration of this feast is recorded in the Bible, it is in connection with an important landmark in the national life (cf. Num. ix.5; Josh. v.10; 2 Kings xxiii.21; 2 Chron. xxx.1ff, xxxv.1ff)."[39]

---

[39]Slotki, *Daniel-Ezra-Nehemiah*, p. 148.

6:21 . . . together with all who had separated themselves . . .

Kidner has pointed to the significance of this verse, which is "crucial for correcting the impression . . . of a bitterly exclusive party. . . . in reality we find that only the self-excluded were unwelcome. The convert found an open door, as Rahab and Ruth had done."[40] "You will seek me and find me when you seek me with all your heart," said the Lord in Jeremiah 29:13.

6:22 . . . Feast of Unleavened Bread . . .

The direct connection between the Passover and this feast is established in Exodus 12:14-20. The Passover was a reminder of how God had saved the firstborn of his people from the power of the death angel in Egypt. The seven-day Feast of Unleavened Bread was directly connected to that event. It was a celebration of the exodus from Egypt that followed immediately after the Passover night. Always joyous, this celebration was particularly so because of God's behind-the-scenes work on their behalf in changing the attitude of the Persian royal house.

. . . the king of Assyria . . .

This reference to the ruler of an empire long departed, succeeded by the Babylonians and then the Persians, is perplexing. One explanation could be scribal error; however, it was in the text from which the LXX was translated. More likely, the author intended to use the expression to recall the beginning of oppression in pre-exilic days that had undergone a dramatic change in the attitude of the contemporary monarch who ruled the region once conquered by the Assyrians (see Neh 9:32).

Implicit in the closing statement of this first part of Ezra is the fact that the God of Israel is in control to accomplish his will and purposes. His people are called to faithfulness to his worship and service even though they are subject to the political control of others. Revolution is not required in order to remain faithful to the God of heaven and of Israel.

The author of Ezra–Nehemiah now skips without notice some sixty years until the arrival of Ezra. We hear nothing more of the earlier leaders, such as Jeshua and Zerubbabel, who would all have died

---

[40]Kidner, *Ezra & Nehemiah*, p. 60.

before Ezra's arrival. Our author is not intent on composing a political history. His concerns are theological, with the underlying hand of God at work to assure the continued existence of his restored people. The only note we have of the silent period is the reference to Xerxes in 4:6. Far from Jerusalem and Yehud, events were occurring in Susa that are recorded in the Book of Esther, but no direct connection is made in it to Jerusalem. The only other window into the situation in Jerusalem is the possibility that Malachi prophesied shortly before the arrival of Ezra. His concerns would reflect the problems that evolved between the joyous dedication of the reconstructed temple and the conditions which Ezra confronted upon his arrival. Those conditions demanded reform, as the next section of Ezra–Nehemiah makes clear.

VIII. EZRA COMES TO JERUSALEM (7:1-10)

A. EZRA'S GENEALOGY (7:1-6a)

¹**After these things, during the reign of Artaxerxes king of Persia, Ezra son of Seraiah, the son of Azariah, the son of Hilkiah, ²the son of Shallum, the son of Zadok, the son of Ahitub, ³the son of Amariah, the son of Azariah, the son of Meraioth, ⁴the son of Zerahiah, the son of Uzzi, the son of Bukki, ⁵the son of Abishua, the son of Phinehas, the son of Eleazar, the son of Aaron the chief priest— ⁶this Ezra came up from Babylon. He was a teacher well versed in the Law of Moses, which the LORD, the God of Israel, had given.**

7:1a After these things,

This vague expression bridges the time between the earlier events relating to the early returnees and those that will follow, related to the returnees led by Ezra.

during the reign of Artaxerxes king of Persia,

This is the same Artaxerxes (I) briefly mentioned in 4:6-23. He was the fifth Persian monarch in the Achaemenid dynasty established by Cyrus.

7:1b-5 Ezra son of Seraiah, . . .

His name is a shortened form of **Azariah**, one of his forebears mentioned in the genealogy (v. 2). The name means, "Ya(hweh) has helped." Ezra's genealogy is abbreviated, and the phrase **son of** signifies "descendant of." This is similar to the abbreviated lineage of Jesus in Matthew 1:1-17. The intent of Ezra's genealogy was to show his lineage reaching back to the high priest, **Aaron**, just as that of Jesus reaches back to King David. Seraiah was the high priest when Zedekiah was king. He was killed at Riblah at the command of Nebuchadnezzar approximately a century earlier than Ezra's mission, and his son, Jehozadak, was deported to Babylon (1 Chr 6:15). This list can be compared with that in 1 Chronicles 6:1-15[5:27-41].

. . . Hilkiah . . .

He was the high priest when Josiah ruled; he discovered the "Book of the Law in the temple of the Lord" (2 Kgs 22:8).

7:6a this Ezra came up from Babylon.

The Hebrew sentence in verse 1, with Ezra as the subject, has been interrupted by the insertion of the lineage of Ezra. Now it is resumed with the repetition of the subject here. Ezra "came up" to Jerusalem, based on the Hebrew verb עָלָה (*ʿālāh*, "go up"). This expression has become a technical term to express the return of Jews to Israel to reside there. To do so is to "make Aliyah."

He was a teacher well versed in the Law of Moses,

Compare the KJV, "a ready scribe," or the NRSV, "a scribe skilled." The NIV veils the identification of Ezra as a scribe. A scribe functioned as "secretary of state" in the Davidic monarchy (2 Sam 20:25), but the ability to write and to copy documents meant that scribes became expert in the studying and interpreting as well as copying of Scriptures (cf. Jer 8:8). Scribes became an important spiritual and intellectual force in Judaism after the return from exile. Scribes dedicated their lives to carefully copying the Law of Moses, interpreting and clarifying its meaning, and teaching it to the people. Jewish tradition regards Ezra as the founder of the class of religious leaders known as the *sopherim*, "sages," "the wise." The word for scribe is the same, סֹפֵר (*sōphēr*). The scribes are mentioned as teachers in the NT (Matt 7:29) and were associated with the Pharisees (Matt 23:2). Ezra is thus identified as both a legitimate priest and a skilled scribe with intimate knowledge of God's word and will for his people Israel.

which the Lord, the God of Israel, had given.

Although known as "the Law of Moses," the instruction (Torah) in the Pentateuch (the Five Books of Moses) is recognized as coming from Yahweh. He, the Lord, is the source and authority — not Moses.

B. EZRA'S PREPARATIONS (7:6b-7)

The king had granted him everything he asked, for the hand of the LORD his God was on him. [7]Some of the Israelites, including priests, Levites, singers, gatekeepers and temple servants, also came up to Jerusalem in the seventh year of King Artaxerxes.

7:6b The king had granted him everything he asked, . . .

There is nothing in the record to indicate what Ezra might have requested. No doubt the initial request was for permission for the project. The long trek with so many people would have required supplies and support. The letter of the king in verses 12-26 should be in part seen as the response to Ezra's requests.

7:7 Some of the Israelites, etc.

Just as in the initial return under Sheshbazzar, laity, priests, and Levites came with Ezra.

. . . in the seventh year of King Artaxerxes.

He ruled from 465–425 B.C.; thus the year was 458.

C. EZRA'S ARRIVAL (7:8-10)

[8]Ezra arrived in Jerusalem in the fifth month of the seventh year of the king. [9]He had begun his journey from Babylon on the first day of the first month, and he arrived in Jerusalem on the first day of the fifth month, for the gracious hand of his God was on him. [10]For Ezra had devoted himself to the study and observance of the Law of the LORD, and to teaching its decrees and laws in Israel.

7:8 Ezra arrived in Jerusalem . . . .

The departure from Babylon is noted here as the first day of the first month (Nisan), March/April. Ezra 8:31 gives the departure date as the twelfth day of the first month. This discrepancy is only supposed; verse 9 literally states **on the first day of the first month** "is the foundation of the ascent." Actual departure from the Ahava Canal was delayed while Levites were sought to accompany the expedition (8:15-20). The arrival **in Jerusalem** was **on the first day of the fifth month** (Ab). So the journey of some nine hundred miles via the ford of the Euphrates at Carchemish took approximately four months to complete. (A direct route of five hundred miles was impossible across a vast desert.)

7:9 . . . the gracious hand of his God was on him.

While the information for the trip has been taken from the underlying Ezra Memoirs, with supplements such as the lineage of Ezra, this is the observation of our author. Here as elsewhere he emphasizes the providence of God in the successful trek of Ezra and those with him from Babylon to Jerusalem. The next verse comments on why the hand of God was on Ezra.

7:10 For Ezra had devoted himself . . .

The literal translation is, "Ezra had set his heart on." His dedication to God's call was threefold: to study, apply it to his personal life, and to teach its decrees and laws to others. No wonder he persevered. Ezra provides a timeless example for every generation of God's people. The disciple, when he or she reaches maturity, will be like the master (Luke 6:40). Such maturity comes with personal devotion to study, application, and teaching.

IX. KING ARTAXERXES' LETTER TO EZRA (7:11-28)

A. THE DECREE OF ARTAXERXES (7:11-26)

[11]**This is a copy of the letter King Artaxerxes had given to Ezra the priest and teacher, a man learned in matters concerning the commands and decrees of the LORD for Israel:**

[12a]**Artaxerxes, king of kings,**

To Ezra the priest, a teacher of the Law of the God of heaven:

Greetings.

[13]**Now I decree that any of the Israelites in my kingdom,**

including priests and Levites, who wish to go to Jerusalem with you, may go. [14]You are sent by the king and his seven advisers to inquire about Judah and Jerusalem with regard to the Law of your God, which is in your hand. [15]Moreover, you are to take with you the silver and gold that the king and his advisers have freely given to the God of Israel, whose dwelling is in Jerusalem, [16]together with all the silver and gold you may obtain from the province of Babylon, as well as the freewill offerings of the people and priests for the temple of their God in Jerusalem. [17]With this money be sure to buy bulls, rams and male lambs, together with their grain offerings and drink offerings, and sacrifice them on the altar of the temple of your God in Jerusalem.

[18]You and your brother Jews may then do whatever seems best with the rest of the silver and gold, in accordance with the will of your God. [19]Deliver to the God of Jerusalem all the articles entrusted to you for worship in the temple of your God. [20]And anything else needed for the temple of your God that you may have occasion to supply, you may provide from the royal treasury.

[21]Now I, King Artaxerxes, order all the treasurers of Trans-Euphrates to provide with diligence whatever Ezra the priest, a teacher of the Law of the God of heaven, may ask of you— [22]up to a hundred talents[b] of silver, a hundred cors[c] of wheat, a hundred baths[d] of wine, a hundred baths[d] of olive oil, and salt without limit. [23]Whatever the God of heaven has prescribed, let it be done with diligence for the temple of the God of heaven. Why should there be wrath against the realm of the king and of his sons? [24]You are also to know that you have no authority to impose taxes, tribute or duty on any of the priests, Levites, singers, gatekeepers, temple servants or other workers at this house of God.

[25]And you, Ezra, in accordance with the wisdom of your God, which you possess, appoint magistrates and judges to administer justice to all the people of Trans-Euphrates—all who know the laws of your God. And you are to teach any who do not know them. [26]Whoever does not obey the law of

your God and the law of the king must surely be punished by death, banishment, confiscation of property, or imprisonment.

ª*12* The text of Ezra 7:12-26 is in Aramaic.   ᵇ*22* That is, about 3 ¾ tons (about 3.4 metric tons)   ᶜ*22* That is, probably about 600 bushels (about 22 kiloliters)   ᵈ*22* That is, probably about 600 gallons (about 2.2 kiloliters)

7:11 This heading is written in Hebrew, even though the letter itself is in Aramaic. It may have been prefixed to the letter for the benefit of those maintaining the royal archives. It would have been written on the exterior of the document containing the letter for ease of identification. That it was in Hebrew rather than Aramaic might have been due to its relation to Jewish affairs. It is also possible that the copy of the letter was kept in the archives of the temple in Jerusalem. The detailed description of Ezra suggests that an informed Jew rather than a non-Jewish Persian bureaucrat wrote the heading.

7:12 In typical royal Persian style, **Artaxerxes** identifies himself, names the recipient, and issues a brief greeting. The self-designation **king of kings** was normal for Persian rulers. They ruled over an empire in which many vassal kings recognized them as overlords. The title appears also in Ezekiel 26:7 and Daniel 2:37.

Rather than the NIV, **a teacher of the Law of the God of heaven**, the literal translation is "the scribe of the Law of the God of heaven." Some commentators have suggested that this was a technical title, the approximate equivalent to "secretary of state for Jewish affairs."[41] Because the letter contains a number of details that only Jews would be familiar with, some scholars doubt its authenticity as a genuine letter of Artaxerxes. The counter to this is that the king had counselors who were experts in particular areas, such as Jewish relations. (Nehemiah is an example of a Jew in a highly responsible position in the Persian court.) He would depend on those assistants to assist in drafting such a letter. Ezra, as both a priest and excellent scribe, may even have provided a draft for the king's use. That would have assured accuracy in such details. Documentary evidence exists of such a general Persian practice.[42]

---

[41]Williamson, *Ezra, Nehemiah*, p. 100.
[42]See Yamauchi, *Persia and the Bible*, pp. 256-257.

7:13 Here implicit permission is given for Ezra to go to Jerusalem. It must have been his first request. Another unstated request must have been for the king to allow Ezra to collect Israelites (laity), priests, and Levites who were willing to go with him. Ezra is clearly to be the leader. The king's permission is in line with earlier royal practice, particularly of Cyrus and Darius.

7:14 You are sent by the king

Not only was Ezra permitted to go, he was commissioned to conduct an inquiry into the religious condition of the Jewish community in Jerusalem and Judah. He was to determine whether or not they were living in accordance with the **Law of your God**, which he possessed. This was probably a "Torah scroll," although the intent may have been, "which you have in your mind, of which you are master."

and his seven advisers

Esther 1:14 also mentions "the seven nobles of Persia and Media who had special access to the king and were the highest in the kingdom." The Greek historian Herodotus also noted that the heads of the seven leading families in Persia comprised a council to advise the king.[43] Ezra's commission was based on the highest authority in Persia.

7:15-17 This section of the letter stipulates authorized sources of funds Ezra is to assemble to take with him. Among these is a freewill offering given by the king and his advisers. We ought not rule out a generous spirit on their part; however, these funds were to be used to purchase sacrificial offerings to be offered up at the Jerusalem temple. At least in part, this was to seek the favor of the God worshiped at that temple on the royal house (cf. 6:10). The specific list of sacrifices indicates a Jewish adviser in the king's presence. Other funds were to be obtained in the province of Babylon, apparently from non-Jews familiar with and friendly to the Jewish community there, as well as freewill offerings from the leaders and people of the Jewish community in Babylonia.

7:18 . . . the rest of the silver and gold . . .

As Williamson has observed, the money spent on the offerings mentioned in verse 17 must have been a one-time celebration, perhaps on the occasion of the successful arrival of the group in Jerusalem (cf.

---

[43]Herodotus III, 31, 71, 83-84, 118.

8:35). Further support of the cultic requirements at the temple is provided for in verses 21-23. Therefore a surplus remained to be used at the discretion of the religious community, informed by the teachings of the Law.

7:19 Deliver . . . all the articles . . . .

These were vessels, perhaps enumerated in 8:27. They were new vessels, perhaps a part of the contribution of the royal house, and not a remnant of those taken by Nebuchadnezzar. Sheshbazzar had returned the latter to Jerusalem (1:7-11).

7:20 In case of contingencies, Ezra was authorized by this letter to obtain additional funds from **the royal treasury**. This did not mean Ezra had access to the vast wealth of the Persian Empire and could access funds in the Persian capitals. These were local and regional "taxes, tribute, and duty" (4:13) collected and used for expenses within satrapies (6:8) with a portion flowing to the Persian treasury in Susa or Ecbatana.

7:21-23 Now I, King Artaxerxes, order all the treasurers . . . .

This section turns aside from Ezra and is addressed directly to these royal appointees. A sufficient number of copies of this order were no doubt provided for distribution to the appropriate governing officials, as 8:36 appears to indicate. The king identifies himself and Ezra, repeating the same description for Ezra as provided in 7:12. The first stipulation (v. 22) is a generous grant. It may have been intended in part to help pay the travel expenses of Ezra and his group during their four-month journey. While generous, the grant was limited. The second stipulation was to free the clergy of tax burdens (v. 24). No limits were placed on this tax freedom. Again, this comprehensive list hints at a Jewish adviser to the king and a Jewish hand assisting him in drafting the letter.

While the grant in verses 22-23 is lavish, "a hundred talents of silver" seems excessive. It would have amounted to approximately three and three-quarter tons. By comparison, Herodotus reported that the annual tribute for the entire Trans-Euphrates province was only 350 talents. While the amount is not impossible, scribal error may have occurred here, in light of the sequence of **a hundred** in the verse.[44] The wheat would amount to some 650 bushels; the wine

---

[44]Williamson, *Ezra, Nehemiah*, p. 103.

and oil would measure about 600 gallons each. These amounts would supply the temple for about two years. See Exodus 29:40 and Hosea 9:4 for references to wine as a drink offering.

7:24 Exempting religious personnel from taxes was not a new Persian royal policy. According to the Gadatas Inscription, Darius relieved the priests of Apollo from paying taxes.[45] Persian rulers recognized the importance of maintaining the good will of religious leaders across their empire, because those leaders were very influential in their communities.

7:25-26 After the diversion of the section addressed to the treasurers, Artaxerxes here turns his attention back to Ezra. The king acknowledges Ezra's qualifications to carry out his orders, because Ezra possesses **the wisdom of your God**. This probably refers to the Pentateuch and Ezra's profound understanding of it. Ezra is ordered to appoint **magistrates and judges**. The distinction between the two functions is unclear, although they may have been similar to the "judges and officials" mentioned in Deuteronomy 16:18. In Deuteronomy, the judges were to decide cases while the officers (NIV "officials") were to enforce the decisions of the judges. Those appointed by Ezra were to deal with problems and injustices within the religious communities of Jews. All those who identified themselves as knowing and bound by the Law of God were to be under the jurisdiction of the magistrates and judges whom Ezra appointed. This included Jews not only in Judah and Jerusalem but also throughout the Trans-Euphrates. There were no doubt communities of Jews throughout greater Syria just as there were such communities in Egypt and in Babylonia. We are to understand that all non-Jews were exempted from this jurisdiction.

Ezra was to function as an envoy of the king for this particular purpose. He was never appointed governor. His authority was specified to governing authorities by this letter. Artaxerxes' policy may seem peculiar to us, but there is historical evidence that two kinds of tribunals existed in the empire. One was a type of social tribunal for dealing with customary laws. Attention in this case is focused on Jewish religious law. Royal tribunals also existed to handle cases related to the

---

[45]Cf. the references in ibid.

state.[46] The concern of the Persian kings for local customary law is illustrated by Darius. In 519 B.C. he ordered a satrap of Egypt to summon wise men from among the religious and ruling authorities to write down the ancient laws of Egypt and specifically mentions "the law of the Pharaoh, of the temples and of the people."[47] It was in the best interests of the crown for subject people to know and observe their own laws, as well as **the law of the king**. Ezra was therefore charged with instructing those who claimed to be Jews and were ignorant of **the law of your God** and (implied) the king's law. The seriousness of the king's intent is seen in the authority granted Ezra to punish those who had been instructed and were yet lawbreakers. Any of four levels of punishment could be used: death, banishment, confiscation of property, or imprisonment. While some of these four possible punishments may be found in the Pentateuch (Lev 24:12; Num 15:34), they were practices of the Persian state (cf. 6:11).

B. EZRA'S THANKSGIVING (7:27-28)

Here the original text reverts to the Hebrew language. The change from third to first person marks this section that continues through the end of chapter 9. They are thus a part of the memoirs of Ezra that our author used as one of his sources. Ezra wrote this expression of praise as he recalled how he felt following his meeting with the king and his advisers. It is a window into the soul of this dedicated servant of God.

[27]Praise be to the LORD, the God of our fathers, who has put it into the king's heart to bring honor to the house of the LORD in Jerusalem in this way [28]and who has extended his good favor to me before the king and his advisers and all the king's powerful officials. Because the hand of the LORD my God was on me, I took courage and gathered leading men from Israel to go up with me.

---

[46]Frye, *The Heritage of Persia*, p. 100.

[47]Roland de Vaux, *The Bible and the Ancient Near East* (Garden City: Doubleday, 1971), p. 74.

7:27 . . . to bring honor to the house of the Lord . . .

Literally, the Hebrew פָּאֵר (*pā'ēr*) is "to beautify, adorn." Probably the totality of what the king authorized came to mind, but perhaps particularly the offerings would enhance the temple.

7:28a Ezra realized that the king's generous arrangements were really due to God's hidden activity at work in the hearts (minds) of the king, his advisers, and powerful officials. God's people ought always to trust in God's providence and loving kindness.

7:28b Because the hand of the Lord my God was on me, . . .

Chapter and verse divisions were not in the original text; therefore some commentators connect this part of the verse to chapter 8. It is a bridge to the next development in Ezra's plan to go up to Jerusalem. He recognized his success before the king was due to divine assistance. This encouraged him to recruit **leading men from Israel**, descendants of exiled ancestors living in Babylonia, to go with him.

X. LIST OF THE FAMILY HEADS
RETURNING WITH EZRA (8:1-14)

¹These are the family heads and those registered with them who came up with me from Babylon during the reign of King Artaxerxes:

²of the descendants of Phinehas, Gershom;

of the descendants of Ithamar, Daniel;

of the descendants of David, Hattush ³of the descendants of Shecaniah;

of the descendants of Parosh, Zechariah, and with him were registered 150 men;

⁴of the descendants of Pahath-Moab, Eliehoenai son of Zerahiah, and with him 200 men;

⁵of the descendants of Zattu,ª Shecaniah son of Jahaziel, and with him 300 men;

⁶of the descendants of Adin, Ebed son of Jonathan, and with him 50 men;

⁷of the descendants of Elam, Jeshaiah son of Athaliah, and with him 70 men;

⁸of the descendants of Shephatiah, Zebadiah son of Michael, and with him 80 men;

⁹of the descendants of Joab, Obadiah son of Jehiel, and with him 218 men;

¹⁰of the descendants of Bani,ᵇ Shelomith son of Josiphiah, and with him 160 men;

¹¹of the descendants of Bebai, Zechariah son of Bebai, and with him 28 men;

¹²of the descendants of Azgad, Johanan son of Hakkatan, and with him 110 men;

¹³of the descendants of Adonikam, the last ones, whose names were Eliphelet, Jeuel and Shemaiah, and with them 60 men;

¹⁴of the descendants of Bigvai, Uthai and Zaccur, and with them 70 men.

ᵃ5 Some Septuagint manuscripts (also 1 Esdras 8:32); Hebrew does not have *Zattu.*   ᵇ*10* Some Septuagint manuscripts (also 1 Esdras 8:36); Hebrew does not have *Bani.*

8:1 These are the family heads . . .

Those named in the list which follows are the **leading men** (7:28b) from Babylonia whom Ezra recruited to go with him. Ezra must have been passionately persuasive. Williamson has made the apt observation that there was little to attract recruits to join Ezra. Those most attracted to a return to the homeland had departed eighty years earlier with the first return. A second and third generation had settled into the easier life in exile. Many of them were no doubt content to respond to Ezra simply by contributing freewill offerings. Even the Levites were uninterested until pressed by Ezra (v. 15). One of the motivations to join Ezra must have been attraction to a second exodus. The way the list of families is arranged — priestly, Davidic, and the remainder laity — "shows clearly that it is regarded as ideal Israel, viewed from a priestly perspective. . . . Though with a somewhat different emphasis from Ezra 1–3, there is nevertheless the definite impression here of a second exodus, with its arduous desert journey and entry into the land. Thus we may find here a further fulfillment of Israel's prophetic hopes for a return from exile . . . ."⁴⁸

---

⁴⁸Williamson, *Ezra, Nehemiah*, p. 111.

8:2-14 Although many of the names duplicate those in Ezra 2-3, noteworthy differences exist between the two lists. Here priests appear first, then Judean royalty, followed by twelve lay families. The earlier list has laity, the priests and Levites, and related personnel. The priests here derive from Aaron; the preceding list has linkages with Zadok. Nothing more is known of Gershom, except a son of Moses also had that name. This Gershom was related to Ezra, who was also of the Phinehas house (7:5). Ithamar was the youngest of Aaron's sons (Exod 6:23).

Hattush was a descendant of David through his great-great-grandfather, Zerubbabel (1 Chr 3:17-22). He should not be confused with the priest of that name in Nehemiah 10:5.

In this list Joab (v. 9) appears independent of the Pahath-Moab line. Apart from Shecaniah (v. 5) and Shelomith (v. 10), the remaining names occur in chapter 2 and Nehemiah 7. (Zattu does not appear in the Hebrew text, as the NIV notes.) This means that all the returnees with Ezra had relatives in Jerusalem. Two other items are worth noting. First, the expression **males** indicates only the men were counted here; in chapters 2-3 females are included in the count. Second, the expression **the last ones** in verse 13 is puzzling. A logical explanation is that these were the last of the family to return to Jerusalem, there to join earlier family migrants.

XI. THE RETURN TO JERUSALEM (8:15-36)

A. THE ORGANIZATIONAL ASSEMBLY AT AHAVA (8:15-20)

[15]**I assembled them at the canal that flows toward Ahava, and we camped there three days. When I checked among the people and the priests, I found no Levites there. [16]So I summoned Eliezer, Ariel, Shemaiah, Elnathan, Jarib, Elnathan, Nathan, Zechariah and Meshullam, who were leaders, and Joiarib and Elnathan, who were men of learning, [17]and I sent them to Iddo, the leader in Casiphia. I told them what to say to Iddo and his kinsmen, the temple servants in Casiphia, so that they might bring attendants to us for the house of our God. [18]Because the gracious hand of our God was on us, they brought us Sherebiah, a capable man, from the descen-**

dants of Mahli son of Levi, the son of Israel, and Sherebiah's sons and brothers, 18 men; [19]and Hashabiah, together with Jeshaiah from the descendants of Merari, and his brothers and nephews, 20 men. [20]They also brought 220 of the temple servants—a body that David and the officials had established to assist the Levites. All were registered by name.

8:15 Nothing more is known of Ahava, which must have been near Babylon along one of the many irrigation canals in the region. The three-day encampment provided a needed opportunity for Ezra to organize the large group. There were some fifteen hundred men, to which women and children would be added. The total number must have been near five thousand. To organize the group for travel required assistants to Ezra, and some of them are named in verse 16. While Ezra was surveying those he had recruited for the journey, he discovered that no Levites were in the group. There were Levites in Jerusalem, so Ezra's concern to have Levites in his group must have been motivated by other interests. Williamson, following Koch, suggests that a second exodus minus Levites participating in the trek would not conform to the pattern of the march in the wilderness of the original exodus (cf. Num 10:13ff).[49]

8:16 So I summoned . . .

Those summoned consisted of two groups: **leaders** and **men of learning**. These leaders (lit. "heads") were not identical with the heads of families listed above; some of the names do not appear in the previous list. **Elnathan** appears three times, which has made the list suspect in the minds of some commentators. But Elnathan ("God has given") was likely a popular name, so three "Elnathans" were as possible then as three "Johns" now. These men and their reputations were well known to Ezra and apparently to the larger Jewish community. He could depend upon them to lead in the recruitment of Levites. The two identified as men of learning were literally "those who cause to understand." They were teachers and interpreters of the Law.[50] Apparently both groups would be useful in

---

[49]Williamson, *Ezra, Nehemiah*, p. 116.

[50]Breneman, *Ezra, Nehemiah, Esther*, pp. 140-141. In Neh 8:8-9 the word מְבִינִים (*m°bînîm*) clearly refers to teaching and interpretation of Scripture.

the effort to persuade reluctant Levites to join the contingent poised
to depart.

8:17-20 and I sent them to Iddo, the leader in Casiphia.

We know nothing more of Iddo nor the location of Casiphia.
The distance between Ahava and Casiphia must not have been great.
Travel to Casiphia, obtaining the new recruits, the time they needed
for closing their affairs and preparing to depart, and returning to
Ezra's camp did not delay his departure by more than a week.

Iddo is identified as the **leader** in Casiphia "the place" (הַמָּקוֹם,
hammāqôm). He was clearly an authority in a Jewish center, and he
may have been a Levite. He may have been the head of a school. The
word *hammāqôm* may also indicate a sanctuary. This would have
been similar to the sanctuary of Yahu at Elephantine in Egypt in the
same period. The connection of the word with a sanctuary can be
seen in Deuteronomy 12:5,11; 14:23; 1 Kings 8:29 and Jeremiah
7:3,6,7. While this suggestion is plausible, it is not proved. The place
might also have been the forerunner of what we later know as the
synagogue (which is a designation based on a Greek word rather
than Persian or Hebrew).

I told them what to say . . .

Ezra was depending on his appointed leaders to accomplish his
purposes. Apparently the press of his larger responsibilities prevented him from leaving Ahava. But as with any competent leader, he
communicated to his envoys the approach they should take to con-
vince Iddo and his associates to recruit men to serve in the Jerusalem
temple. Artaxerxes had authorized Ezra to recruit all those who
wished to go with him. One wonders why no Levites had responded
to the general word that must have circulated throughout the Jewish
population in Babylonia. The underlying reasons were probably
those noted by Kidner, ". . . it was only natural for these men to
shrink from a prospect which was doubly daunting: not only the
uprooting which all the pilgrims faced, but the drastic change from
ordinary pursuits to the strict routines of the Temple."[51]

What is surprising is that they were able to recruit thirty-eight
Levites from two families in such a short time. **Sherebiah** traced his
ancestry back to **Mahli**, a grandson **of Levi** through Merari (Exod

---

[51]Kidner, *Ezra & Nehemiah*, p. 65.

6:16-19). According to Numbers 3:33-37; 4:29-33, the Merarites carried the Tent of Meeting in the wilderness, so it was particularly providential for Ezra that this family of Levites agreed to go with him. Sherebiah is described as **a capable man**. He subsequently appears as a leader or instructor of people in Jerusalem (Ezra 8:24; Neh 8:7; 9:4-5; 10:12; 12:8,24). **Hashabiah**, **Jeshaiah**, and their relatives were also Merarites. Hashabiah also is mentioned later in Ezra–Nehemiah. A surprisingly large contingent of temple servants was also enlisted. Ezra had asked only for Levites. Myers suggested "that the decision of such a large number of temple slaves to accompany Ezra was a factor in persuading the Levites to go."[52] Ezra checked the family connections of the new recruits and registered them by name.

Because the gracious hand of our God was on us . . . .
As we would expect, Ezra recognized that success in recruiting the Levites and receiving the bonus of temple servants was only possible because of God's extraordinary grace. This evidence of God's continuing participation in the enterprise must have brought joy and renewed energy to Ezra.

B. SPIRITUAL PREPARATION FOR THE JOURNEY (8:21-23)

[21]**There, by the Ahava Canal, I proclaimed a fast, so that we might humble ourselves before our God and ask him for a safe journey for us and our children, with all our possessions. [22]I was ashamed to ask the king for soldiers and horsemen to protect us from enemies on the road, because we had told the king, "The gracious hand of our God is on everyone who looks to him, but his great anger is against all who forsake him." [23]So we fasted and petitioned our God about this, and he answered our prayer.**

8:21 . . . I proclaimed a fast . . .
Despite the elation he must have felt with the arrival of the Levites and temple servants, and the recognition of God's hand in it, Ezra would not presume upon God's continued grace. He proclaimed a

---

[52]Jacob M. Myers, *Ezra-Nehemiah*, The Anchor Bible, vol. 14 (Garden City, NJ: Doubleday, 1965), p. 70.

fast. By fasting and praying, the entire entourage sought God's protection against the hazards of the journey ahead. They humbled themselves before God. They realized the enormity of the journey ahead of them and the unseen factors that could bring disaster, save for the benevolent hand of God. They were leaving the security of a settled, comfortable life for a four-month journey during the heat of the summer, often traveling through desert regions. Some five thousand required food and water daily, not to mention their animals. The logistics of supplying these needs and efficiently moving this large group forward each day and setting up camp each night seems overwhelming. Ezra must have been a master in organization with a cadre of wise assistants to direct and coordinate the pilgrimage. But all human ingenuity and wisdom are insufficient in the face of the unexpected. Then only God's grace is sufficient.

Fasting is seldom mentioned in the OT, and the only required annual fast was the Day of Atonement. Following the exile, the number of fasts was increased. Zechariah 8:19 refers to four fast days, those of the fourth, fifth, seventh, and tenth months. In Esther 4:16 a three-day fast is observed. The example of Ezra (here and in 10:6) was instructive to his fellow Jews in Jerusalem (Neh 9:1) and through generation after generation of the faithful.

8:22 I was ashamed to ask the king . . .

The focus of the spiritual preparation was to petition God for a safe trip, particularly in light of Ezra's decision when he was before King Artaxerxes not to ask for an armed guard to accompany him. Ezra's decision and his explanation provide another insight into his deep faith and dependence upon God. Surely such testimony (set in quotations) was a powerful factor in convincing the king and his advisers to respond positively to Ezra's requests.

8:23 . . . and he answered our prayer.

This is likely in retrospect, completely realized only after their safe arrival in Jerusalem (v. 31). The journey was a walk by faith. The safe progress each day was an assurance for that day of the hand of God. To trust in God is to experience each day as an adventure in faith, trust that **the gracious hand of our God is on everyone who looks to him**.

C. CONSIGNMENT OF THE TEMPLE TREASURES
TO THE PRIESTS AND LEVITES (8:24-30)

[24]Then I set apart twelve of the leading priests, together with Sherebiah, Hashabiah and ten of their brothers, [25]and I weighed out to them the offering of silver and gold and the articles that the king, his advisers, his officials and all Israel present there had donated for the house of our God. [26]I weighed out to them 650 talents[a] of silver, silver articles weighing 100 talents,[b] 100 talents[b] of gold, [27]20 bowls of gold valued at 1,000 darics,[c] and two fine articles of polished bronze, as precious as gold.

[28]I said to them, "You as well as these articles are consecrated to the LORD. The silver and gold are a freewill offering to the LORD, the God of your fathers. [29]Guard them carefully until you weigh them out in the chambers of the house of the LORD in Jerusalem before the leading priests and the Levites and the family heads of Israel." [30]Then the priests and Levites received the silver and gold and sacred articles that had been weighed out to be taken to the house of our God in Jerusalem.

[a]26 That is, about 25 tons (about 22 metric tons)   [b]26 That is, about 3¾ tons (about 3.4 metric tons)   [c]27 That is, about 19 pounds (about 8.5 kilograms)

8:24 Then I set apart twelve of the leading priests . . .

After the spiritual preparation, Ezra provided for the transportation of the contributions intended for the Jerusalem temple. He appointed twelve priests and twelve Levites to the responsibility. According to Numbers 3:8,31; 4:5ff., it was the priests' responsibility to handle the sacred objects and the Levites' to transport them. This was doubtless a major reason why Ezra sought Levites to join the group.

8:25-27 and I weighed out to them . . .

The Hebrew verb for weighed is שָׁקַל (šāqal), the basis also for the word "shekel." This word originally designated a particular weight of silver or gold. After coinage began it came to designate a certain weight of silver or gold coin. Although coinage was in use in Ezra's time, apparently the offerings were weighed and an accurate written account was made (cf. v. 34). This careful accounting reveals

the meticulous attention to detail and appropriate procedures on
Ezra's part. Such practices assured the integrity of all involved.
Much damage to Christ and his church caused by financial scandals
could be avoided by following Ezra's example in handling contributions dedicated to God.

When we read the NIV footnotes for the modern equivalents of
the Persian weights and values, they may seem unbelievable. D.J.A.
Clines has computed that the total value "would represent the annual income of, say, between 100,000 and 500,000 men."[53] Some scholars have suggested that a textual error has resulted in the substitution of "talents" for "minas." The phrase **silver articles weighing
100 talents** more accurately reads "100 silver vessels weighing . . . talents." The number indicating value has dropped out. Williamson,
following earlier commentators, allows for the missing number to be
two, i.e. "weighing two talents."[54] Despite these problems, the total
was a very large amount of precious metals. What is known is that
the Persian kings were extremely wealthy.[55] The amount contributed
by the court could be substantial. Considering Artaxerxes' contribution, Kidner has observed, "If the God of the Jews were no more
than a name (he might have [mentally] argued), the whole exercise
was pointless; but if He existed, He would expect tangible courtesies
from a king–and the scale of them should reflect the donor's power
and majesty."[56] We should recall as well that Babylonian Jewry had
lived there for a century and a half. They were well established and
prospering. Archaeology has provided evidence that the Murashu
family of Nippur was well established in banking with some eighty
of their clients bearing Jewish names.[57] So the resources of the Jews
of Babylon should not be underestimated.

Assuming the weight of treasure at approximately thirty tons, a
large number of pack animals would have been necessary to transport that weight. A modest amount could have been carried by
Levites with the assistance of 220 temple servants.

---

[53]David J. Clines, *Ezra, Nehemiah, Esther*, New Century Bible (Grand
Rapids: Eerdmans, 1984), p. 113.
[54]Williamson, *Ezra, Nehemiah*, p. 119.
[55]Frye, *The Heritage of Persia*, p. 110.
[56]Kidner, *Ezra & Nehemiah*, p. 66.
[57]*ABD*, IV:928.

8:28-30 I said to them, . . .

Ezra, the priest, here instructs the twenty-four priests and Levites and emphasizes that both they and the offerings were consecrated to the Lord. The **you** of verse 29 is plural. Individually and collectively they were responsible for this sacred offering until they, in turn, weighed it out to the priests, Levites, and family heads in the לִשְׁכוֹת (liškôth), **chambers**, of the temple in Jerusalem. The chambers were storerooms around the temple, described in 1 Kings 6:5. The appointed priests and Levites accepted the responsibility.

D. DEPARTURE FROM BABYLON AND ARRIVAL IN JERUSALEM (8:31-36)

[31]On the twelfth day of the first month we set out from the Ahava Canal to go to Jerusalem. The hand of our God was on us, and he protected us from enemies and bandits along the way. [32]So we arrived in Jerusalem, where we rested three days.

[33]On the fourth day, in the house of our God, we weighed out the silver and gold and the sacred articles into the hands of Meremoth son of Uriah, the priest. Eleazar son of Phinehas was with him, and so were the Levites Jozabad son of Jeshua and Noadiah son of Binnui. [34]Everything was accounted for by number and weight, and the entire weight was recorded at that time.

[35]Then the exiles who had returned from captivity sacrificed burnt offerings to the God of Israel: twelve bulls for all Israel, ninety-six rams, seventy-seven male lambs and, as a sin offering, twelve male goats. All this was a burnt offering to the LORD. [36]They also delivered the king's orders to the royal satraps and to the governors of Trans-Euphrates, who then gave assistance to the people and to the house of God.

8:31-32 The assignment of responsibility for the offering freed Ezra to arrange the final details for departure. **On the twelfth** of Nisan (late April) they set out. This was later than originally intended, the first of Nisan (7:9), due to delays in obtaining the contingent of Levites.

. . . he protected us from enemies and bandits along the way.

The long trek is summarized so briefly by Ezra: departure, God's protection en route, arrival. Ezra was well aware of the potential hazards of the journey, the enemies and bandits. Whether God saved them from experiencing such attacks or rescued them when attacks occurred is unclear. In either case, their arrival was evidence of answered prayer for a safe journey (v. 21). What is untold is the enormity of conducting this caravan over some nine hundred miles, traveling at about nine miles per day, to reach their destination. What would be needed? Food and water for people and animals, partially carried with them and partially purchased along the way; arrangement of the line of march; scouts sent ahead to locate suitable campgrounds each day; others responsible for locating, bargaining for, and buying needed supplies, including water when they were away from the Euphrates; the effort to break camp and get on the road in a timely fashion each day — these are but a few of the realities of the journey that Ezra and his subordinates had to anticipate and accomplish. But with God, nothing shall be called impossible. So they arrived in Jerusalem; they deserved the three days of rest.

8:33-34 On the fourth day . . .

The treasure was weighed **into the hands of Meremoth**, who is mentioned again in Nehemiah 3:4,21. He may have been the temple treasurer. Eleazar appears again in Nehemiah 12:42, Jozabad in Nehemiah 11:16, and Binnui in Nehemiah 3:24. These were witnesses to the accuracy of the accounting. The care with which it was done is evident. They weighed each item, confirming its weight with its item number, and totaled their combined weights. Every item was verified. That part of the mission — accomplished.

8:35-36 Then the exiles . . .

This section is written in the words of our author rather than being a direct quote from Ezra, as in the preceding section where "we" occurs. He reports on the fulfillment of the other two parts of Ezra's mission: sacrifices (7:17) and delivery of the king's orders to local and regional officials (7:21-24). The offerings are representative of all Israel: ninety-six equals eight rams per tribe. Seventy-seven is the perfect number magnified (cf. Jesus' words to Peter, Matt 18:22). Normally the priests ate a part of the sin offerings (cf. Lev

4:22 ff). In this special case all were completely consumed on the altar. The sin offerings were for ritual defilement inevitably contracted on the long journey.

The plural **satraps** poses a problem; each satrapy was administered by a single satrap. Trans-Euphrates was a single satrapy with a number of provinces under different governors. A possible solution is that the king's orders were also given to the satrap of Egypt where Jewish communities existed, allowing Ezra to teach and apply Jewish law in them. The governors of regions in Syria-Palestine followed the king's command and **gave assistance to the people and to the house of God**. They could hardly refuse.

XII. EZRA'S PRAYER ABOUT INTERMARRIAGE (9:1-15)

We should note here that commentators generally agree that Ezra 9 and 10 are all a part of a single event. It began with the visit of the deputation of leaders who came to Ezra and subsequent developments until the settlement of the matter by the first day of Nisan (10:17).

A. EZRA INFORMED ABOUT ASSIMILATION (9:1-5)

[1]**After these things had been done, the leaders came to me and said, "The people of Israel, including the priests and the Levites, have not kept themselves separate from the neighboring peoples with their detestable practices, like those of the Canaanites, Hittites, Perizzites, Jebusites, Ammonites, Moabites, Egyptians and Amorites. [2]They have taken some of their daughters as wives for themselves and their sons, and have mingled the holy race with the peoples around them. And the leaders and officials have led the way in this unfaithfulness."**

[3]**When I heard this, I tore my tunic and cloak, pulled hair from my head and beard and sat down appalled. [4]Then everyone who trembled at the words of the God of Israel gathered around me because of this unfaithfulness of the exiles. And I sat there appalled until the evening sacrifice.**

⁵Then, at the evening sacrifice, I rose from my self-abasement, with my tunic and cloak torn, and fell on my knees with my hands spread out to the LORD my God

The author returns here to the Ezra Memoirs.

9:1-2 After these things had been done,

Ezra came to Jerusalem prepared by his study and observance of the Law of the Lord to teach its decrees and laws in Israel (7:10). After taking care of the delivery of the offerings to the temple and the decrees to the government officials, he received this report. Williamson and others, however, believe that ". . . the present passage is left without adequate introduction and the motivation for the leaders' confession remains unexplained."[58] He and others believe that Ezra's reading of the law took place between the events at the end of chapter 8 and the beginning of chapter 9. The compiler of Ezra–Nehemiah moved that segment into Nehemiah for theological purposes, to form a part of the climax he has provided for the work of both Ezra and Nehemiah. These views of the *historical* sequence of events are strongly argued and may indeed be valid. However, the person who wrote Ezra–Nehemiah was not writing history as such, he was drawing on the historical resources available to him in order to write a *theological* statement for the benefit of his people. While we are interested in the history incorporated in the narrative, it is appropriate to read his story as he has woven it together. That is what we are attempting to do.

Four months had passed between the arrival of Ezra in Jerusalem in the fifth month and the present episode in the ninth month (10:9). The text provides no indication of Ezra's activity during that third of a year. It is difficult to believe that Ezra was inactive during this period because his passion was to teach and practice the Law of God. It also seems apparent that he would have had some awareness of the intermarriage problem by the time the leaders came to him. These leaders may have come under conviction about the problem as a result of Ezra's teaching. Reference to "in accordance with the counsel of my lord" (10:3) hints at this while Nehemiah 8 provides an example of what Ezra consistently taught. Rather than force an

---

[58]Williamson, *Ezra, Nehemiah*, p. 128.

unwilling community to do his will, Ezra allowed the word of God, which he taught, to reach fruition in the hearts of his hearers. At last his teaching was changing lives.

the leaders . . .

Who הַשָּׂרִים (*haśśārîm*, "the chiefs, rulers") were is not specifically stated; possibly they were some of the heads of families of long-time residents. It is unlikely that they were leaders of those who had recently returned with Ezra, for they would have been enlightened in their communities in Babylon.

The people of Israel . . .

Here the expression signifies the laity and the religious leaders. Through the long period after the initial return, families of the exile and those who had freely associated with them in order to seek the Lord (6:21) had begun to intermarry with their non-Jewish neighbors. Marriage then was not a boy-meets-girl romantic affair. It was a family alliance formed with bride-price and dowry arranged by family leaders for economic and status benefits. Note that marriages between Jewish men and non-Jewish women are mentioned, not the opposite. The distinction of who is a Jew has historically been determined by the Jewishness of the mother. That relationship can be proven but, until the recent discovery of DNA, paternity could be questioned.

The danger in such alliances was twofold. First, they had failed to maintain a separate and distinct identity as the people of Israel. They had mingled the holy race with the (unholy) people around them. Second, they were open to the influence of the detestable religious practices considered normal by their neighbors. Those neighbors are characterized as directly connected to the peoples of Canaan in ancient times, even though by Ezra's time all had disappeared from history except the Ammonites, Moabites, and Egyptians. The warnings against intermarriage in the Pentateuch were as valid for the renewed community as they were for the Israelites of old (e.g., Exod 34:11-16; Deut 7:1-4). The history of their forefathers was a bleak testimony to the effects of ignoring the will of God in this respect. Following the first exodus, God had called Israel to be "my treasured possession. . . . a kingdom of priests and a holy nation" (Exod 19:5-6). Now, following the second exodus, from Babylon, the holiness of the remnant descendants was being defiled.

This tendency to assimilate did not begin at the bottom of society and move upward, it began at the top and infiltrated the followers. **The leaders and officials . . . led the way.** The distinction between leaders (cf. v. 1) and officials (הַסְּגָנִים, *hass⁺gānîm*) is unclear. The latter word is Akkadian in origin and may be translated "magistrates" (NEB), "rulers" (KJV), or "chiefs." All leaders bear responsibility for what they do and teach by actions and attitudes. This is particularly true of religious leaders.

9:3-4 Ezra may have had a prior inkling of this unfaithfulness, but now with the report of the leaders he publicly displayed his reaction to their report. No details of the report are given, but it was so serious that his reaction was to mourn over the situation as one would mourn for the dead. Spiritually, the community had so ignored the revealed will of God that they deserved death. Ezra not only tore his outer garment, the depth of his grief is shown in the tearing also of his inner garment. The partial or complete shaving of the head or beard was another aspect of mourning (cf. Job 1:20; Isa 22:12, etc.). In that critical moment, Ezra symbolized this by pulling hair from his head and his beard. Then he just sat in stunned silence (cf. Job 2:13; Ezek 26:16). Soon around him gathered those who trembled at the disrespect shown to the God of Israel by the unfaithfulness of so many. They were strict observers of the law. They sat in sympathetic silence, as did the mourners who came to Job in his grief (2:13). The time for the evening sacrifice was three o'clock in the afternoon. Acts 3:1 calls it "the time of prayer," a fitting time for Ezra to end his silence by breaking into prayer.

9:5 I rose . . . and fell on my knees . . .

There is no preferred position for prayer. Ezra chose to rise from his sitting position, then to kneel with outstretched hands, a sign of humility and supplication, similar to that of Solomon (1 Kgs 8:54). Like Solomon, too, Ezra would pray for all his people.

B. EZRA'S PRAYER (9:6-15)

This is one of the great biblical prayers. It moves from a general recognition of sin and just punishment (vv. 6-7) to recognition of God's current favor (vv. 8-9) to confession of current sin (vv. 10-12) to acknowledgment of the grossness of their sin and the greatness of God's grace (vv. 13-14) to a humble doxology (v. 15).

⁶**and prayed:**

> **"O my God, I am too ashamed and disgraced to lift up my face to you, my God, because our sins are higher than our heads and our guilt has reached to the heavens. ⁷From the days of our forefathers until now, our guilt has been great. Because of our sins, we and our kings and our priests have been subjected to the sword and captivity, to pillage and humiliation at the hand of foreign kings, as it is today.**
>
> ⁸**"But now, for a brief moment, the LORD our God has been gracious in leaving us a remnant and giving us a firm place in his sanctuary, and so our God gives light to our eyes and a little relief in our bondage. ⁹Though we are slaves, our God has not deserted us in our bondage. He has shown us kindness in the sight of the kings of Persia: He has granted us new life to rebuild the house of our God and repair its ruins, and he has given us a wall of protection in Judah and Jerusalem.**
>
> ¹⁰**"But now, O our God, what can we say after this? For we have disregarded the commands ¹¹you gave through your servants the prophets when you said: 'The land you are entering to possess is a land polluted by the corruption of its peoples. By their detestable practices they have filled it with their impurity from one end to the other. ¹²Therefore, do not give your daughters in marriage to their sons or take their daughters for your sons. Do not seek a treaty of friendship with them at any time, that you may be strong and eat the good things of the land and leave it to your children as an everlasting inheritance.'**
>
> ¹³**"What has happened to us is a result of our evil deeds and our great guilt, and yet, our God, you have punished us less than our sins have deserved and have given us a remnant like this. ¹⁴Shall we again break your commands and intermarry with the peoples who commit such detestable practices? Would you not be angry enough with us to destroy us,**

leaving us no remnant or survivor? [15]O LORD, God of Israel, you are righteous! We are left this day as a remnant. Here we are before you in our guilt, though because of it not one of us can stand in your presence."

9:6-7 I . . . our . . .

Ezra begins the prayer as an individual and soon transforms it into a communal prayer. Although he personally does not share the guilt of the faithlessness that calls forth this prayer, he does not distance himself but identifies with his people. Ezra, too, "trembled at the words of the God of Israel" (v. 4) and recognized the magnitude of this sin. It so shamed him that he could not lift his head toward heaven as he prayed, for a mountain of sin and guilt reaching to heaven stood between them and God. The current deviation was equal to and the same as the iniquities of their forefathers. The history of their people, which resulted in destruction, exile, and foreign domination, the effects under which they still lived, was due to their sins. This prayer will have a powerful effect on those at Ezra's side. His spiritual anguish must have been heart-wrenching, because it was to move those around him to action.

9:8-9 But now, for a brief moment . . .

Less than a century had passed since the first return; more recently a few thousand more had arrived with Ezra, but in historical perspective it was but a moment of time and only a remnant of what had been a nation. Yet it was a moment in which God's grace was evident. Even the existence of a remnant was a mark of God's favor. **Firm place** is literally, "a tent peg." God has provided security for his remnant in the reestablishment of his holy temple. Ezra recognizes that what God has wrought in Jerusalem in the restoration has brightened his people's eyes in an otherwise gloomy situation. The reference to bondage is recognition that they were under the political control of others. The restoration was still incomplete as long as they lacked political self-determination, no matter the benevolent policies of the Persian throne.

The reestablished community and the rebuilt temple were a restoration of life and evidence that God had not deserted them. The **wall of protection in Judah and Jerusalem** may be a metaphor for the protection of the Persian king. The word for **wall** is גָּדֵר

(*gādēr*), the wall around a vineyard, as in Isaiah 5:1-7. Nehemiah had not yet restored the wall of Jerusalem; nor was there ever a wall built around Judah.

9:10-12 But now . . .

Turning from acknowledging the goodness of God, Ezra contrasts their current disregard for God's commandments. God knows what they have done, but recognition that one is aware of what God knows is essential. Contrition and confession should follow. Ezra recalls some of those commands from the inspired words of Scripture. The words that come to his mind are applicable to the current situation. They are a composite taken from various passages: Leviticus 18:25ff; 2 Kings 16:3; Deuteronomy 7:1-3; 11:8; 2 Kings 21:16; Isaiah 1:19 and possibly Deuteronomy 23:6, in reference to "Do not seek a treaty of friendship with them," that is, the Ammonites and Moabites. Ezra makes no distinction here between the law and the prophets, recognizing that all were composed under prophetic inspiration. This was a public prayer, a "sermon prayer." Recalling God's commandments about intermarriage and assimilation not only was right before God, it was something the audience needed to hear.

9:13-14 The convicting power of Ezra's sermon prayer reaches its climax here. The calamities of the past were the result of evil deeds resulting in an enormous burden of guilt. Guilt is real, even when not acknowledged. Yet God had not punished the nation to the degree merited. Rather than complete annihilation, by his mercy a remnant had survived in exile and had now returned. But for the restored community, having broken his commandments and indulged in intermarriage, would this not mean an utter end to them? This rhetorical question expects an answer of "Yes!" As Slotki notes, "The whole passage strikingly, recalls Deut. vii.4, xi.17; Josh. xxiii.16."[59]

9:15 In his closing words, Ezra utters absolutely no special pleading. The **God of Israel** is **righteous**, that is, justified in his treatment of his people. To paraphrase, "We are a remnant, evidence of your righteousness and grace, but an utterly guilty remnant. Because of this, not a single one of us can stand guiltless before you." With that,

---

[59]Slotki, *Daniel, Ezra and Nehemiah*, p. 168.

Ezra threw himself to the ground in dramatic confirmation of what
he had stated. (Recall there were no original chapter divisions. Ezra
10:1 follows without interruption.) Not only did Ezra identify himself
with the people, all of them were bound up together in responsibility for the nation's guilt. Unspoken but implicit in this final statement
is that their only salvation in this situation was the grace of God.

One cannot doubt the deep conviction and sincerity expressed
by Ezra in this prayer. At the same time, it is apparent that his prayer
was not intended solely to influence God's appropriate judgment on
them. His intent also was to produce a psychological effect on those
who heard him. Proof that he succeeded in moving the audience is
evident in what happened next.

XIII. THE PEOPLE'S CONFESSION OF SIN (10:1-17)

Observant readers will note the change from first person to third
person even though chapter 10 continues the sequence of events
from chapter 9. Scholars propose varied explanations for this pecu-
liarity.[60] One view is that for chapter 10 the author has drawn from
a different source, not from Ezra's Memoirs. Another suggestion is
that two separate sources, a first-person and a third-person, have
been combined. The more compelling reason, which we adopt here,
is that the author drew on the first-person Ezra Memoirs but changed
this part to the third person because he abbreviates in some places
and inserts comments in others.

A. EFFECT OF EZRA'S PRAYER (10:1-6)

[1]**While Ezra was praying and confessing, weeping and throwing
himself down before the house of God, a large crowd of Israelites—
men, women and children—gathered around him. They too wept
bitterly. [2]Then Shecaniah son of Jehiel, one of the descendants of
Elam, said to Ezra, "We have been unfaithful to our God by marrying foreign women from the peoples around us. But in spite of**

---

[60]Space does not permit a presentation of all the arguments; they are ably
marshaled in Williamson, *Ezra, Nehemiah*, pp. 145-149.

this, there is still hope for Israel. ³Now let us make a covenant before our God to send away all these women and their children, in accordance with the counsel of my lord and of those who fear the commands of our God. Let it be done according to the Law. ⁴Rise up; this matter is in your hands. We will support you, so take courage and do it."

⁵So Ezra rose up and put the leading priests and Levites and all Israel under oath to do what had been suggested. And they took the oath. ⁶Then Ezra withdrew from before the house of God and went to the room of Jehohanan son of Eliashib. While he was there, he ate no food and drank no water, because he continued to mourn over the unfaithfulness of the exiles.

10:1 . . . a large crowd of Israelites . . . gathered around him. . . .

A group of those who "trembled at the words of the God of Israel" had been with Ezra before his prayer, as he sat in stunned silence. As he prayed, weeping and casting himself prostrate, others gathered until there was a crowd. **Before the house of God** must have been in an outer court or an area where women and children were allowed. The emotional condition of Ezra was contagious. Soon they were weeping uncontrollably (lit., "wept much weeping"). This was a natural human reaction once they were informed about the grave situation that explained why this respected community leader was prostrate on the ground sobbing.

10:2a Then Shecaniah son of Jehiel . . .

He was from a family of the first returnees (2:7). It was primarily this group that had intermarried with the local population. **Jehiel** may be the person mentioned in verse 26. If so, Shecaniah denounced his own father, an indication of the zeal kindled by Ezra. Kidner comments, "Instead of whipping a reluctant people into action, Ezra has pricked their conscience to the point at which they now urge *him* to act."[61]

10:2b We have been unfaithful to our God

Shecaniah[62] is not listed among those who had intermarried (vv. 18-43); therefore, his confession, like that of Ezra, was not per-

---

[61]Kidner, *Ezra & Nehemiah*, pp. 69-70.

[62]His exact identification is problematic; eight people are so named in

sonal but collective, on behalf of the entire community. How important it is for God's people in every age to observe communal unity.
This was the core of the prayer of Jesus (John 17) and Paul's instruction to a fragmented church in Corinth (1 Cor 12:14-26).

by marrying foreign women

The Hebrew נֹשֶׁב (*nōšeb*, literally, "caused to dwell") is used only
here and in Nehemiah 13 for "to marry." It implies, "provided with
a home." Shecaniah recognized that by bringing foreign women into
their homes they had broken faith with God. But Shecaniah thought
that they could escape the inevitable disaster Ezra had envisioned in
his prayer. The hope for Israel involved the action he proposed.

10:3 Now let us make a covenant . . .

He does not propose to bargain with God, but to renew the
covenant God had made with Israel by taking a solemn oath **before
our God**, with God as their witness. Words without action can be
meaningless. Shecaniah proposes to reverse the situation by sending
away **all these women and their children**. "To send away" in
Hebrew is literally "to cause to go out." As with the word for marriage, לְהוֹצִיא (*lᵉhôṣî'*) is not the usual word for divorce. Perhaps this
was due to the situation. As Fensham notes, "Foreign women were
married contrary to the law of God. The marriages were illegal from
the outset. The sending away of the women is to guard the exiles
against the continuation of an illegal act. . . . Even the children born
from the illegal marriages must be sent away. This proposal is harsh
in the light of modern Christian conceptions. Why should innocent
children be punished? We must remember that the religious influence of the mothers on their children was regarded as the stumbling
block. [There is no indication of conversion in these marriages.] To
keep the religion of the Lord pure was the one and only aim of Ezra
and the returned exiles. As a small minority group, the repatriates
lived in the Holy Land among a large population of influential people who were followers of various polytheistic religions. Against
such larger numbers they had to defend themselves and their religious identity. Thus the drastic measures are understandable."[63]

---

the Bible, six of them lived in the 6th–5th centuries B.C. See *ABD*, V:1173-
1174.
[63]Fensham, *The Books of Ezra and Nehemiah*, p. 135.

Nothing is said in the text about the outcome for these women and children. The author/editor could not swerve from his main focus to deal with such matters. However, these were arranged marriages. The women would have returned to their paternal families with their children. With them they would have taken their dowries and any other property they had brought into the marriage or acquired. With them also would go the animosity against the Jewish community that may have contributed to antagonisms Nehemiah was to confront.

. . . with the counsel of my lord . . .

The reference is clearly to Ezra, showing the high esteem with which Shecaniah held Ezra. Nowhere in the preceding chapter was there a hint of what Shecaniah urges. This suggests that Ezra had been teaching about the problem before the report occurred that set off this chain of events. Whatever the specifics in Ezra's counsel may have been, the general theme was echoed in Shecaniah's words, **Let it be done according to the Law.** He may have been referring to the prohibition of mixed marriages (Deut 7:3) or to divorce procedures (Deut 24:1ff).

10:4 Rise up; . . . take courage and do it.

These imperatives call for Ezra to act now. With encouragement such as this, Ezra arose to the challenge, the responsibility, and the hope.

10:5 . . . And they took the oath.

The taking of an oath here is the equivalent of making a covenant, offered above by Shecaniah. Once the leaders swore to follow through, obedience could be expected from the rest of the people.

10:6 Then Ezra withdrew . . . and went . . .

Ezra went into one of the rooms around the perimeter of the temple courts, that of Jehohanan the son of Eliashib. A high priest named Eliashib is mentioned in Nehemiah 3:1. Some commentators say that he was the father of this Jehohanan. They then argue that Ezra obviously came after Nehemiah, ca. 400 B.C. The arguments are various and involved; they are sufficiently explored by Williamson, so we will not repeat them here.[64] Since Jehohanan was a popular

---

[64]Williamson, *Ezra, Nehemiah*, pp. 151-154.

name, and since his father, Eliashib, is not here identified as high priest, we will assume that this Jehohanan has no direct connection to the Eliashib of Nehemiah 3:1. However, he was a friend and fellow priest with Ezra. Our attention ought rather to be focused on Ezra. Despite the initiative he had taken, he was still deeply concerned for his people. How easily they had forgotten why they had grown up in exile and had fallen into the very sins of their forefathers. In private he continued to mourn and fast about the gravity of what his people had done.

B. THE CALL TO CONVENE (10:7-8)

⁷A proclamation was then issued throughout Judah and Jerusalem for all the exiles to assemble in Jerusalem. ⁸Anyone who failed to appear within three days would forfeit all his property, in accordance with the decision of the officials and elders, and would himself be expelled from the assembly of the exiles.

10:7-8 A proclamation was then issued . . .

We should assume that after Ezra finished fasting and praying in Jehohanan's room, he conferred with the leaders who had taken the oath and developed a plan of action. A summons from **the officials and elders** was sent throughout Jerusalem and Judah to assemble in Jerusalem. We can assume that only the men were required to come. The time limit was sufficient, because the region of Yehud (including Benjamin, v. 9) was relatively small. No one was forced to attend, but failure to do so was severe — confiscation of property and total excommunication. Banishment would have serious social, economic, and religious consequences. **Forfeit** translates a Hebrew word related to חֵרֶם (ḥērem), "banned, devoted [to God]." The confiscated property would come into the temple treasury (cf. Lev 7:21). The authority to impose such penalties had been given to Ezra by Artaxerxes (7:26).

The purpose of the assembly was for the entire community to become informed about the crisis and to agree to the proposed resolution of it. Only a small part of the male population had been in front of the temple at the time of Ezra's prayer; the rest were uninformed.

C. THE ASSEMBLY OF THE RETURNEES (10:9-17)

⁹Within the three days, all the men of Judah and Benjamin had gathered in Jerusalem. And on the twentieth day of the ninth month, all the people were sitting in the square before the house of God, greatly distressed by the occasion and because of the rain. ¹⁰Then Ezra the priest stood up and said to them, "You have been unfaithful; you have married foreign women, adding to Israel's guilt. ¹¹Now make confession to the LORD, the God of your fathers, and do his will. Separate yourselves from the peoples around you and from your foreign wives."

¹²The whole assembly responded with a loud voice: "You are right! We must do as you say. ¹³But there are many people here and it is the rainy season; so we cannot stand outside. Besides, this matter cannot be taken care of in a day or two, because we have sinned greatly in this thing. ¹⁴Let our officials act for the whole assembly. Then let everyone in our towns who has married a foreign woman come at a set time, along with the elders and judges of each town, until the fierce anger of our God in this matter is turned away from us." ¹⁵Only Jonathan son of Asahel and Jahzeiah son of Tikvah, supported by Meshullam and Shabbethai the Levite, opposed this.

¹⁶So the exiles did as was proposed. Ezra the priest selected men who were family heads, one from each family division, and all of them designated by name. On the first day of the tenth month they sat down to investigate the cases, ¹⁷and by the first day of the first month they finished dealing with all the men who had married foreign women.

10:9 . . . all the men of Judah and Benjamin had gathered in Jerusalem. . . .

The third day was the twentieth of Kislev (Nov./Dec.), a little over four months since Ezra's arrival and in the midst of the rainy season. All the men were sitting, not on chairs but on the stone pavement, likely in the broad space in front of "the Water Gate" (Neh 3:26; 8:1). They were **greatly distressed**, literally "trembling," for two reasons. Without was the heavy, cold rain; within was anguish over this crisis situation. We may surmise that inner distress for some focused on the guilt of "faithlessness." Some may have been distressed over the thought of sending away a wife and children.

10:10-11 No indication is given of the time of day the men assembled nor how long they waited in the rain before Ezra arose and addressed them. His remarks were short and direct, yet sufficient to inform his audience. By marrying foreign women, they had disobeyed God's will and had added **to Israel's guilt**. Rather than living thankfully and faithfully, in light of the catastrophe their forefather's guilt had caused, the restored community had added to that guilt by their own disloyalty. What to do? First, **make confession**, literally, "to give thanks/praise." God is praised in the human act of confession, which acknowledges the righteousness of God in contrast to the guilt of the confessor. Doing God's will, keeping his law will follow true confession. This required separation from the people of the land and from their foreign wives. Only this sacrifice would atone for their sin in intermarrying.

10:12-14 . . . You are right! . . .

The response was immediate, positive, and vocal. But the combination of the nasty weather and the length of time needed to investigate the circumstances for each man required a more protracted arrangement. An appropriate procedure was suggested, likely by a few leaders. A commission of **officials**, (הַשָּׂרִים, *haśśārîm*, the same word as used in 9:1) would be in charge of the matter. They would remain in Jerusalem, and at appointed times individuals would appear before them, accompanied by local officials. The latter would no doubt have made preliminary investigations. This process would continue until all cases had been resolved. Only then the disaster of God's fierce anger might be averted.

10:15 Only . . . opposed this.

On that rainy day, the opposition to this plan was extremely limited; only four men are listed, and one was a Levite. The nature of their opposition is unclear in the original. Did they oppose the plan, desiring for immediate resolution of the matter? Did they oppose the required divorce? It may be that our author has left out details in which we would be interested but which were not included for the sake of brevity and focus. The point is that any opposition was minute.

Meshullam

If he was the same person mentioned in verse 29, we could understand his opposition, because he was forced to give up his foreign wife. But there are at least ten Meshullams in Ezra–Nehemiah. It is doubtful that this was the Meshullam who had arrived with Ezra less than a year earlier (8:16), unless he was opposed to lengthening the process of resolving the problem.

10:16-17 The proposed plan was adopted, and Ezra appointed the commission. There is no evidence that he involved himself intimately in their work. He appointed them and rightly assumed they would pursue the plan responsibly. Master administrator that he was, no doubt he consulted others in the process of making the appointments. His wisdom is also evident in that commission members were heads of all the families. The text indicates that all of them were designated by name. The names were likely listed in Ezra's Memoirs, but the author decided not to include them here, again for the sake of brevity. Fensham notes that it took about three months to complete the investigation.[65] From the list below, that would amount to less than two cases a day; however, there must have been a number of cases investigated in which divorce was not required. Conversions could have occurred in which the foreign women would have become a part of the Jewish community.

Ezra's concern, and that of the commission, was to establish the authenticity of every Jewish family. Williamson observes, "The commission itself is thus presented in the Memoir as the fulfillment of Ezra's primary duty according to the edict of Artaxerxes. Surprising as this may seem at first sight, it probably conforms rather more closely to what Artaxerxes intended than is generally recognized . . . ."[66] Interestingly, they completed the work one year to the day from Ezra's intended departure from Babylon (7:9).

XIV. THOSE GUILTY OF INTERMARRIAGE (10:18-44)

This section lists 110 (or 111, depending on the reading of v. 40) men who had taken foreign wives: seventeen priests, ten Levites,

---

[65]Fensham, *Ezra and Nehemiah*, p. 142.
[66]Williamson, *Ezra, Nehemiah*, p. 157.

and eighty-three (or eighty-four) from lay families. We can assume it
was drawn from temple archives and/or from Ezra's Memoirs.

A. GUILTY PRIESTS (10:18-22)

[18]**Among the descendants of the priests, the following had married foreign women:**

> **From the descendants of Jeshua son of Jozadak, and his
> brothers: Maaseiah, Eliezer, Jarib and Gedaliah. [19](They all
> gave their hands in pledge to put away their wives, and for
> their guilt they each presented a ram from the flock as a
> guilt offering.)**
> [20]**From the descendants of Immer:**
> **Hanani and Zebadiah.**
> [21]**From the descendants of Harim:**
> **Maaseiah, Elijah, Shemaiah, Jehiel and Uzziah.**
> [22]**From the descendants of Pashhur:**
> **Elioenai, Maaseiah, Ishmael, Nethanel, Jozabad and
> Elasah.**

10:18 . . . Jeshua son of Jozadak . . .

This ancestor had been a contemporary of Zerubbabel and a
coleader in the return under Cyrus (2:2). The high priestly family is
mentioned first, in reverse order of chapter 2. This arrangement
emphasizes that "unfaithfulness" (9:2) was found within the leading
religious family in Jerusalem.

10:19 Once the commission had established the guilt of a man,
he followed this procedure. While this is mentioned only of the
priests, it was likely required of all the other groups. Leviticus 5:14-
16 indicates that even inadvertent sins require atonement, so it is
reasonable to assume that all these guilty parties were required to
present a sacrifice.

10:20-22 Three other priestly families had members who had
intermarried with non-Jewish families.

B. GUILTY LEVITES (10:23-24)

[23]Among the Levites:

Jozabad, Shimei, Kelaiah (that is, Kelita), Pethahiah, Judah
and Eliezer.
[24]From the singers:
Eliashib.
From the gatekeepers:
Shallum, Telem and Uri.

10:23-24 Next down the hierarchical ladder are the Levites and
related temple personnel. This grouping follows the order of 2:40-
42. Kelaiah appears in Nehemiah 8:7 and 10:11 as Kelita.

C. OTHER GUILTY ISRAELITES (10:25-44)

[25]And among the other Israelites:

From the descendants of Parosh:
Ramiah, Izziah, Malkijah, Mijamin, Eleazar, Malkijah and
Benaiah.
[26]From the descendants of Elam:
Mattaniah, Zechariah, Jehiel, Abdi, Jeremoth and Elijah.
[27]From the descendants of Zattu:
Elioenai, Eliashib, Mattaniah, Jeremoth, Zabad and Aziza.
[28]From the descendants of Bebai:
Jehohanan, Hananiah, Zabbai and Athlai.
[29]From the descendants of Bani:
Meshullam, Malluch, Adaiah, Jashub, Sheal and Jeremoth.
[30]From the descendants of Pahath-Moab:
Adna, Kelal, Benaiah, Maaseiah, Mattaniah, Bezalel, Binnui
and Manasseh.
[31]From the descendants of Harim:
Eliezer, Ishijah, Malkijah, Shemaiah, Shimeon, [32]Benjamin,
Malluch and Shemariah.
[33]From the descendants of Hashum:
Mattenai, Mattattah, Zabad, Eliphelet, Jeremai, Manasseh
and Shimei.

³⁴**From the descendants of Bani:**

Maadai, Amram, Uel, ³⁵Benaiah, Bedeiah, Keluhi, ³⁶Vaniah, Meremoth, Eliashib, ³⁷Mattaniah, Mattenai and Jaasu.

³⁸**From the descendants of Binnui:ᵃ**

Shimei, ³⁹Shelemiah, Nathan, Adaiah, ⁴⁰Macnadebai, Shashai, Sharai, ⁴¹Azarel, Shelemiah, Shemariah, ⁴²Shallum, Amariah and Joseph.

⁴³**From the descendants of Nebo:**

Jeiel, Mattithiah, Zabad, Zebina, Jaddai, Joel and Benaiah.

⁴⁴**All these had married foreign women, and some of them had children by these wives.ᵇ**

ᵃ*37,38* See Septuagint (also 1 Esdras 9:34); Hebrew *Jaasu ³⁸and Bani and Binnui,*   ᵇ*44* Or *and they sent them away with their children.*

10:25-43 And among the other Israelites:

These are the non-temple-related people, the laity. The names in the list occur in chapter 2, but the order is not exactly the same.

The appearance of two individuals with identical names (Malkijah) from the same extended family should cause no problem. First Esdras 9:26, however, lists Hashabiah in place of the second Malkijah.

The family name Bani occurs in both verses 29 and 34. Williamson holds the opinion that one occurrence must be a corruption. Noting the list in chapter 2, he suggests substituting "Bigvai" (2:14) for one family name in this list, a reasonable adjustment.⁶⁷ Compare the footnote in the NIV for verse 38 in which Bani occurs in the original, but the indicated emendation has been used to solve the textual problem.

10:40 Macnadebai is strikingly unusual for a biblical personal name; there is an obvious textual problem here. It is difficult to resolve, but a likely solution is to emend the text to read וּמִבְּנֵי (*ûmibᵉnê*) "of the sons/descendants of" plus a family name. In 1 Esdras 9:24, one reads "from the descendants of Ezora." The latter name is of little help, but it points toward the possibility of "Zaccai" from 2:9. Williamson has used "Azzur," following 1 Esdras; Fensham has employed "Zaccai."⁶⁸

---

⁶⁷Williamson, *Ezra, Nehemiah*, p. 144.
⁶⁸Ibid., p. 142; Fensham, *The Books of Ezra and Nehemiah*, p. 143.

10:44 The NIV translators have struggled with this verse, as the footnote indicates. There are grammatical peculiarities in the Hebrew, for one thing, particularly with the last clause. Literally it translates, "and there were of them wives, and they put children." The Greek text of 1 Esdras 9:36 translates, "and they sent them and the children away," but 2 Esdras 10:44 in the LXX follows the Hebrew. Fensham notes this and follows 1 Esdras: "and they sent the wives and children away."[69]

After a careful examination of the options, Williamson translates, "and some of the women had even borne children." He also notes, "If it is true that in the original list v 19 or its equivalent was repeated at the end of each of the list's main sections, then perhaps its equivalent once stood after this verse, too. . . . MT [the Hebrew] may stand as an indication that the narrator was not insensitive to the personal tragedies he was recording."[70]

But this is a peculiar way to end the narrative about Ezra before continuing with Nehemiah. It suggests at the least that the end of the manuscript may have been damaged or lost in the course of transmission.

The story of the revived community in Jerusalem and Yehud pauses here. Our author/editor will pick up for his readers the thread of the narrative with the return of Nehemiah more than a decade later.

---

[69]Fensham, *The Books of Ezra and Nehemiah*, pp. 143-144.
[70]Williamson, *Ezra, Nehemiah*, pp. 143-145, 159.

XV. NEHEMIAH'S PRAYER (1:1-11)

The account of the hand and power of God at work to restore his people in Jerusalem is continued by the author/editor of Ezra–Nehemiah in this part of his narrative. The name of the book is appropriate, because Nehemiah is the main human figure in the story. Scholars almost universally agree that much of the book, and in particular the first-person sections in the story, come from the Nehemiah Memoirs, which the author had at hand, just as with the memoirs of Ezra. Likely these were deposited in the archives in the restored temple in Jerusalem, along with other records and documents, such as genealogical lists. Just as Ezra is remembered for rescuing the Jewish community in Jerusalem from assimilation and establishing the Law of Moses as the rule of faith and practice, Nehemiah is remembered as God's agent for rebuilding the city and its security. Both were moved by faith in the God of heaven and concern for God's people in Jerusalem and Yehud.

A. REPORT FROM JERUSALEM (1:1-4)

¹The words of Nehemiah son of Hacaliah:

In the month of Kislev in the twentieth year, while I was in the citadel of Susa, ²Hanani, one of my brothers, came from Judah with some other men, and I questioned them about the Jewish remnant that survived the exile, and also about Jerusalem.

³They said to me, "Those who survived the exile and are back in the province are in great trouble and disgrace. The wall of Jerusalem is broken down, and its gates have been burned with fire."

⁴When I heard these things, I sat down and wept. For some days I mourned and fasted and prayed before the God of heaven.

1:1a The words of Nehemiah son of Hacaliah:

The compiler of the history that follows introduces the subject with this brief title.

The name Nehemiah means, "the Lord has comforted." The same root occurs in the name of Nahum the prophet and in the famous phrase from Isaiah 40:1, "Comfort, comfort my people."

The name was popular; another Nehemiah is referred to in 3:16 and a third in Ezra 2:2 // Nehemiah 7:7. His father's name is otherwise unknown in the OT.[71] Because almost a century and a half had passed since Nebuchadnezzar's conquest and the beginning of the exile, Hacaliah would have been born in exile and probably his father as well. But family memories persisted through the generations; Nehemiah mentioned to the king that Jerusalem was the place where his forefathers were buried (2:3,5).

It is interesting that Nehemiah is remembered and praised in the Wisdom of Jesus Son of Sirach (Eccl 49:13), while Ezra is not mentioned. In another book of the Apocrypha, Nehemiah is referred to in respect of "the festival of fire" (2 Macc 1:18-36) as well as founding a library (2:13).

1:1b In the month of Kislev

"Now it came to pass" in KJV translates וַיְהִי (way ̊hî), a frequently used expression that the NIV leaves untranslated, since it adds nothing essential to the content.

There is a question as to what calendar Nehemiah was using. The first month of the year beginning in the spring was Nisan, so Kislev would have been the ninth month; however, a fall New Year in Tishri would make Kislev the third month. This latter is likely the dating Nehemiah is using, for in 2:1 he mentions Nisan as also in the twentieth year of Artaxerxes.

in the twentieth year

It seems peculiar that the name of the king is not mentioned here. It may have appeared in the sources the editor was using, but for the sake of brevity and because this section follows immediately after that in Ezra in which Artaxerxes had been identified as the ruler in his seventh year (7:8), he chose not to name him here. Artaxerxes I was clearly the king under whom Nehemiah served. His twentieth year was 445 B.C.

while I was in the citadel of Susa,

The city of Susa (Shushan) was the winter residence of the Persian rulers. It was south of Ecbatana, the summer capital, and

---

[71]A Hacaliah was an Egyptian (Jewish) general (Josephus *Ant.* 13.10, 13), and a slave by that name is known from the Wadi Daliyeh Papyri, ca. 331 B.C. (Frank Cross, "The Discovery of the Samaria Papyri," *BA* 26 [1963]: 111f.).

about 150 miles north of the Persian Gulf. Darius I had built a palace there during 518–512 B.C. The citadel was situated on the highest part of the city and was a fortress walled off from the rest of the city for the sake of royal security. Events in Esther occurred in Susa, and it figured in the vision of Daniel (8:2).

1:2 Hanani, one of my brothers,

Although the word "brother" does not have to connote a family relationship, Hanani apparently was Nehemiah's blood brother. In 7:2 he is mentioned again by the same designation and is given a major responsibility by Nehemiah.

came from Judah with some other men,

Hanani (shortened form of Hananiah, "Yahweh has been gracious") and the men with him arrived in Susa after the thousand-mile journey from Jerusalem. Hanani had either immigrated to Judah previously or had traveled there to see at firsthand what conditions were.[72] The family of Hacaliah may have owned property there; as noted above, the tomb of their ancestors was still there. What is clear is that Jews living in Persia could and did travel to and from "the old home country."

and I questioned them . . .

Something of Nehemiah's character already begins to appear here with his concern for the condition of others of "the household of faith." The people of his concern are literally identified as "the Jews, the escaped, who remain of the captivity." To whom does Nehemiah refer? Those who had returned from Babylon to Jerusalem or the descendants of those who had never been taken into exile? The NIV's use of **remnant** is based on the greater probability that Nehemiah refers to those who had returned to the homeland from exile.

Nehemiah wanted to know the economic, social, and religious circumstances of the Jews in Judah. He also asked about the physical condition of Jerusalem itself.

---

[72]Hanani and those with him may have been a delegation coming directly to Artaxerxes in Susa in order to bypass the dominant and unfriendly Samaritans who had blocked attempts to rebuild Jerusalem. Cf. *ABD*, III:46.

1:3 The response to Nehemiah's inquiries is reported succinctly; much greater detail would certainly have been given as the men talked with Nehemiah. The heart of their report is given here: the remnant **who . . . are back in the province** (not just the city) **are in great trouble**, that is, in great poverty. The causes for these conditions were at least twofold, deteriorating religious devotion (cf. Hag 1:5-6; Mal 3:6-12) and Persian economic policies.

> "Artaxerxes 1 continued Xerxes' policy of non-taxation for Persians; accordingly, Artaxerxes increased taxes throughout the rest of the empire . . . [he thereby] . . . significantly depleted the money supply. Coined money was rare, and loan sharks became common. Local landowners became bankrupt and lost their land . . . ."[73]

The condition of Jerusalem was deplorable, too. The report of the broken-down walls and burned gates does not refer to the destruction caused by Nebuchadnezzar one hundred and forty years earlier. What is only hinted at in Ezra 4:12 must have resulted in destructive activity on the part of "the enemies of Judah and Benjamin" (Ezra 4:1) after they received the response from this same King Artaxerxes early in his reign. At that time the western fringe of the Persian Empire was under stress from revolts, including that of Egypt with the assistance of Greece. Even the satrap of Trans-Euphrates, Megabyzus, rebelled briefly in 448 B.C.[74]

1:4 Nehemiah's response to the report reflects his spiritual sensitivity and compassion. It is not true that strong men do not cry. Similar to the response of Ezra to the news brought to him when he sat in stunned silence then wept (Ezra 9–10:1), Nehemiah **sat down and wept**. Devout Jews still sit *shivah*, in mourning for seven days after the death of a close relative. Nehemiah continued to mourn, fast, and pray. He does not disclose the content of those days of prayer, but they must have included the concerns he recorded in this first of nine prayers in the book.

---

[73]Jon L. Berquist, *Judaism in Persia's Shadow: A Social and Historical Approach* (Minneapolis: Fortress Press, 1995), p. 106.
[74]Ibid., p. 107.

B. THE PRAYER OF NEHEMIAH (1:5-11)

⁵Then I said:

"O LORD, God of heaven, the great and awesome God, who keeps his covenant of love with those who love him and obey his commands, ⁶let your ear be attentive and your eyes open to hear the prayer your servant is praying before you day and night for your servants, the people of Israel. I confess the sins we Israelites, including myself and my father's house, have committed against you. ⁷We have acted very wickedly toward you. We have not obeyed the commands, decrees and laws you gave your servant Moses.

⁸"Remember the instruction you gave your servant Moses, saying, 'If you are unfaithful, I will scatter you among the nations, ⁹but if you return to me and obey my commands, then even if your exiled people are at the farthest horizon, I will gather them from there and bring them to the place I have chosen as a dwelling for my Name.'

¹⁰"They are your servants and your people, whom you redeemed by your great strength and your mighty hand. ¹¹O Lord, let your ear be attentive to the prayer of this your servant and to the prayer of your servants who delight in revering your name. Give your servant success today by granting him favor in the presence of this man."

I was cupbearer to the king.

The elements of this prayer are (a) invocation, verse 5; (b) plea to be heard, verse 6a; (c) confession of sin, verses 6b-7; (d) petition for God to remember his promises and his people, verses 8-10); (e) a personal request, verse 11a.

1:5 O Lord, God of heaven, . . .

יהוה אָנָּא (*'ānnāh YHWH*), literally, "Ah, now, Yahweh," addresses the Lord almost with a groan of entreaty. **God,** (אֵל, *'ēl*) signifies the divine attribute of power. Nehemiah recognizes that the God of heaven is virtually beyond human description, worthy of all reverential awe, echoing Deuteronomy 7:21. His faithfulness endures through all generations, showing covenant love (חֶסֶד, *ḥesed*) to those who love (אֹהֵב, 'ohēb) him and keep his commands. The term ḥesed, "faith, loyalty," reflects Deuteronomy 7:9. It is used frequently in the OT concerning God's covenant relationship with his people. The word 'oheb is the more common word for human love; the Shema (Deut 6:4-5), the creed of Judaism, commands the faithful to love God, and Jesus noted love of God as the greatest commandment (Matt 26:37).

1:6-7 your ear . . . your eyes

Nehemiah's request that God will heed his prayer reminds us of Solomon's petition (1 Kgs 8:52). God is not human with ears and eyes, but we have no other means of addressing him but with human language. Prayer can degenerate into vain repetitions, but Nehemiah's consistent and persistent prayers have poured forth from a burdened heart. In the parable of the persistent widow, Jesus taught that persevering prayer is effective (Matt 18:1-8).

Nehemiah's prayers have been **for your servants, the people of Israel**, rather than for himself alone. Although he is about to confess their disloyalty, yet he identifies them as God's servants. Although the sins he confesses are not specified, he includes himself and his family as also guilty, perhaps following the example of Moses in the case of the golden calf (Exod 34:9). The reference to **commands** (מִצְוֹת, miṣwōth), **decrees** (חֻקִּים, ḥuqqîm), and **laws** (מִשְׁפָּטִים, mišpāṭîm) is comprehensive in its coverage of the Mosaic legislation.

1:8 Remember . . .

זְכָר (zᵉkor) is followed in the original by a particle of entreaty, נָא (nā'), a shortened form of the one noted in verse 5, rendered in KJV, "I beseech thee." This adds a touch of the passionate humility, which is Nehemiah's attitude throughout the prayer. What God is called to remember is set off in quotation marks in the NIV; however, no precise quotation can be found in the OT. Nehemiah here incorporates phrases from passages such as Leviticus 26:33; Deuteronomy 4:27,29; 30:4-5.

1:9 If . . . , but if . . . , then even if . . .

Nehemiah asks the God of heaven to recall his promise of restoration despite the history of his people's unfaithfulness. As far as they might be from the land of promise, remember your promise to gather them and bring them back, **even** from **the farthest horizon**.

KJV translates בִּקְצֵה הַשָּׁמַיִם (*biqṣēh haššāmayim*) literally, "unto the uttermost part of the heaven"; NRSV renders "under the farthest skies." The expression recalls Deuteronomy 30:4. Since there were those who had been brought back living in the environs of Jerusalem, Nehemiah may have sensed that something was still lacking in the return, thus the reference to **the place I have chosen as a dwelling for my Name**. Williamson notes that this expression "implies the Divine Presence dwelling with the restored community. It is precisely that, according to Nehemiah, which the currently prevailing conditions show yet to lie in the future."[75] In Ezekiel's vision, the glory of the Lord departed from the Jerusalem temple (11:22-24) and the Sovereign Lord promised, "Although I sent them far away among the nations and scattered them among the countries, yet for a little while I have been a sanctuary for them in the countries where they have gone" (11:16). This suggests that "the divine glory is present among the exiles in Babylon."[76] The unanswered question is, "Did the divine glory return to the rebuilt Jerusalem temple?"

1:10 They are your servants and your people . . .

The expression refers to those whom Nehemiah mentioned in verse 6, "your servants, the people of Israel." In light of verse 3, the reference is to those of the exile who were back in Judah in dire straits. They had returned to God, and he had returned them to the land. They were not aliens, but his own people, with all the unexpressed hope that is thereby implied.

1:11 Having prayed for the Jewish remnant, Nehemiah pleads for the Lord to hear his own request. This time he uses both forms of the particles of entreaty, *'annāh* and *nā'*, noted previously, indicating a passionate plea. The Lord knew the desire of his heart; Nehemiah had prayed about the condition of Jerusalem since he had heard the report of its sorry state. Apparently he was aware of others who were praying about the general matter as well, **your servants who delight in revering your name**. Reference to the "name" is equivalent to God. In the course of time Jewish reverence for God

---

[75]Williamson, *Ezra, Nehemiah*, p. 173.

[76]Robert R. Wilson, "Ezekiel," *Harper's Bible Commentary*, James L. May, gen. ed. (San Francisco: Harper & Row, 1988), p. 669.

caused them to refrain from pronouncing YHWH; instead they spoke of him as HaShem, "The (divine) name."

The petition is straightforward but general. Nehemiah knew that **today** was the day, but he did not presume to advise God as to how he should proceed to assure Nehemiah's success before the king. The expression **this man** does not belittle the king. It does recognize that the monarch was a human being with whom Nehemiah had to deal. Only God could establish the environment in which Nehemiah could find favor before the king.

The possibility that Artaxerxes would not be favorable certainly existed. We noticed above the unsettled situation on the western borders of the empire. Not too many years earlier he had prevented further construction in Jerusalem. Why would he change his policy now? It has been suggested that the strengthening of the small province of Yehud, populated with Jews loyal to the empire, would counteract the tendencies toward rebellion in the region.[77] It would be a pro-Persian anchor in the region.

I was cupbearer to the king.

Nehemiah had not so identified himself earlier, but here he inserts the information as a preface to the events that follow. His position not only permitted him access to the king, but also required his presence. Persian kings, as with monarchs in every age, were always faced with the possibility that someone would attempt to poison them. The cupbearer not only brought the king's wine to him, but on occasion might be required to sip from the cup to guarantee it was not lethal. This was a position of the highest trust.[78] Possessing recognized high Jewish morals and being a non-Persian with no pretense to the throne would have made Nehemiah an excellent choice for the office. The confidential relationship between the cupbearer and the king often established a warm bond between the two. A cupbearer could attain a high level of influence with his sovereign. The Book of Tobit mentions that a certain Ahikar was cupbearer, keeper

---

[77]Artaxerxes may have altered his policy and allowed the refortification of Jerusalem by Nehemiah because he would have a proven supporter in charge of a small, but loyal region in a strategic location. This would have been particularly true after the resolution of Megabyzus' rebellion. Cf. Berquist, *Judaism in Persia's Shadow*, pp. 112-113.

[78]Solomon's cupbearers are mentioned in 1 Kgs 10:5 and 2 Chr 9:4.

of the signet (ring), and a treasurer for the Assyrian ruler Esarhaddon (1:22).

Some commentators suggest that Nehemiah was a eunuch, since there is no indication that he had a family and since cupbearers were sometimes eunuchs.[79] However, this suggestion is highly unlikely, since castration would have made him unacceptable as a leader in the Jewish community (Deut 23:1).[80]

XVI. ARTAXERXES SENDS NEHEMIAH TO JERUSALEM (2:1-10)

A. NEHEMIAH'S REQUEST (2:1-5)

[1]In the month of Nisan in the twentieth year of King Artaxerxes, when wine was brought for him, I took the wine and gave it to the king. I had not been sad in his presence before; [2]so the king asked me, "Why does your face look so sad when you are not ill? This can be nothing but sadness of heart."

I was very much afraid, [3]but I said to the king, "May the king live forever! Why should my face not look sad when the city where my fathers are buried lies in ruins, and its gates have been destroyed by fire?"

[4]The king said to me, "What is it you want?"

Then I prayed to the God of heaven, [5]and I answered the king, "If it pleases the king and if your servant has found favor in his sight, let him send me to the city in Judah where my fathers are buried so that I can rebuild it."

2:1 In the month of Nisan . . .

The date in Nisan (March/April), the first month of their calendar, is not indicated. Williamson suggests that Nehemiah may have chosen to show his forlorn face at the start of the new year, during a festive occasion when the king was inclined to deny no requests to

---

[79]E.g., Fensham, *The Books of Ezra and Nehemiah*, p. 157; Myers, *Ezra–Nehemiah*, p. 96; *The Eerdman's Bible Commentary*, p. 404.

[80]E. Yamauchi, "Was Nehemiah the Cupbearer a Eunuch?" *ZAW* 92 (1980): 132-143, provides a comprehensive treatment of the question.

those present.[81] Perhaps Nehemiah had chosen the day; that is the implication of **Give your servant success today** in the prayer above.

I took the wine . . .

Envision the king eating with others, Nehemiah near him. A subordinate brought the wine to Nehemiah, who then tasted it and offered it to the king. The cupbearer then was adjacent to the king and fully visible to him.

. . . sad . . .

The Heb literally reads, רַע (ra‘), "bad," similar to our usage, "you look bad" for "you look ill." Nehemiah had been serving the king regularly but had masked his troubled heart. On this day he chose to reveal his true feelings. There was a certain danger in doing this — to appear worried or agitated in the king's presence might be interpreted as due to disloyal thoughts about him.

2:2 . . . This can be nothing but sadness of heart.

The king's expression, רֹעַ לֵב (rōa‘ lēb), literally, "badness of heart," must have disquieted Nehemiah. In that instant, fear stabbed at his heart. To arouse even the slightest suspicion could endanger the servant of a despot. "A king's wrath is a messenger of death" (Prov 16:14).

2:3 . . . May the king live forever! . . .

This common greeting for the king occurs also in Daniel 2:4 and 1 Kings 1:31. Despite the tug of fear he experienced, Nehemiah went on to explain why he was sad. No mention is made of Jerusalem; to do so might have reminded the king of his recent decree to stop all building in the city. Concern for the burial place of one's forefathers was not limited to Jews. The tomb of Cyrus was at Pasargadae, Cambyses near Persepolis, Darius and Xerxes, father and grandfather of Artaxerxes at Naqsh-i Rustam, three and a half miles north of Persepolis. There Artaxerxes himself would be buried.[82] As Slotki notes, "The appeal to be allowed to show respect for the dead would touch the sense of ancestral piety which was strong in the oriental heart."[83]

---

[81]Williamson, *Ezra, Nehemiah,* p. 178.

[82]Yamauchi, *Persia and the Bible,* p. 182.

[83]Slotki, *Daniel, Ezra and Nehemiah,* p. 188.

2:4 The king said to me, "What is it you want?" Then I prayed . . .

The king's question must have been asked in a tone of voice that hinted that he would hear Nehemiah with favor. As a devout person, his natural response was to pray. He did not record this prayer, as he had the earlier one, but it must have been a silent word of thanksgiving that the king seemed favorably disposed toward allowing him a request. It may have also been for divine guidance in stating his request.

2:5 . . . If it pleases the king . . .

It had pleased the heavenly king to answer Nehemiah's request that he might be granted favor in the presence of the king. Emboldened, Nehemiah makes a forthright request, **let him send me**. The request was not stated, "Allow me to go," but diplomatically suggested that the king take the initiative to send him **to the city in Judah**. Again Jerusalem is not explicitly named, although both Nehemiah and the king knew that was the city to which he requested to go. Nehemiah must have been sensitive to the impact the mention of Jerusalem might have on the king's courtiers who sat at table with him; they were well aware of the king's past policies and directives. Nehemiah was careful not to embarrass the king. Having mentioned the core of what he envisioned, **so that I can rebuild it**, he allowed the king to react and respond.

B. ARTAXERXES' RESPONSE (2:6-8)

[6]**Then the king, with the queen sitting beside him, asked me, "How long will your journey take, and when will you get back?" It pleased the king to send me; so I set a time.**

[7]**I also said to him, "If it pleases the king, may I have letters to the governors of Trans-Euphrates, so that they will provide me safe-conduct until I arrive in Judah?** [8]**And may I have a letter to Asaph, keeper of the king's forest, so he will give me timber to make beams for the gates of the citadel by the temple and for the city wall and for the residence I will occupy?" And because the gracious hand of my God was upon me, the king granted my requests.**

2:6 . . . with the queen sitting beside him . . .

The word for **queen**, שֵׁגַל (šēgal), is not the usual מַלְכָּה (malkāh).

It occurs in Psalm 45:9[10] and in Daniel 5:2 and seems to refer to the leading ladies of the harem. This woman may have been Damasias, the favored consort of Artaxerxes according to an ancient historian. The Book of Esther is evidence that a Persian queen could have considerable influence over the king's policies. This brief note without further explanation, that she was sitting beside the king as Nehemiah spoke with him, seems peculiar. But brevity is a hallmark of biblical writers. Here there is a hint that her presence was beneficial to Nehemiah's interchange with the king. That the queen was sitting beside the king, rather than on a chair at his feet as depicted in a bas relief, implies the possibility that Nehemiah has telescoped two meetings into this one report. The proposed scenario is that his initial conversation with the king took place at a large banquet, but the details were worked out in a private dinner with the queen present. The private dinner arranged by Esther provides an example of the latter setting.

. . . It pleased the king to send me, . . .

Williamson adds "when I had told him how long I should be" to make explicit what is implicit in the statement.[84] Once the time of departure, length of stay, and time of return were determined, the king approved. It is highly unlikely, however, that the king would grant a favorite cupbearer permission to be gone for twelve years, the period during which he was governor (5:14). The time was no doubt much shorter. Kidner makes the astute suggestion that "He is more likely to have reported back after the dedication of the walls, within the year, and then to have had his appointment as governor renewed."[85]

2:7 . . . may I have letters . . .

is in the passive mode in the original, literally, "let letters be given to me." Despite his gentle tone, Nehemiah was specific in his request. He asked for letters of safe-conduct. He was well aware of the hostile environment toward the Jews in the vicinity of Jerusalem. Hananiah and those with him must have revealed to him much more

---

[84]Williamson, *Ezra, Nehemiah*, p. 176.
[85]Kidner, *Ezra & Nehemiah*, p. 81. Since there is no reference to his appointment as governor here, we may suggest his return to Susa, within a year, his report to the king, and his subsequent appointment as governor.

than is recorded. Further, coming from Susa his mission would threaten the political security of local governors such as Sanballat. Letters from the king would allow him to pass safely through Trans-Euphrates to his destination.

2:8 And may I have a letter to Asaph, . . .

The verb of request is not repeated as he continues to specify his needs. Nehemiah knew intimately the affairs of the empire from his advantageous position, including the name of this important official. Further, the name is Semitic rather than Persian; Asaph may have been a fellow Jew. The word translated **forest** is פַּרְדֵּס (pardēs), a Persian word in origin (paridaida). In Hebrew it signifies a park; the Greek paradeisos is the basis for English "paradise." It occurs also in Song of Solomon 4:13 and Ecclesiastes 2:5. The location of this forest is unknown. It most likely was in Lebanon, the major source of timber for the empires of the ancient Near East. And it was the source of the timbers for rebuilding the temple (Ezra 3:7). Another possibility would be a source nearer Jerusalem. The mountains of Palestine were more heavily forested in antiquity than at present.

Nehemiah specifies three projects requiring timber in the construction. **The gates of the citadel** would consist of two thick plank doors constructed to swing inward and secured by a heavy cross-beam on the inside when closed. The citadel was no doubt located on the northwestern corner of the temple area, the highest point.[86] Gates and related towers in **the city wall** required timbers for construction as well. The third item in his list was **for the residence which I shall occupy**. This would either be an existing building that would be refurbished for his residence or a completely new construction. There may have been family property in Jerusalem. It may also have been a Persian governor's house previously provided for Zerubbabel (cf. Hag 1:1,14; 2:2,21).[87] An official from the Persian court would not be expected to live in a squalid hovel.

---

[86]The citadel is mentioned again in 7:2. The strategic point saw further construction by the Hasmoneans (1 Macc 13:52) and a major rebuilding by Herod the Great, converting it into the Fortress of Antonia (cf. Acts 21:37).

[87]Excavations at biblical Lachish revealed a small palace constructed in the Persian period designated "the Residency" by the excavators. Cf. OEANE, 3:322.

And because the gracious hand of my God was upon me, . . .

Note the discussion at Ezra 7:6. Nehemiah had prayed persistently as well as briefly. He had envisioned what he would do to remedy the sad situation in Jerusalem were he to go there. We would expect such a man of faith and vision to recognize the hand of God in fulfilling his desire. God had given him favor with the king. He is an example of what James had in mind when he advised, "If it is the Lord's will, we will do this or that" (4:15).

C. NEHEMIAH'S ACTION AND THE
OPPONENTS' REACTION (2:9-10)

⁹**So I went to the governors of Trans-Euphrates and gave them the king's letters. The king had also sent army officers and cavalry with me.**
¹⁰**When Sanballat the Horonite and Tobiah the Ammonite official heard about this, they were very much disturbed that someone had come to promote the welfare of the Israelites.**

2:9 Reminiscent of Ezra, who recorded nothing of the journey, Nehemiah simply mentions the deliverance of **the king's letters** to **the governors** as he made his way toward Judah. Apparently no problems occurred.

Note that Nehemiah had not asked for an armed escort; it was the king's initiative to send **army officers and cavalry** with him. The king would not have traveled without such an escort; neither would he allow his cupbearer to do so. The king had sent him on official Persian business. He was armed with official documents and a military cohort that demanded due respect from governors and commoners.

2:10 When Sanballat the Horonite and Tobiah the Ammonite . . .

Sanballat was the governor of Samaria and Tobiah was apparently a political leader in the region allied to Sanballat. One of the letters from Artaxerxes no doubt was addressed to Sanballat and delivered to him by Nehemiah. The negative reaction of Sanballat and Tobiah to the sudden news that a highly ranked Jew from the imperial court had come to **promote the welfare of the Israelites** must have been clearly evident.

The name Sanballat comes from Babylonian *Sin-uballiṭ*, "Sin (the moon god) gives life." Babylonian connections in his family may have reached back to the Assyrian resettlement of people in Samaria (2 Kgs 17:24). He apparently adhered to a form of Yahwistic religion, because he had two sons — Delaiah and Shelemiah — whose names ended in a shortened form of YHWH, like that of Nehemiah. It is also possible that he simply took a Babylonian name as had Zerubbabel. He is identified as **the Horonite**, a geographical designation. Both upper Beth-Horon and lower Beth-Horon are candidates for the place, about five miles northwest of Jerusalem on the descent from the highlands to the coastal plain (cf. Josh 16:3,5).

Sanballat is mentioned numerous times in Nehemiah (2:10,19; 4:1[3:33]; 4:7[1]; 6:1,2,5,12,14; and 13:28). He is identified as governor (*paḥat šmryn*) of Samaria in an Aramaic document among the Elephantine Papyri, dated to 408 B.C., although he would have been quite old then and he had delegated governing power to his two sons. A Sanballat was still governor when Alexander conquered the region (Josephus *Ant.* 11), so a descendant named after the family ancestor was in the governorship. The family lineage has been partially reconstructed on the basis of available sources.[88]

Tobiah the Ammonite official is, literally, "Tobiah, the servant, the Ammonite." Slotki conjectured that he was employed by Sanballat and "may have been a renegade Jew, judging by his name, and the term used by Nehemiah in contempt."[89] He is one of several individuals in the Bible bearing the name Tobiah, which means, "YHWH is good." The designation **the Ammonite** is parallel to **the Horonite**, and thus is geographical rather than ethnic. The Tobiad family had a long connection with Transjordan. At the archaeological site of Araq el-Emir the name was found carved in stone. The Tobiads were influential in Jerusalem in support of Greek culture in the period before the Maccabean Revolt[90] This particular Tobiah was friendly with the elite of Jerusalem, posing a problem with which Nehemiah had to deal over a decade later (13:4-9). Eskenazi has drawn attention to a possible connection between Tobiah the Ammonite and the Tobiah family among the first returnees who

[88]*ABD*, V:973-975.
[89]Slotki, *Daniel, Ezra and Nehemiah*, p. 190.
[90]Josephus, *Ant.* 12.160-236.

could not prove that their families were descended from Israel (Ezra 2:60). "Although the list of names does not specify the consequences, it is conceivable that the uncertain genealogy of these families forms the backdrop for the later tensions."[91]

XVII. NEHEMIAH INSPECTS JERUSALEM'S WALLS (2:11-20)

A. NEHEMIAH'S NOCTURNAL TOUR (2:11-16)

[11]**I went to Jerusalem, and after staying there three days [12]I set out during the night with a few men. I had not told anyone what my God had put in my heart to do for Jerusalem. There were no mounts with me except the one I was riding on.**

[13]**By night I went out through the Valley Gate toward the Jackal[a] Well and the Dung Gate, examining the walls of Jerusalem, which had been broken down, and its gates, which had been destroyed by fire. [14]Then I moved on toward the Fountain Gate and the King's Pool, but there was not enough room for my mount to get through; [15]so I went up the valley by night, examining the wall. Finally, I turned back and reentered through the Valley Gate. [16]The officials did not know where I had gone or what I was doing, because as yet I had said nothing to the Jews or the priests or nobles or officials or any others who would be doing the work.**

[a]*13 Or Serpent or Fig*

2:11-12 . . . after staying there three days . . .

Like Ezra (8:32), Nehemiah rested for three days after his lengthy journey. He probably met with the Jewish leaders also. The **few men** who accompanied him on his night inspection trip are not identified. They may have been personal attendants who came with him from Susa, along with a local person or two that he could trust and who were familiar with the city. The night inspection trip allowed him to secretly look over the condition of the walls and gates. It is highly likely that it was a moonlit night; otherwise, in an era long before street lights, starlight would have been insufficient

[91]*ABD,* VI:584.

COLLEGE PRESS NIV COMMENTARY

to see the way or to inspect the walls. **What my God had put in my heart** is a translation that veils the process by which an inspired plan was developing in Nehemiah's mind. Williamson catches the immediacy of the action expressed by a present participle, "what my God was prompting me to do."[92] He was forming the plan in his mind as he went, convinced that his thoughts were being framed by God.

The detail that only one animal was along, the one on which he rode, indicates the care he took to keep from arousing those sleeping nearby as he went. It was likely a donkey, sure-footed and quieter than a horse. Several horses would have made considerable noise.

It is clear that Nehemiah anticipated trouble and interference, particularly after he had noted the attitudes of Sanballat and Tobiah. As a new arrival in Jerusalem, he could not know whom to trust and whom to view with suspicion. After all, those two officials were well known and had well-established authority among the people in and round about Jerusalem. By keeping his inspection and plans secret, he could move forward with opposition considerably delayed.

2:13-15 the Valley Gate . . . the Valley Gate

Despite the detailed description Nehemiah gives of his counter-clockwise inspection of the city walls, extremely limited archaeological remains from the Persian period have survived. This is due in large part to subsequent destructions and reconstructions over two millennia of continuous occupation. The suggested locations of the various features are primarily educated guesses. Mare has provided a reasonable description on that basis.[93] What is clear is that the occupied area in Nehemiah's time was considerably less than that of pre-exilic Jerusalem. It was confined to the ridge and western slope of the City of David, the Temple Mount, and a modest area north of it. "The city developed on the crest of the narrow spur of the City of David, over an even smaller area than in the tenth century BCE."[94] Nehemiah's Jerusalem covered approximately twelve acres.

Ruins of the **Valley Gate** were likely discovered by J.W. Crowfoot in 1927 on the west side of the City of David on the eastern slope of

---

[92]Williamson, *Ezra, Nehemiah*, p. 185.

[93]W. Harold Mare, *The Archaeology of the Jerusalem Area* (Grand Rapids: Baker, 1987), pp. 121-128.

[94]"Shiloh," *NEAEH*, 2:709. On the use of "BCE," see p. 19, fn. 11.

the Central (Tyropoeon) Valley[95] about 500 yards from the **Dung Gate**. The Dung Gate was located south of the Valley Gate, likely as an exit into the Hinnom Valley near where it joins the Kidron Valley. It may have been known as the Potsherd Gate prior to the exile (Jer 19:2). Its name indicates its use as an exit for disposing of refuse. The **Jackal Well** (note the NIV footnote with the alternate translations) was located somewhere along the valley between the two gates. Debris has filled the Tyropoeon over the centuries so that all trace of it has been lost. The **Fountain** [Spring] **Gate** at the southeast corner of the city wall apparently allowed access to the spring En-Rogel, about 240 yards south of the junction of the Hinnom and Kidron Valleys.

From this southernmost point, Nehemiah turned north toward the Fountain Gate and the **King's Pool**. The gate could have given access to the Pool of Siloam, the King's Pool (?) from the Kidron Valley. Or there may have been a pool in the valley outside the walls into which overflow from the Siloam Pool emptied. It is also possible, and more likely, that the Fountain Gate allowed access to the Gihon Spring in the Kidron Valley. But Nehemiah was unable to ride to these two locations. The eastern wall of the city was on the eastern slope of the hill rather than in the Kidron Valley. So much destruction debris blocked his way that he could not follow the line of the wall and was forced to dismount, go down the slope into the valley, and walk north in it as he continued his inspection from a distance. At some point, probably opposite the south end of the temple mount, he turned around and retraced his route until he had returned to the Valley Gate. Since Kathleen Kenyon discovered a short line of a wall constructed in the Persian period on the eastern crest of the City of David, it is clear that Nehemiah had decided to abandon the earlier wall down the eastern slope, with all the debris, and established a new line of wall where construction would not be hampered.

2:16 The officials did not know . . .

Here Nehemiah restates what he had noted in verse 12, but here

---

[95]J.W. Crowfoot and G.M. Fitzgerald, *Excavations in the Tyropoeon Valley, Jerusalem, 1927* (London: Annual of the Palestine Exploration Fund for 1927, 1929), pp. 12-23.

specifying four groups: Jews, priests, nobles, and officials. סְגָנִים (s°gānîm, noted earlier, Ezra 9:2), **officials**, occurs twice here. The first occurrence may refer to watchmen (cf. LXX). For the second usage, Nehemiah may have had in mind some other local functionaries. **The Jews** were the general population (cf. 4:1-2). **The priests** are specified because in the restored community without a king, they took on greater governing responsibilities in the Persian era. And here, as the primary religious leaders, they would play a significant role in supporting the efforts of Nehemiah. The word for **nobles**, חֹרִים (ḥōrîm), may also be rendered as "freemen," or "citizens." The distinction between these groups is difficult to ascertain, but they probably involved recognized and varied functions in the Jerusalem community. The thrust of the verse is to reemphasize the care with which Nehemiah kept his ideas and activities from everyone else until the time was right to divulge them.

B. JEWISH ACTION AND THEIR OPPONENTS' REACTION (2:17-20)

[17]**Then I said to them, "You see the trouble we are in: Jerusalem lies in ruins, and its gates have been burned with fire. Come, let us rebuild the wall of Jerusalem, and we will no longer be in disgrace." [18]I also told them about the gracious hand of my God upon me and what the king had said to me.**

They replied, "Let us start rebuilding." So they began this good work.

[19]**But when Sanballat the Horonite, Tobiah the Ammonite official and Geshem the Arab heard about it, they mocked and ridiculed us. "What is this you are doing?" they asked. "Are you rebelling against the king?"**

[20]**I answered them by saying, "The God of heaven will give us success. We his servants will start rebuilding, but as for you, you have no share in Jerusalem or any claim or historic right to it."**

2:17-18 The lapse of time between the night inspection and when Nehemiah revealed his plans is not indicated but, man of action that he was, it was likely the following day. Succinct as his written recollection of what he said is, he pointed out first **the trouble we are in**. As with Ezra, by using "we" he identifies himself directly with the Jerusalemites, even though he had arrived but a few days earlier. As he reviews their current situation, he uses the same words that had troubled him in Susa when he had been informed by Hanani what the situation was in Jerusalem (1:3), **trouble** and **disgrace**. The word חֶרְפָּה (*ḥerpāh*), **disgrace**, can be rendered "reproach" (KJV), or "held in derision."[96] The disgrace of the exile had only partially been removed by the restoration of a Jewish presence and temple. The dilapidated condition of the holy city was a continuing cause of the contempt of the surrounding peoples.

Brutal frankness may open eyes too long glazed by inaction. But opened eyes need a new vision. Nehemiah gave them renewed hope by calling them to a plan of action and inspiring them with his personal testimony. Not only was God's favor evident in what he had done to bring Nehemiah to Jerusalem, the king had told him that he could go and rebuild the city's walls and gates.

So challenged and inspired, the response of the leaders and the people was enthusiastic. The KJV captures the sequence of the Hebrew verbs, "Let us rise up and build." And they were true to their word. They literally "strengthened their hands for the good (work)." This response must have reconfirmed for Nehemiah that the gracious hand of God was still on him.

2:19 Geshem the Arab

An alternate form of his name, Gashmu, occurs in 6:6. A third opponent joined Sanballat and Tobiah in deriding the initial efforts of rebuilding. Geshem is designated as the Arab(ian), just as Sanballat and Tobiah had been associated with geographical regions. He apparently had been given imperial authority over certain Arab tribes extending from Kedar in north Arabia across the Sinai and into the delta region of Egypt. Extrabiblical sources throw additional light on Geshem. A fifth-century Aramaic inscription on a silver vessel at Tell el-Mashkuta in the eastern delta refers to "Qaynu, the son of Gashmu, the king of Kedar." An inscription written in Lihyanite found at biblical Dedan, a major oasis in northwest

---

[96]Myers, *Ezra–Nehemiah*, p. 103.

Arabia, mentions Geshem.[97] The area of his dominance was thus some distance from Jerusalem, and a strengthened Jewish center there would have posed no threat to him. He must have simply joined his friends in ridiculing the effort out of personal loyalty.

But when [they] heard about it . . .

Williamson has plausibly proposed that "the speed . . . with which Nehemiah's opponents reacted to events in Jerusalem suggests that they had sympathizers there who kept them informed of developments."[98]

The letter from the king that Nehemiah presented to Sanballat had given no indication that he would reconstruct the walls. No one knew of the plans until Nehemiah revealed them immediately before the reconstruction began.

Besides ridicule, they thought to deter the work by questioning the motivation for rebuilding. **Are you rebelling against the king?** No doubt they had an historical memory that a similar tactic had brought earlier reconstruction efforts to a halt (Ezra 4:12), so they attempted to repeat the effort.

2:20 I answered them . . .

Something of the measure of Nehemiah can be taken from his response to his hecklers. First, he expressed confidence that he and his associates would succeed because of the God of heaven. He spoke with confidence because of his deep and abiding faith and because he knew, and they did not, that the gracious hand of God had been on him until this moment. Second, in the face of *your* opposition, *we*, God's servants, will proceed to rebuild. Third, you all (who are not God's servants) have no **share** (חֵלֶק, *ḥēleq*), i.e. allocation of land; nor **claim** (צְדָקָה, *ṣᵉdāqāh*), no legal authority; nor **historic right** (זִכָּרוֹן, *zikkārôn*), traditional claim, in Jerusalem. Kidner sums it up: "In the three words . . . he dismisses the past, present, and future of these unenviable outsiders."[99]

---

[97]*ABD,* II:995.
[98]Williamson, *Ezra, Nehemiah,* pp.191-192.
[99]Kidner, *Ezra & Nehemiah,* p. 84.

XVIII. BUILDERS OF THE WALL (3:1-32)

Despite our inability to currently establish accurately the locations listed in this chapter, approximations are possible. What the list provides is evidence of the active participation of all segments of the Jews in Jerusalem and the province of Yehud in the reconstruction of the walls and gates. This reflects Nehemiah's organizational abilities and his talent for encouraging others to participate. In light of typical historical recollection, too, it is refreshing to see recorded the names of the individuals and families that actually did the hard work, i.e., that of assembling, shaping, lifting, and laying the stones for the walls and cutting, hewing, transporting, raising, and fitting the timbers for the towers, rather than just the names of a few leaders. Congregations might take note and benefit later generations by keeping good records of the people who contribute to the life and edifying of the local church.

A. THE NORTH WALL (3:1-5)

[1]Eliashib the high priest and his fellow priests went to work and rebuilt the Sheep Gate. They dedicated it and set its doors in place, building as far as the Tower of the Hundred, which they dedicated, and as far as the Tower of Hananel. [2]The men of Jericho built the adjoining section, and Zaccur son of Imri built next to them.

[3]The Fish Gate was rebuilt by the sons of Hassenaah. They laid its beams and put its doors and bolts and bars in place. [4]Meremoth son of Uriah, the son of Hakkoz, repaired the next section. Next to him Meshullam son of Berekiah, the son of Meshezabel, made repairs, and next to him Zadok son of Baana also made repairs. [5]The next section was repaired by the men of Tekoa, but their nobles would not put their shoulders to the work under their supervisors.[a]

[a]5 Or *their Lord* or *the governor*

3:1-2 Eliashib the high priest . . .

The name means, "God will restore," which seems particularly appropriate for the leading role he plays in the reconstruction of the

walls. According to 12:10 he was the son of Joiakim and grandson of
Jeshua, the high priest and contemporary of Zerubbabel (Ezra 3:2;
Hag 1:1). He and the other priests apparently initiated the reconstruction, beginning at the **Sheep Gate**. This was located in the
northeast corner of the temple area and is mentioned in John 5:2 as
near the Pool of Bethesda. It probably received its name because
animals for sacrifice were brought into the temple area through it.
The priests thus had a particular interest in rebuilding it. The translation **They dedicated it and set its doors in place** is problematic.
Myers believes a scribal error has resulted in קִדְּשׁוּהוּ (*qiddᵉšûhû*)
rather than the more likely קֵרוּהוּ (*qērûhû*), "they repaired" (NIV
"they laid its beams"), as in verse 6.[100] Williamson renders "they
boarded it" on similar grounds.[101] A similar error would then appear
when the same word for **dedicated** occurs. An alternative explanation is to leave the Hebrew without change and to note that the dedication is only in connection with the reconstructions of the high
priest and his colleagues. Later, there is a celebration and dedication
of the entire wall (12:27-47).

The **Tower of the Hundred** would have been the second gate in
the north wall. Guesses as to the reason for the name include: it was
approached by a hundred steps, or it was a hundred cubits high, or
it could accommodate one hundred defenders. The RSV, following
the KJV, through association collapse both dedications into one:
"They consecrated it and set its doors; they consecrated it as far as
the Tower of the Hundred, as far as the Tower of Hananel." The
Tower of Hananel was apparently the third tower set into the north
wall. We have no indication of the distance between these three towers, but strong defenses on the north were required since it was
most vulnerable to attack from that direction. Elsewhere around the
city, walls and gates supplemented the natural defenses of surrounding valleys. We may assume that the three towers on the north
were within easy bowshot of one another, to provide full coverage
in defense of the wall against an attacker. The Tower of Hananel
[perhaps "the citadel by the temple" (2:8)] is mentioned again in
12:39, in Jeremiah 31:38 and in Zechariah 14:10. It may have stood

[100]Myers, *Ezra–Nehemiah*, p. 107, n. a.
[101]Williamson, *Ezra, Nehemiah*, pp. 194-195.

on the highest point along the north wall. Both of these towers may have been incorporated by subsequent constructions into the protective fortress at the northwest corner of the temple grounds.

. . . Zaccur son of Imri . . .

The name Zaccur is mentioned again in 10:13; 12:35; and 13:13.

3:3 The Fish Gate is mentioned again in 12:39; Zephaniah 1:10; and 2 Chronicles 33:14. Apparently it was the gate through which the Tyrian dealers brought fish for sale (13:16) into a business area or, more likely, into the gate area in which the selling took place. The fish would have come from the Mediterranean Sea; Phoenicians controlled the coast south at least to Joppa in the Persian era. **Hassenaah** may be a place name, since the first element (**Ha**) is the word "the" in Hebrew. **Senaah** comes at the end of a list of places in Ezra 2:35 and the parallel list in Nehemiah 7:38. But a personal name spelled **Hassenuah** is in 11:9 and 1 Chronicles 9:7.

3:4 Meremoth son of Uriah . . . .

This is the priest into whose hands Ezra had weighed the temple offerings (8:33); he is mentioned again in verse 21. The word **repaired** is repeated several times. This indicates that the line of the wall was still visible and some of the older fortification was still standing. In this area the wall required strengthening and the reconstruction of the upper levels with stone.

3:5 The next section was repaired by the men of Tekoa, . . .

Located about ten miles southeast of Jerusalem, it had been the home of the prophet Amos. Tekoa was near the region dominated by Geshem the Arab, and fear of reprisals from him might have been a factor in **their nobles** not supporting the rebuilding efforts in Jerusalem. It is also possible that they resented the new leadership provided by Nehemiah. Literally, these leaders "did not put their necks to the work of their lords." The metaphor arises from oxen plowing. The NIV's **supervisors** is an interpretation of "their lords." As the footnote indicates, it may be a reference to God using the plural of "majesty," as in the KJV. Despite this lack of cooperation, the men of Tekoa more than redeemed the reputation of their hometown; they repaired two sections of the wall (see v. 27). Nevertheless, this verse is "a valuable reminder that sharp differences of opinion within the wider Jewish community were never far beneath the surface."[102]

B. THE WEST WALL (3:6-12)

[6]The Jeshanah[a] Gate was repaired by Joiada son of Paseah and Meshullam son of Besodeiah. They laid its beams and put its doors and bolts and bars in place. [7]Next to them, repairs were made by men from Gibeon and Mizpah—Melatiah of Gibeon and Jadon of Meronoth—places under the authority of the governor of Trans-Euphrates. [8]Uzziel son of Harhaiah, one of the goldsmiths, repaired the next section; and Hananiah, one of the perfume-makers, made repairs next to that. They restored[b] Jerusalem as far as the Broad Wall. [9]Rephaiah son of Hur, ruler of a half-district of Jerusalem, repaired the next section. [10]Adjoining this, Jedaiah son of Harumaph made repairs opposite his house, and Hattush son of Hashabneiah made repairs next to him. [11]Malkijah son of Harim and Hasshub son of Pahath-Moab repaired another section and the Tower of the Ovens. [12]Shallum son of Hallohesh, ruler of a half-district of Jerusalem, repaired the next section with the help of his daughters.

[a]6 Or *Old*   [b]8 Or *They left out part of*

3:6 The **Jeshana Gate** opened from the Old City to the west. After the expansion of the city to occupy the western hill in the time of Hezekiah and Manasseh, the new sector called the Mishneh was also enclosed in the cities fortifications. Thereafter the Jeshana Gate opened into the Mishneh, the "second," district of the city. It was identical to the Corner Gate of 2 Kings 14:13, some six hundred feet north of the Ephraim Gate (cf. Jer 31:37; Zech 14:10).

3:7 Moving south along the western wall, **men from Gibeon and Mizpah** made the repairs. Gibeonites were among the first returnees with Zerubbabel (cf. 7:25). The ruins of Gibeon lie under modern Tell el-Jib five miles northwest of Jerusalem. Mizpah (Tell en-Nazbeh)

---

[102]Williamson, *Ezra, Nehemiah*, p. 204. Cf. Fensham, *The Books of Ezra and Nehemiah*, p. 174.

lies about eight miles north of Jerusalem. **Meronoth** must have been a village near Mizpah. It is unclear what is meant by **places under the authority of the governor of Trans-Euphrates**, literally "(belonging to) the seat of the governor . . .". Apparently Mizpah in particular continued to serve as the place to which the satrap of Trans-Euphrates or his designate would occasionally come. After the destruction of Jerusalem, it had become the seat of government and the residence of Zedekiah, Nebuchadnezzar's appointee (2 Kgs 25:22-23). The men from Gibeon and Mizpah were outside the jurisdiction of Yehud, therefore, and under no obligation to help restore the walls of Jerusalem. By joining in the work, they identified themselves with the reconstruction effort and were worthy of particular mention in the records.

3:8 Repairs to the wall were continued southward by members of two guilds. The **goldsmiths** and the **perfume-makers** were likely among the middle-class of the population, inhabitants of Jerusalem with a vested interest in the project. The NIV footnote for **They restored** points to a textual problem. The root meaning of וַיַּעַזְבוּ (wayya'az°bû) is "to forsake, leave." The translation "They left out" would indicate that a part of the former city, now abandoned, was left out of the new line of the wall. However, the translation "restored" is possible on the basis of a second Hebrew root with the same consonants, עזב ('zb), and the meaning "to prepare, to make" (Exod 23:5). The **Broad Wall** was apparently located in a particularly vulnerable area between the "Tower of the Ovens" and "the Gate of Ephraim" (12:38-39). It would have been thicker (as much as twenty-four feet wide) and stronger than the rest of the wall.

3:9 Rephaiah is identified as **ruler of a half-district of Jerusalem**. In verse 12 we find the ruler of the other half-district was Shallum, and the word "ruler," (שַׂר, śar) occurs in verses 14,15,16,17, and 18. The word for "district" is פֶּלֶךְ (pelek). Since it is used elsewhere in the Bible with the meaning "spindle whorl," the word here likely derives from Akkadian pilku, "region, district." The way pelek is used in reference to "the ruler of the district of Mizpah" (v. 15), compared to "the ruler of Mizpah" (v. 19), suggests that the districts and half-districts were locales adjacent to but outside the city proper.

3:10 Those who had houses **opposite**, that is, adjacent to the city walls, such as **Jedaiah** (cf. vv. 23,28-30), would naturally be interested in strengthening the wall for their own security as well as that of others.

3:11 Malkijah son of Harim had been guilty of intermarriage (Ezra 10:31), but had corrected that problem. The **Tower of the Ovens** was apparently adjacent to the city's bakeries.

3:12 Shallum, noted above, apparently had no sons. But contrary to the presuppositions about the role of women in Israelite society, **with the help of his daughters** he repaired the section between the Tower of the Ovens and the Valley Gate. If he had no sons, his daughters would have inherited his property (Num 27:1-11).

Some commentators take the word for **daughters** (בָּנוֹת, *bᵉnôth*) as a reference to villages surrounding a biblical city, a well-known usage (cf. 11:25, 27), and translate "men from the small towns."[103] This is unnecessary and misses the point that all segments of the population were involved in the project.

C. THE SOUTHWEST WALL (3:13-14)

[13]**The Valley Gate was repaired by Hanun and the residents of Zanoah. They rebuilt it and put its doors and bolts and bars in place. They also repaired five hundred yards**[a] **of the wall as far as the Dung Gate.**

[14]**The Dung Gate was repaired by Malkijah son of Recab, ruler of the district of Beth Hakkerem. He rebuilt it and put its doors and bolts and bars in place.**

[a]*13* Hebrew *a thousand cubits* (about 450 meters)

3:13 The Valley Gate was repaired by Hanum and the residents of Zanoah. . . . (cf. 2:13-15)

This was the chief entrance through the west wall of the city and was opposite the Water Gate in the eastern wall. The latter gave access to the waters from the Spring Gihon. The Valley Gate may have permitted easy access to that water source for the inhabitants in the Mishneh prior to the destruction of Jerusalem by the Chaldeans.

---

[103]Fensham, *The Books of Ezra and Nehemiah*, p. 176.

They also repaired five hundred yards of the wall as far as the Dung Gate.

This long section of the wall must have remained largely intact, allowing a smaller crew to repair it. The **residents of Zanoah** were from a village about two miles south and slightly east of Beth-Shemesh, at the base of the central highlands west of Jerusalem. The modern name is Khirbet Zanu (or Zanukh)[104]

3:14 The Dung Gate . . .

was noted above (2:13-15). **Beth Hakkerem**, although identified by some with Ain Karim southwest of Jerusalem and the traditional birthplace of John the Baptist, is more properly placed at Ramat Rachel on the height between Bethlehem and Jerusalem.[105]

D. THE SOUTHEAST WALL (3:15-27)

[15]**The Fountain Gate was repaired by Shallun son of Col-Hozeh, ruler of the district of Mizpah. He rebuilt it, roofing it over and putting its doors and bolts and bars in place. He also repaired the wall of the Pool of Siloam,[a] by the King's Garden, as far as the steps going down from the City of David. [16]Beyond him, Nehemiah son of Azbuk, ruler of a half-district of Beth Zur, made repairs up to a point opposite the tombs[b] of David, as far as the artificial pool and the House of the Heroes.**

[17]**Next to him, the repairs were made by the Levites under Rehum son of Bani. Beside him, Hashabiah, ruler of half the district of Keilah, carried out repairs for his district. [18]Next to him, the repairs were made by their countrymen under Binnui[c] son of Henadad, ruler of the other half-district of Keilah. [19]Next to him, Ezer son of Jeshua, ruler of Mizpah, repaired another section, from a point facing the ascent to the armory as far as the angle. [20]Next to him, Baruch son of Zabbai zealously repaired another section, from the angle to the entrance of the house of Eliashib the high priest. [21]Next to him, Meremoth son of Uriah, the son of**

---

[104]*ABD,* VI:1039.

[105]Avraham Negev, ed., *The Archaeological Encyclopedia of the Holy Land,* rev. ed. (Nashville: Thomas Nelson, 1986), p. 57.

Hakkoz, repaired another section, from the entrance of Eliashib's house to the end of it.

²²The repairs next to him were made by the priests from the surrounding region. ²³Beyond them, Benjamin and Hasshub made repairs in front of their house; and next to them, Azariah son of Maaseiah, the son of Ananiah, made repairs beside his house. ²⁴Next to him, Binnui son of Henadad repaired another section, from Azariah's house to the angle and the corner, ²⁵and Palal son of Uzai worked opposite the angle and the tower projecting from the upper palace near the court of the guard. Next to him, Pedaiah son of Parosh ²⁶and the temple servants living on the hill of Ophel made repairs up to a point opposite the Water Gate toward the east and the projecting tower. ²⁷Next to them, the men of Tekoa repaired another section, from the great projecting tower to the wall of Ophel.

ᵃ15 Hebrew *Shelah*, a variant of *Shiloah*, that is, Siloam   ᵇ16 Hebrew; Septuagint, some Vulgate manuscripts and Syriac *tomb*   ᶜ18 Two Hebrew manuscripts and Syriac (see also Septuagint and verse 24); most Hebrew manuscripts *Bavvai*

3:15 On **The Fountain Gate** see 2:13-15. An alternative translation is the Spring Gate, giving access to the Rogel spring. The NIV has noted a modest textual problem, translating הַשֶּׁלַח (*hašelaḥ*) as **Siloam**. Both the RSV and NRSV have "the Pool of Shelah." The NIV translation receives some support from "the waters of Shiloah" in Isaiah 8:6. The **City of David** is the small eastern hill, which the walls under repair enclosed, along with the Temple Mount to the north.

Apparently **Shallun**, after repairing the Fountain Gate, "started work on the new wall, following the line of the steps up the hill into what had formerly been part of the city itself."[106] This was to replace the old wall that ran north along the eastern slope of the City of David. It lay buried beneath enormous debris.

A careful reader will note that the section of the account that begins here differs somewhat from the previous description. The landmarks are now primarily houses and other buildings instead of gates. The obvious explanation for this is that the new line of wall was being built along the eastern crest of the hill.

[106]Williamson, *Ezra, Nehemiah*, p. 208.

3:16 This **Nehemiah** is the son of Azbuk, at work on the project initiated by Nehemiah son of Hacaliah. Beth Zur was a town about fifteen miles south of Jerusalem on the southern border of Judah. It is identified with Khirbet el-Tubeiqeh.

The tombs of David, that is, the place where David and his successors were buried, cannot be identified now, although they were still visible in NT times (Acts 2:29). Extensive quarrying in the Roman era may have obliterated them. What appear to be rock-cut tombs in the southeastern part of the City of David have been tentatively identified with David's tombs, but they can also be understood as cisterns.

The **artificial pool** is different from the Pool of Siloam. While both were man-made, this one may have been the same as the King's Pool noted in 2:14. It was likely a plastered reservoir to catch rainwater. The storage and use of rainwater was common practice in Jerusalem in antiquity and currently continues on a lesser scale.

The **House of Heroes** may have been a barracks dating back to David's time, built to house his heroes (2 Chr 23:8ff).

3:17 Now a section of the new wall is constructed by Levites and priests. **Hashabiah** is of particular interest. While a Levite, he is also **ruler of half the district of Keilah**. It is identified with Khirbet Qila, about eight miles east of Beth Guvrin toward Hebron. Williamson remarks that some of the Levites "who remained in the land during the exile turned to this [civil administration] in the absence of any form of temple service."[107]

3:18 Working adjacent to Hashabiah was the **ruler of the other half-district of Keilah, Binnui son of Henadad**. The NIV footnote draws attention to a spelling problem in the Hebrew text. The translated form is supported by verse 24 where he is mentioned working on another section.

3:19-21 The angle was likely a point of deviation in the line of the wall. Another angle is mentioned in verses 24-25. The KJV renders "the turning *of the wall*," although these points are clearly different from "the corner" (v. 24).

Exceptional effort was noticed by Nehemiah. **Baruch son of**

---

[107]Ibid.

Zabbai worked **zealously**; this is ignored in the RSV but noted in the KJV. Nehemiah wisely assigned homeowners to repair the walls adjacent to their homes, but **Eliashib the high priest** appropriately worked in the temple area while others worked on the walls next to his house.

3:22-27 . . . priests from the surrounding region. . . .

Not all the priests lived in Jerusalem (cf. Zechariah, John the Baptist's father, Luke 1:39-40). Here those living outside the city are distinguished from those living within it. In verse 24, **the corner** must have been a more significant change of direction than the angle, yet the general direction of construction along the crest of the ridge was northward.

Verse 25 mentions the remnant of parts of the palace complex that were still partially standing. It appears to have been just south of the slope overlooking the Gihon Spring at the base of the hill. Jeremiah 32:2 locates the **court of the guard** in the palace. What is described here is the incorporation of the remnants of the palace and its towers into the new wall at the crest of the hill. In verse 26, the construction continued on the crest of the hill above the **Water Gate.** That gate was a part of the old wall adjacent to the Gihon Spring. Its ruins have recently been discovered. We do not know if a gate was installed in the new wall above the spring, to allow access to it, but it seems likely that at least a postern gate, less than a yard wide, would have been built. **Ophel** has a derivation related to swelling. Thus it was the name for a rise in the hill toward the temple mount. The **wall of Ophel** was not a section of the wall under construction. Rather, it seems to have run east-west and to have been the northern wall of the city until Solomon incorporated the temple mount to the north into his city.

E. THE NORTHEAST WALL (3:28-32)

[28]Above the Horse Gate, the priests made repairs, each in front of his own house. [29]Next to them, Zadok son of Immer made repairs opposite his house. Next to him, Shemaiah son of Shecaniah, the guard at the East Gate, made repairs. [30]Next to him, Hananiah son of Shelemiah, and Hanun, the sixth son of Zalaph,

repaired another section. Next to them, Meshullam son of Berekiah made repairs opposite his living quarters. ³¹Next to him, Malkijah, one of the goldsmiths, made repairs as far as the house of the temple servants and the merchants, opposite the Inspection Gate, and as far as the room above the corner; ³²and between the room above the corner and the Sheep Gate the goldsmiths and merchants made repairs.

3:28-32 The location of the **Horse Gate** is problematic. References in 2 Kings 11:16 and 2 Chronicles 23:15 place a horse gate between the temple and the palace. But Jeremiah 31:40 indicates it was a gate in the city wall not far from the temple area. The priests lived up the natural elevation above the gate and adjacent to the temple compound.

The East Gate was in the east wall of the temple compound (cf. Ezek 10:19). It was likely located approximately where the Golden Gate is now situated. **Shemaiah**, as one guarding an entrance into the holy place, was likely a Levite. The repairs he was making were not at the gate, but just to the south of it.

The Inspection Gate is also translated "Muster Gate" (RSV). The KJV simply transliterates the Hebrew, "Miphkad." Fensham, thinks that "at this tower the people or men were mustered for conscription."[108] It may be identified with the Benjamin Gate (Jer 37:13; 38:7; Zech 14:10) and would have been the northernmost entrance on the east side.[109] Verse 32 indicates clearly that **the room above the corner** is the northeast corner of the wall. Westward from that corner to the Sheep Gate, **the goldsmiths and the merchants** made the repairs. Their shops may have been in that area.

XIX. OPPOSITION TO THE REBUILDING
(4:1-23[3:33–4:17])

The preceding chapter was not intended to chronicle the completion of the reconstruction of the walls of Jerusalem. It represented primarily the initiation of the project. The people involved and

---

[108]Fensham, *The Books of Ezra and Nehemiah*, p. 179.
[109]Williamson, *Ezra, Nehemiah*, p. 211.

the segments of the construction upon which they were assigned to work was given. In the Hebrew text, the account continues with verses 33-35 and its chapter 4 begins with our 4:7. By a direct continuation, the Hebrew connects the reaction of the adversaries directly to the early progress of the project.

A. SAMARIAN SCORN AND AMMONITE DISDAIN (4:1-3[3:33-35])

¹**When Sanballat heard that we were rebuilding the wall, he became angry and was greatly incensed. He ridiculed the Jews, ²and in the presence of his associates and the army of Samaria, he said, "What are those feeble Jews doing? Will they restore their wall? Will they offer sacrifices? Will they finish in a day? Can they bring the stones back to life from those heaps of rubble—burned as they are?"**

³**Tobiah the Ammonite, who was at his side, said, "What they are building—if even a fox climbed up on it, he would break down their wall of stones!"**

4:1 When Sanballat heard that we were rebuilding the wall, . . .

When Sanballat had first heard that Nehemiah had arrived to promote the welfare of the Israelites, when Nehemiah had delivered the letter from the king to him, he and his buddy, Tobiah the Ammonite, had been "very much disturbed" (2:10). Later, after Sanballat, Tobiah, and Geshem got word that the Jews had started to rebuild the walls, "they mocked and ridiculed" them. Now, when word had arrived that they were continuing to rebuild the walls, Sanballat **became angry and was greatly incensed.** His irritation with the continuing developments was increasing. His frustration was growing in intensity. Although he wanted to stop the reconstruction, he could not because the king had authorized Nehemiah's activities. The Hebrew words reflected in the NIV translation indicate the growing aggravation of Nehemiah's enemies. Sanballat is mentioned first in each instance, indicating that he is the main instigator of the opposition.

He ridiculed the Jews,

The Hebrew root לעג (*l'g*) may also be translated "mocked"

(RSV), "jeered" (NEB), and "derided."[110] Exactly what he said is reported in verse 2.

4:2 and in the presence of his associates . . .

Literally, the word for "associates" means "brethren," as in the KJV, but blood relationship is not intended. The expression **army of Samaria** implies more than we should expect. Samaria was not a military colony, but each district might be called upon to supply military units to assist the imperial army when needed. Sanballat likely had with him a contingent of armed men, perhaps his personal bodyguards. He had come to personally see how much had been done rather than to threaten military action at this time.

The five questions asked were intended to have a twofold effect. First, by asking them within the hearing of Nehemiah and the Jews, he ridiculed them. Second, "Sanballat uses ridicule as a means of avoiding loss of face in the presence of his supporters and subordinates."[111] The first question is one of disdain, emphasizing the feebleness of the Jews in contrast to the enormity of what they are attempting to do. The word for feeble, אֲמֵלָלִים (*'ămēlālîm*), occurs only here in the Bible, but a related form is used in 1 Samuel 2:5 and Psalm 6:3. The root, מלל (*mll*), is used to indicate the fading or withering of a plant (Isa 16:8; 24:7, etc.) and of people without hope (Isa 19:8; Hos 4:3). This choice of words struck at the morale of the Jews who, under Nehemiah's leadership, were just beginning to throw off a sense of disgrace (2:17).

The following four rhetorical questions expect a "No!" answer. They drip with sarcasm. The Hebrew here rendered **Will they restore their wall?** is problematic, resulting in these varied translations: "Will they fortify themselves?" (KJV), "Will they restore things?" (RSV), "Do they mean to reconstruct the place?" (NEB), "Will they commit their cause to God?" (Williamson)[112] Despite translation difficulties, it is clear that Sanballat was casting doubt on the wisdom of the project. The question, **Will they offer sacrifices?** implies that they do not have the resources to do the job and they

---

[110]Myers, *Ezra–Nehemiah*, p. 121.

[111]Williamson, *Ezra, Nehemiah*, p. 216.

[112]Ibid., p. 213. He provides a comprehensive study of the translation options and reasons for his translation.

will attempt to wheedle God for help through sacrifices. Kidner paraphrases: "Are these fanatics going to *pray* the wall up?"[113] Myers has combined three questions, "Can they renovate them, offer sacrifices and complete them in a day?"[114]

The last question mentions bringing **stones back to life . . . burned as they are**. So destructive had been the fires that consumed Jerusalem many years before, that the limestone had been calcined and weakened. Sanballat pours scorn on the reuse of such resources.

4:3 Tobiah's contribution to the ridicule grows out of Sanballat's last question. He jests at what he sees as the inferior quality of the reconstruction. The image of the wall breaking under the feet of a fox adds insult to injury. The figure of a fox/jackal among Jerusalem's ruins is used in Lamentations 5:18.

B. NEHEMIAH'S REACTION (4:4-6[3:36-38])

[4]Hear us, O our God, for we are despised. Turn their insults back on their own heads. Give them over as plunder in a land of captivity. [5]Do not cover up their guilt or blot out their sins from your sight, for they have thrown insults in the face of[a] the builders.

[6]So we rebuilt the wall till all of it reached half its height, for the people worked with all their heart.

[a]5 Or *have provoked you to anger before*

4:4-5 Nehemiah faced ridicule with prayer. It was always his customary reaction to problem situations (1:4; 2:4). A number of additional brief prayers are included in his record of these events. They are evidence of his deep, personal dependence upon God, and they serve as an example to all destined to read and appreciate both his deeds and his words. Similarities have been drawn between this prayer and psalms of lament. Sabourin has identified these elements in psalms of lament: (1) Invocation, a cry to God for help, often in the imperative mode of speech; (2) Main section consisting of some or all of the following — complaint, supplication, identity of suppli-

---

[113]Kidner, *Ezra & Nehemiah*, p. 90.
[114]Myers, *Ezra–Nehemiah*, p. 121.

cants, expression of trust in God; (3) Conclusion (or none), with either a blessing, expression of trust, or thanksgiving.[115] However applicable the similarities, it is but natural for a person of faith to pray in patterns of expression learned from childhood in a community of faith.

The prayer begins with the imperative, **Hear us, O our God**. This is a prayer of the community, apparently lifted to heaven by their devout leader. The complaint is **for we are despised** (בוּזָה, *bûzāh*), "an object of contempt." That contempt is specified in the last line of the prayer, **they have thrown insults in the face of the builders.** This is an indication that many of the builders were present with Nehemiah and heard the derision of Sanballat and Tobiah, and no doubt the hoots of the troops. Williamson argues for and translates that line, "for they have provoked you [God] to anger right in the presence of the builders," arguing that the verb, הִכְעִיסוּ (*hikʾîsû*), "to provoke, anger," with לְנֶגֶד (*lᵊneged*), "in front of," can be used to express the provoking of God to anger.[116] This translation makes the point that it is not the builders alone but God who is being slandered by these adversaries. It is similar to the KJV, "for they have provoked *Thee* to anger *before* the builders."

Nehemiah calls on God to let the adversaries experience exile as had the Jews. He asks God to rightly punish them for their attempt to frustrate and sneer at what is clearly his divine will. (Similar imprecations are found, for example, in Jer 11:18-20; 15:15; 17:18; 18:19-23.)

Was this a silent prayer expressed to God at that moment? Or was it a public prayer? There is no definite indication. However, if it was public, as I am inclined to believe, it was a resolute answer to the threatening visitors, and a powerful encouragement to the builders.

4:6 So we rebuilt the wall . . .

Both the continued favor of God on the project, in answer to prayer, and the determination of the laborers are evident in the progress noted here. To finish all parts of the wall to half the intended height was clearly wiser than building some sections to full height

---

[115]Leopold Sabourin, S.J., *The Psalms: Their Origin and Meaning* (New York: Alba House, 1974), pp. 215-218.

[116]Williamson, *Ezra, Nehemiah*, pp. 213-214.

while others languished. The translation, **for the people worked with all their hearts**, is clear; the KJV is memorable: "for the people had a mind to work."

C. THREATS OF ARMED CONFLICT AND INTERNAL DISSENT (4:7-12[4:1-6])

[7]**But when Sanballat, Tobiah, the Arabs, the Ammonites and the men of Ashdod heard that the repairs to Jerusalem's walls had gone ahead and that the gaps were being closed, they were very angry. [8]They all plotted together to come and fight against Jerusalem and stir up trouble against it. [9]But we prayed to our God and posted a guard day and night to meet this threat.**

[10]**Meanwhile, the people in Judah said, "The strength of the laborers is giving out, and there is so much rubble that we cannot rebuild the wall."**

[11]**Also our enemies said, "Before they know it or see us, we will be right there among them and will kill them and put an end to the work."**

[12]**Then the Jews who lived near them came and told us ten times over, "Wherever you turn, they will attack us."**

4:7-8 Sanballat and his henchmen had apparently withdrawn after making their disparaging comments, confident that the work on the walls would come to a halt. When they **heard that the repairs to Jerusalem's walls had gone ahead** they reacted angrily. This time Sanballat and his underling, **Tobiah**, had been joined by **the Ammonites and the men of Ashdod**. The opponents to the reconstruction of the walls now represented the complete encirclement of Yehud. To the north were the Samarians, to the east across the Jordan River were the Ammonites, to the south were the Arabs, and to the east the Ashdodites. Ashdod here refers to the province. The name had been given to the former Philistine territory by the Assyrians, after their takeover in 711 B.C. The Philistines had lost their distinctiveness and had assimilated into the predominant Canaanite culture.

The expression, **the repairs to Jerusalem's walls had gone ahead** in Hebrew is literally, "healing had risen to the walls of Jerusalem."

The metaphor is drawn from a wound that has healed by rebuilding the flesh.

Sanballat and his allies conspired to come and fight and to **stir up trouble against it**. The word for **trouble** is תּוֹעָה (*tô'āh*), "to wander, stray in bewilderment." The RSV translates, "to cause confusion," which ensuing events indicate happened.

4:9 When Nehemiah became aware of this renewed threat, his reaction was as we would expect, prayer and action. Prayer was never a last resort for this godfearing man. The guard would help prevent a surprise attack, even one that might be launched at night.

4:10 The continued threats of opponents combined with the bone-wearying work was wearing down the enthusiasm of the workers. They had been working for about a month, and the wall was only about half the height intended. Some one or few of the workers had composed a ditty that expressed their state of mind, and it was picked up and repeated throughout the work force. The song is in the meter (3+2, 3+2) of a lament, a *qinah*, expressive of one limping along in sorrow in a funeral procession. Myers has attempted to express this in his translation:

The strength of the burden-bearer is drooping,
    The rubbish heap so vast;
And we are unable by ourselves
    To rebuild the wall.[117]

Besides finding reusable stones, hoisting them up and laying them, they had to remove the debris left from that long-ago destruction. And as the wall increased in height, the upper courses required more and more effort to raise the stones.

4:11-12 Enthusiasm may be contagious, but discouragement tends to be destructive. To add to the growing malaise about the work, the adversaries continued their psychological warfare, sowing rumors of a surprise attack with the intent to **kill them and put an end to the work**. Nehemiah was facing a crisis among his people.

Verse 12 has a number of problems, probably the result of copyists errors or damaged manuscripts in the process of transmission.

---

[117]Myers, *Ezra–Nehemiah*, p. 122.

Fensham notes that the text is so corrupt that it is impossible to restore it properly. He translates, "'When the Jews who lived near them came, they said ten times to us: "From everywhere they are coming against us."'"[118] Williamson has thoroughly reviewed suggested solutions to the textual problems and has offered his own solution, translating, "'When the Jews who lived near them came and said to us time and again from all sides, 'You must return to us . . . .'" What is happening is that the workers who come in from the outlying areas near the borders with the adversaries were reporting time and again what they were hearing. No doubt the opposition to a refortified Jerusalem wanted their words and activities reported to Nehemiah and all those who worked on the wall. A part of the message was that the focus was on Jerusalem and its wall-builders. Apparently groups of concerned relatives and friends were coming to Jerusalem to encourage their husbands and sons to leave the work and return home where they would be unmolested and safe. Nehemiah faced mass desertion unless he acted forthrightly.

D. NEHEMIAH'S RESPONSE (4:13-23[4:7-17])

[13]Therefore I stationed some of the people behind the lowest points of the wall at the exposed places, posting them by families, with their swords, spears and bows. [14]After I looked things over, I stood up and said to the nobles, the officials and the rest of the people, "Don't be afraid of them. Remember the Lord, who is great and awesome, and fight for your brothers, your sons and your daughters, your wives and your homes."

[15]When our enemies heard that we were aware of their plot and that God had frustrated it, we all returned to the wall, each to his own work.

[16]From that day on, half of my men did the work, while the other half were equipped with spears, shields, bows and armor. The officers posted themselves behind all the people of Judah [17]who were building the wall. Those who carried materials did their work with one hand and held a weapon in the other, [18]and each of

---

[118]Fensham, *The Books of Ezra and Nehemiah*, pp. 183, 185.

the builders wore his sword at his side as he worked. But the man
who sounded the trumpet stayed with me.

[19]Then I said to the nobles, the officials and the rest of the people, "The work is extensive and spread out, and we are widely separated from each other along the wall. [20]Wherever you hear the
sound of the trumpet, join us there. Our God will fight for us!"

[21]So we continued the work with half the men holding spears,
from the first light of dawn till the stars came out. [22]At that time I
also said to the people, "Have every man and his helper stay inside
Jerusalem at night, so they can serve us as guards by night and
workmen by day." [23]Neither I nor my brothers nor my men nor the
guards with me took off our clothes; each had his weapon, even
when he went for water.[a]

[a]*23* The meaning of the Hebrew for this clause is uncertain.

4:13 This verse is full of problems as well. Rather than **I stationed
some of the people behind the lowest points**, Williamson continues
from verse 12, "then I took up a position in the lowest parts of the
space behind the wall . . . ." The point is that Nehemiah called all his
workers from the walls and assembled them before him **by families,
with their swords, spears and bows**. The word translated "families"
means extended families, clans. This arrangement recalls the organization of ancient Israel by clans to fight a "holy war."[119] Their basic
arms were for hand-to-hand combat, except for the bows, which were
likely composite. (Such bows might send an arrow as much as 700
yards, but with an effective range of 300-400 yards.)

Nehemiah's actions accomplished two ends. First, despondent
men who had been working in small groups all around the wall
would be encouraged when they were in the midst of the large,
armed group, prepared to defend themselves under the strong leadership of Nehemiah. Second, the marshaled forces were a visual

[119]As noted by Williamson, Kellermann has observed in 4:1-14 relationships to "holy war": the enemy band together against Jerusalem; the people
pray before arming themselves; the human resources for defense are slen-
der; the forces are a conscript militia rather than a standing army; the leader
proclaims God's involvement in the battle and calls for faith and fearless-
ness; the enemy is discouraged; and the trumpet blast is the signal for battle (*Ezra, Nehemiah*, p. 224).

message to any observers of the opposition that this group was ready to defend itself.

4:14 After I looked things over, . . .

The Hebrew simply states, "And I looked . . . ." As any military commander would, Nehemiah looked over the assembled "army." He may have moved around among them, instructing and encouraging each clan. Then he addressed the entire group. His words echoed those of Israel's past. **Don't be afraid of them** recalls, for example, Moses (Exod 14:13-14) and Joshua (Josh 10:25). He encouraged them by reminding them of the great and awesome Lord (the one who had fought for their forefathers). Then he challenged them to fight for **your brothers, your sons and daughters, your wives and your homes**. Kidner wisely notes that "There is less danger of excess and distortion in the call to fight [for these] than in some higher-sounding, ideological battle-cry."[120]

4:15 Nehemiah's response to the plot was effective, and he rightly gave God the credit. The adversaries realized a surprise attack was no longer possible and any attack could cost them heavily. Behind their frustrated plans, again by the hidden activity of God which underlies this entire project, was the awareness that a military adventure on their part would not be looked upon favorably by the Persian court, since Nehemiah was authorized to refortify the city.

With the crisis somewhat abated, **we all returned to the wall, each to his own work**.

4:16-18 This section provides in some detail the defensive precautions Nehemiah set in place when the entire workforce had assembled (v. 14).

Mention is made of **half of my men**, (נְעָרַי, *nᵉʿāray*), literally, "youths." The RSV, following the KJV, translates the word, "servants." This is a special group of young men, perhaps Nehemiah's own bodyguard (cf. 5:10,16; 13:19). Note that they are better armed than the other men (cf. v. 13). The **armor** was likely a chest covering made of tough leather rather than metal scales.

It is obvious that the cavalry detachment that escorted Nehemiah to Jerusalem was not permanently assigned to him. They saw to his

---

[120]Kidner, *Ezra & Nehemiah*, p. 93.

safe arrival and then, we can assume, they returned to Susa. Other-wise they would have been a potent deterrent to Sanballat and his henchmen. After his arrival Nehemiah may have recruited these young men to serve him in numerous ways. They had been working on the construction and may have been supervising work on sec-tions of the wall. Now at any time half of them were at the ready for an armed attack while the other half continued to work.

The officers were the leaders of each of the clan groups at work on the wall, watching over the wall in their areas of responsibility to warn of any approaching attackers coming in their direction. **Those who carried materials**, probably baskets of rubbish as well as stones, also carried **a weapon**, which would seem very hard to do. The word for weapon is הַשֶּׁלַח (*haššālaḥ*), "the weapon," possibly a knife or javelin which could be carried along with the handle of a basket, etc. The majority of the workers had both hands free to work, with a **sword** strapped to their sides. The trumpeter was needed because workers were scattered over a wide area and could not be reached by shouting.

4:19-20 We may assume that these instructions were given to the entire assembled group (v. 14) prior to their return to work on the walls. The plan shows the practical wisdom and creativity of Nehemiah. He and the trumpeter would quickly move to the endangered area, the trumpet would be sounded, and everyone would rush to the point of attack.

. . . Our God will fight for us!

This is an added detail of what he had reminded them in verse 14. If an attack came, they would have to fight, but they would be fighting for the cause of God, and he would be on their side. This again echoed words from the ancient history of Israel, as in Exodus 14:14; Deuteronomy 1:30; 3:22; 20:4; Joshua 10:14,42; and 23:10.

4:21-23 Nehemiah realized that every minute counted. In an era long before the invention of artificial lights, other than oil lamps, work was necessarily restricted to daylight hours, including dusk and dawn.

Some of the workers came each day to and from their home vil-lages, often a considerable distance away. By instituting the new rule that everyone must **stay in Jerusalem at night**, Nehemiah accomplished two significant improvements. One, it would allow the workers to use "travel time" to work on the walls. Second, it would prevent the tendency in any individual to reduce his commitment to the work by staying home. We can assume that guard duty was by shifts.

Nehemiah and those closest to him set the example of constant vigil for the rest of the work force. **My brothers** were probably blood relatives. **My men** were the young men mentioned in verse 16; we have no idea of how many there were. Exactly who **the guards** were is unclear; it may refer to the officers who posted themselves behind all the people of Judah (v. 16). These were always ready for defensive action at a moment's notice.

The last segment of verse 23 does not make sense in the original. Literally it reads, "a man his weapon the water." The KJV connects it to the preceding idea of not putting off one's clothes, "*saving that* every one put them off for washing." The RSV has, "each kept his weapon in his hand." The NEB similarly renders, "each keeping his right hand on his weapon." From the context, these last two seem to approximate the intended meaning.

XX. NEHEMIAH HELPS THE POOR (5:1-19)

As if the problems caused by Sanballat and his allies were not enough, to which can be added the loss of morale among the workers, all of which we have noted previously, a serious internal problem arose while the reconstruction of the walls was in progress. In the first part of this chapter Nehemiah had to address sociological and related economic problems that threatened to tear the community apart. If the problems had been left unresolved, no doubt the work on the walls would have languished and died. Later in the chapter, Nehemiah looks back over his governorship from a later vantage point to recall his own deeds, always motivated by his religious faith, in contrast to those who had governed before him.

A. ECONOMIC AND SOCIAL OPPRESSION (5:1-5)

¹Now the men and their wives raised a great outcry against their Jewish brothers. ²Some were saying, "We and our sons and

daughters are numerous; in order for us to eat and stay alive, we must get grain."

³Others were saying, "We are mortgaging our fields, our vineyards and our homes to get grain during the famine."

⁴Still others were saying, "We have had to borrow money to pay the king's tax on our fields and vineyards. ⁵Although we are of the same flesh and blood as our countrymen and though our sons are as good as theirs, yet we have to subject our sons and daughters to slavery. Some of our daughters have already been enslaved, but we are powerless, because our fields and our vineyards belong to others."

5:1 The outcry was from **the men,** but literally, "the people," that is, the common people as distinct from the wealthy elite. It is exceptional that **their wives** are also mentioned as protesting conditions. This may have been because they were so conscious of desperate conditions at home; they bore the major responsibility there while their husbands were engaged in constructing the walls.

The outcry was against **their Jewish brothers,** that is, the nobles and officials mentioned in verse 7; it was not against Nehemiah. He had encouraged the project, but the decision to proceed had been made by the entire community (2:16-18). **Outcry** is the identical word used in Exodus 3:9 when the Israelites cried out under Egyptian oppression.

Three subgroups are identified in the verses that follow by the repeated expression, **some were saying** (וְיֵשׁ אֲשֶׁר אֹמְרִים, *weyēš 'ăšer 'ōmᵉrîm*).

5:2 Some with large families were short of food, verging on starvation. Grain was their staple food. The KJV and NEB read "corn"; however, the meaning is small grain rather than the maize of the Americas.[121] Apparently this group consisted of day laborers who depended for their livelihood solely upon their daily earnings. Since the men had been engaged in rebuilding the walls for at least a month, and there is no indication that anyone was receiving compensation for the construction work, their families were becoming destitute.

---

[121]Corned beef receives its name because the meat was preserved with small grains (corns) of salt.

5:3 Another group owned property but were forced to mortgage their fields, or vineyards, or homes in order to obtain food **during the famine**. The context does not indicate whether this was a natural famine or one caused by political and economic conditions. It may have been a combination of factors. On the northern fringe of desert, the region was always vulnerable to droughts with subsequent crop loss (cf. Hag 1:6; 2:16). At this time Judah and Jerusalem were also surrounded by antagonistic neighbors, bringing regional economic activities to a virtual standstill. And the men were in Jerusalem working on the walls during a part of the harvest season.

The main problem this group faced was not the inability to mortgage their property, but the inability to repay mortgages, resulting in the loss of their property. In this period, interest rates were between 40-50%.[122]

5:4 Another group of landowners were apparently able to provide food for their families, but they **had to borrow money to pay the king's tax on our fields and vineyards**. (For a discussion of taxes, see Ezra 4:13.) The heavy burden of the royal taxes is implied in 9:37. Conquests were driven by the love of money. The Babylonians imposed property taxes, and the Persians continued the practice. In the time of Artaxerxes taxes were heavy across the Persian Empire. Referring to the province of Yehud, Stern states that "In contrast to the liberal approach of the Persian rulers towards the conquered people in matters of cult and administration, in questions of economy and taxation it was rather severe."[123] While local projects might be financed from these taxes (Ezra 6:8; 7:20), Olmstead notes that "little of this vast sum was ever returned to the satrapies."[124]

5:5 Although we are of the same flesh and blood as our countrymen . . . .

Jews owed their debts to fellow Jews, goes the argument, so why should the sons and daughters of those in debt be sold into slavery to

---

[122]Yamauchi, *Persia and the Bible*, p. 275.

[123]Ephraim Stern, *The Cambridge History of Judaism I: Introduction: The Persian Period*, eds. W.D. Davies and L. Finkelstein (Cambridge: Cambridge University Press, 1984), p. 113.

[124]A.T. Olmstead, *History of the Persian Empire* (Chicago: Univeristy of Chicago Press, 1948), p. 298.

pay their Jewish debtors when their children were in no way inferior to those of their debtors? And the law regarded all Jews as brothers.

As difficult as it may be for us to comprehend, families such as these were sometimes forced to resort to debt slavery. A common practice in the ancient Near East, it was controlled but not prohibited in Israel (Exod 21:1-11). The children of those unable to pay their debts became servants to the lender to work until the debt was paid (cf. 2 Kgs 4:1).

Some of our daughters have already been enslaved, . . .

What was in the process of happening to some had already become a reality for others, and they had no resources to redeem their enslaved daughters. In some cases the daughter might become the wife of the lender or of one of his sons. Williamson notes that the word translated "enslaved" (נִכְבָּשׁוֹת, *nikbāšôth*), has sexual overtones in Esther 7:8 and that the daughters are mentioned in particular here because "they were having to gratify the creditors' lusts as payment for delaying foreclosure on the loans."[125]

Selling sons and daughters into debt slavery was the lesser of two evils. Without doing so, the family would lose its source of income and any hope of an early redemption of the enslaved. Sadly, this sorry state of affairs was due to the avarice of the elite of the society, wealthy enough to avoid the heart-wrenching circumstances of their Jewish brethren but covetous enough to take advantage of their desperate situations.

B. NEHEMIAH'S RESPONSE AND REBUKE (5:6-11)

[6]**When I heard their outcry and these charges, I was very angry. [7]I pondered them in my mind and then accused the nobles and officials. I told them, "You are exacting usury from your own countrymen!" So I called together a large meeting to deal with them [8]and said: "As far as possible, we have bought back our Jewish brothers who were sold to the Gentiles. Now you are selling your brothers, only for them to be sold back to us!" They kept quiet, because they could find nothing to say.**

---

[125]Williamson, *Ezra, Nehemiah*, p. 238.

⁹So I continued, "What you are doing is not right. Shouldn't you walk in the fear of our God to avoid the reproach of our Gentile enemies? ¹⁰I and my brothers and my men are also lending the people money and grain. But let the exacting of usury stop! ¹¹Give back to them immediately their fields, vineyards, olive groves and houses, and also the usury you are charging them—the hundredth part of the money, grain, new wine and oil."

5:6-7 When I heard their outcry and these charges, . . .

Here the outcry is distinguished from the charges. This suggests that these people had come to Nehemiah with bitter tears and anguished groans, with weeping and wailing and gnashing of teeth. Then they poured out these **charges.** דְּבָרִים (dᵉbārîm, "words, things") is variously translated as "words" (KJV/RSV), "complaints" (NRSV), and "the story they told" (NEB). Verses 2-5 contain the gist of what Nehemiah heard over and over. The result was, **I was very angry.** These are the exact words used to describe Sanballat's ire in 4:1.

What stirred him to such intense anger was the degree to which the bonds of Jewish brotherhood were ignored in the face of the dire circumstances which the community faced. The breakdown of the fabric of society was in its own way a greater danger to the survival and success of the Jewish province than that of the immediate threat of the adversaries. If it persisted, not only would their disgrace (2:17) not be removed, it would be compounded.

So Nehemiah writes, **I pondered them in my mind.** Literally, the Hebrew expression is, "my heart took counsel upon me." The NEB has, "I mastered my feelings," suggesting that with difficulty he controlled his emotions, but the NRSV captures well the idea with, "After thinking it over." Nehemiah knew that this was a crisis that must be resolved, and after considering what he should do, he formulated his plan. The situations of the poor Jews must be reversed. So he confronted directly those who were creditors, receivers of debt slaves, and foreclosers of mortgages — **the nobles and officials.**

Nehemiah **accused** them, that is, he brought a lawsuit against them. That is the underlying connotation of רִיב (rîb). Thus the RSV renders, "I brought charges." The specific charges follow. They were exacting **usury,** "the practice of exacting a rate of interest beyond what is allowed by law."[126] It is not clear, however, that the Hebrew מַשָּׁא . . . נשָׁאִים (maššā'. . . nōšîm) means "to lend for interest."

Slotki renders, "Ye lend upon pledge."[127] Williamson, on the basis of his study of this word, translates, "Each of you is acting the creditor against his own brother."[128] The word, used in Deuteronomy 24:10, is translated "pledge." A pledge is something promised as security for a loan. Exodus 22:25 and Deuteronomy 24:10 speak to such loan arrangements, indicating a need on the part of the lender to have a generous and kindly attitude toward the borrower. One could not take a millstone pledged for a debt because it was essential for preparing a family's daily bread (Deut 24:6), nor could a cloak taken as a pledge be kept overnight because it was needed by the owner as protection against the chill of the night (Exod 22:26-27; Deut 24:12-13). The nobles and officials were ignoring the desperate plight of those to whom they had loaned money, and were taking the pledged property despite their situation. That loans were permissible was not the problem; Nehemiah had been making loans of money and grain as well (v. 10).

Since this was a matter involving the entire community, Nehemiah held a mass meeting to explain the charges and to hear the judgment of the people. This was a wise plan. The alienation of these leaders would do no good, and their continuing support was needed for completion of the primary project and for subsequent activities. With the assembly as witness, the creditors could hardly back away from the resolution of the problem offered and the pledge they were soon to make.

5:8 Nehemiah provided an important context by which all present could view the current situation. The focus of his remarks was on debt slavery, but as a stock example it had application to all the cases he had heard about (vv. 2-5). The Jewish community had been struggling to redeem poor Jews who had sold themselves into debt slavery to Gentiles. (It is unclear if this is a reference to indentured Jews in Persia and Babylonia or to the local situation, but probably the latter.) This was important; if at all possible, no Jew should be sold to foreigners, and those sold should be redeemed, for the Lord

---

[126]*Funk & Wagnall's New International Dictionary of the English Language* (Chicago: J.G. Ferguson, 1996), p. 1383.

[127]Slotki, *Daniel, Ezra and Nehemiah*, p. 210.

[128]Williamson, *Ezra, Nehemiah*, pp. 231, 233.

God had said, "the Israelites belong to me as servants" (Lev 25:55). And redeeming them required precious resources from the community. The current situation was absurd: **now you are selling your brothers, only for them to be sold back to us!** The nobles and officials answered not a word; nothing they might have said would have freed them of guilt.

5:9 After a pause to allow the accused opportunity to reply, and after their silence, Nehemiah continued. Shifting attention from the level of social responsibility, Nehemiah states flatly that what they have been doing **is not right**. The Hebrew word is "good." It is not good because it is morally wrong. The question, **Shouldn't you walk in the fear of our God?** casts their practices in a different light. The people of God ought to live their lives in reverence of God, and so order their ways. הלך (*hlk*, "to walk") is the basis of *halakhah*, the Jewish tradition of ordering one's life according to God's will. The practices of these creditors testified to a shallow view of **our God** (rather than "your God"). While pointedly shaming the accused nobles and officials, by the use of "our," Nehemiah did not ostracize them. They were still a part of the people of God along with Nehemiah and the assembled community. What they, a part of God's people, had been doing was bound to bring **reproach** from their Gentile enemies. Once the neighboring peoples heard about the merciless treatment of Jew by Jew, they would pour out scorn and derision (Ps 79:4) on them, disparaging their God in the process. This will be the result of thoughtless actions by the people of God in any age.

5:10 I and my brothers and my men . . .

In a remarkably honest and candid way, Nehemiah states that he and his close associates have also been **lending the people money and grain**. This statement reveals that Nehemiah came from a family possessing some wealth in Jerusalem and Yehud. It also reveals his sympathetic concern for the less fortunate members of that community. Seeing people's needs, he had responded to them. The nobles and officials benefited from Nehemiah's revelation also. What they had done, Nehemiah had done, although not exactly. Nehemiah has said nothing about debt slavery in his confession. What the situation demanded and that for which he called was the abandonment of this system of loans.

5:11 Not only should old practices cease, he calls also for the restoration of the pledged property which the lenders had taken when the borrowers were unable to pay the loans. So important is the healing of this social wound that he demands that the restoration be done **immediately**, literally, "today." Among the properties to be restored to their owners were **olive groves**. These had not been mentioned in the complaints about which Nehemiah had previously written (vv. 3-4), but they were an important segment of agricultural production in Judah.

The last part of the verse is difficult to interpret. Literally it reads, הַכֶּסֶף וּמְאַת (ûm⁽ə⁾ath hakkeseph), "the hundred of the silver." It might refer to interest, an annual rate of 12 percent, which was much lower than the minimum 20 percent per annum rate among the Persians in this period. The NEB translates "the income in money," taking the phrase to refer to the income made off the pledged property that the lenders had seized. Whereas the RSV has "the hundredth of money," the NRSV reads, "the interest on money."

Despite this minor problem of interpretation, the overall intent is clear. Whatever was taken from those in dire straits, it must be returned immediately. No debt slaves are mentioned, but in this context it is clear that they also would be restored to their families. Williamson reasons that the cancellation of the debts is implied and notes Kidner's observation that Nehemiah "sees now that the depth of poverty had called for gifts, not loans."[129] Breneman's observation is also valid: "In times of crisis or at any time the well-being of the community of faith is more important than the comfort and security of the affluent; they must be willing to sacrifice (cf. Prov 22:16)."[130]

C. REPENTANCE AND RESTORATION (5:12-13)

[12]"We will give it back," they said. "And we will not demand anything more from them. We will do as you say."

Then I summoned the priests and made the nobles and officials take an oath to do what they had promised. [13]I also shook out

---

[129]Ibid., p. 241.
[130]Breneman, *Ezra, Nehemiah, Esther*, p. 205.

the folds of my robe and said, "In this way may God shake out of his house and possessions every man who does not keep this promise. So may such a man be shaken out and emptied!"

At this the whole assembly said, "Amen," and praised the LORD. And the people did as they had promised.

5:12 The nobles and officials responded to the twofold demand of Nehemiah. They agreed to give **it** back. The Hebrew is one word, נָשִׁיב (nāšîb), "We will restore." The object(s) to be restored are understood. They are exactly what Nehemiah had listed. The second part of their response was to assure him before the assembly that they would make no further claims against those to whom they had made loans.

Promises made under the pressure of momentary circumstances may not always be kept. Nehemiah **summoned the priests** (out of the assembly) to take the oath of the nobles and officials that they would do as they had said. Oaths were normally taken by priests (Num 5:19). Rather than swearing on a scroll, God is invoked as witness and guarantor of the oath, with the expectation that an unfulfilled oath would be punished by God. The seriousness with which vows were held is detailed in Ecclesiastes 5:2-7, and the same gravity of oaths was current in the NT (Matt 26:63).

5:13 I also shook out the folds of my robe . . .

This symbolic act combined with the related curse further emphasized the seriousness of the promises to all who witnessed it. The "fold" (singular in the original) was the sash around his waist that kept his long, flowing robe in place. This provided a place to carry personal items. As he shook it out, those items would cascade to the ground. Together act and anathema implied that God would shake any promise breaker out of his possessions. The entire assembly, including the promise-makers, said **"Amen."** (The English word is a direct transliteration of Hebrew, אָמֵן, 'āmēn, "truly," or "let it be so.") Then they praised the Lord for what had happened. The oppressed were relieved at the outcome, and even the creditors were pleased that the problem had been satisfactorily resolved. And Nehemiah was no doubt relieved so that they could go back to work on the walls. It was his primary passion.

And the people did as they had promised.

Looking back as he recalled this incident, Nehemiah acknowledges that the nobles and officials did as they had promised. The word translated **people** is fluid enough in its usage to allow this interpretation.

D. NEHEMIAH'S EXAMPLE OF GENEROSITY (5:14-19)

When Nehemiah was writing his record of events during his time in Jerusalem, probably at a time during his second and last period as governor (13:6-7), he found this as an appropriate place to insert this summary. His concern for all the people led him to be very careful not to be a burden on them. The other side of the coin of concern was generosity.

[14]**Moreover, from the twentieth year of King Artaxerxes, when I was appointed to be their governor in the land of Judah, until his thirty-second year—twelve years—neither I nor my brothers ate the food allotted to the governor. [15]But the earlier governors—those preceding me—placed a heavy burden on the people and took forty shekels[a] of silver from them in addition to food and wine. Their assistants also lorded it over the people. But out of reverence for God I did not act like that. [16]Instead, I devoted myself to the work on this wall. All my men were assembled there for the work; we[b] did not acquire any land.**

[17]**Furthermore, a hundred and fifty Jews and officials ate at my table, as well as those who came to us from the surrounding nations. [18]Each day one ox, six choice sheep and some poultry were prepared for me, and every ten days an abundant supply of wine of all kinds. In spite of all this, I never demanded the food allotted to the governor, because the demands were heavy on these people.**

[19]**Remember me with favor, O my God, for all I have done for these people.**

[a]*15* That is, about 1 pound (about 0.5 kilograms)   [b]*16* Most Hebrew manuscripts; some Hebrew manuscripts, Septuagint, Vulgate and Syriac *I*

5:14 . . . when I was appointed to be their governor . . .

Nehemiah had not mentioned earlier that he had been appointed governor by Artaxerxes. That appointment would have been for the years 445 to 432. We should assume that he made one or more trips back to the seat of the empire to confer with the king during that long period. His appointment as governor over Yehud would have displaced the former authority of Sanballat over the region. Sanballat, whose governmental center was in the city of Samaria, must have been informed of this change by the letter Nehemiah conveyed to him from King Artaxerxes. This would have been a major blow to his prestige and pride, thus contributing to his animosity toward Jerusalem.

At the same time, mention is made below of governors in Jerusalem preceding Nehemiah. We lack a clear picture of the relationship of their authority to that of Sanballat, but it probably was one of subservience. Williamson even suggests that "after the forcible stopping of building work in Jerusalem (Ezra 4:23), Tobiah, a junior colleague of Sanballat, may have been appointed to temporary authority over Jerusalem until Nehemiah's arrival."[131]

Under Persian practice, the governor had a right to receive a portion of the royal taxes collected from the people to support his personal and governmental expenses. It amounted to forty shekels of silver per day (v. 15), about one pound. The value in modern terms is difficult to assess; purchasing power then was much greater than now. Nehemiah waived his right to receive these taxes out of his consideration of the heavy tax burden they already carried. His ability to do so is another indication that his family owned considerable wealth-producing property in Yehud.

5:15a But the earlier governors . . .

Apart from Sheshbazzar and Zerubbabel, extrabiblical information has provided the names of three governors who preceded Nehemiah. With approximate dates they were: Elnathan (515), Yeho'ezer (490), and Aḥzai (470). Another governor, later than Nehemiah, is also known from the Elephantine Papyri, Bagohi (408).[132] Given the time

---

[131]Williamson, *Ezra, Nehemiah*, p. 243.
[132]Shemaryahu Talmon, "Ezra and Nehemiah," *IDB Supplementary Vol.* (Nashville: Abingdon, 1976), p. 327.

span, this is clearly an incomplete list, and they were not considered important enough to be mentioned by the biblical writers. The former governors placed an extra burden on the subsistence farmers. After collecting the required silver for taxes, they took **food**, literally, "bread," that is, grain with which to make bread, and wine. Further oppressing the populace, **their assistants also lorded it over the people.** The word (נַעַר, *na'ar*) translated **assistants** here was translated "men" in 4:16. These governors allowed their aides to lord it over the people. All too frequently, bureaucracy breeds contempt for the common man. Fensham suggests that this is probably in reference to tax-collecting. "The minor officials levied the taxes in a harsh manner in order to collect enough for the Persian king, the satrap, themselves, and the governor."[133]

5:15b Nehemiah acted differently than his predecessors **out of reverence for God**, the identical expression to that of verse 9. In these verses "He reveals his twofold motivation: first, filial reverence for God, which restrained him from 'lording it over the people' (15b), and made heaven's verdict all-important to him (19); and second, brotherly compassion, 'because the servitude was heavy upon this people' (18). In his own brusque style he exemplified the two great commandments, and anticipated the cheerful disregard of one's entitlements which Paul would expound in 1 Corinthians 9."[134] He exemplified "the royal law found in Scripture" (Jas 2:8).

5:16 . . . All my men . . .

Both Nehemiah and his assistants had no interest in or time for personal enrichment. Their obsession was the completion of the wall. And neither Nehemiah nor his associates had acquired land by means of unpaid loans.

5:17 . . . ate at my table . . .

Nehemiah underwent significant personal expense to provide food and drink daily to so many people. This was in line with the Persian custom where the noblemen often ate at the table of the king. Identified here are **Jews and officials**. These were apparently men who worked under him in the administration of the city and

---

[133]Fensham, *The Books of Ezra and Nehemiah*, p. 197.
[134]Kidner, *Ezra & Nehemiah*, p. 98.

province. Next mentioned are **those who came to us from the surrounding nations**. Some of these would be general visitors, perhaps Jews from outlying villages; some might be Jews immigrating into Yehud from surrounding territories; and some visiting government dignitaries, Nehemiah's hospitality, too, may reflect the continuing influence of Middle Eastern desert hospitality, always provided by the tribal sheik.

5:18 Despite the heavy expenses he bore for this hospitality, he **never demanded the food** (literally, "bread") **allotted to the governor** out of concern for the burdens the common people were bearing.

5:19 Remember me with favor, O my God, . . .

Rather than a prayer breathed in the moment of crisis, this is Nehemiah's prayer as he looks back over all his efforts and sacrifices on behalf of his people. He asks God to remember literally "for good." Most translations render "for my good," which misses the point. Nehemiah is not asking God for personal reward, but to be remembered for the good he has done. By promoting the welfare of God's people, he was advancing the cause of God. Rather than suspecting him of self-glorification, we should view this prayer in light of the fact that at that time "Nehemiah and the Jews were the sole bearers of the true religion."[135]

XXI. FURTHER OPPOSITION TO THE REBUILDING (6:1-14)

As Nehemiah recalled the chain of events in the story of the reconstruction of Jerusalem's walls, he had interrupted the account of the outside opposition. While dealing with Sanballat's strategies, an internal crisis had developed with which he had to deal. Chapter 5 contained his report on the internal controversies that threatened to tear the Jewish community apart. He also informed his readers how he had resolved the problem. In chapter 6, Nehemiah returns to the ongoing saga of outside opposition.

---

[135]Fensham, *The Books of Ezra and Nehemiah*, p. 199.

A. SANBALLAT'S SCHEMES AND NEHEMIAH'S RESPONSE
(6:1-9)

¹When word came to Sanballat, Tobiah, Geshem the Arab and the rest of our enemies that I had rebuilt the wall and not a gap was left in it—though up to that time I had not set the doors in the gates— ²Sanballat and Geshem sent me this message: "Come, let us meet together in one of the villagesᵃ on the plain of Ono."

But they were scheming to harm me; ³so I sent messengers to them with this reply: "I am carrying on a great project and cannot go down. Why should the work stop while I leave it and go down to you?" ⁴Four times they sent me the same message, and each time I gave them the same answer.

⁵Then, the fifth time, Sanballat sent his aide to me with the same message, and in his hand was an unsealed letter ⁶in which was written:

> "It is reported among the nations—and Geshemᵇ says it is true—that you and the Jews are plotting to revolt, and therefore you are building the wall. Moreover, according to these reports you are about to become their king ⁷and have even appointed prophets to make this proclamation about you in Jerusalem: 'There is a king in Judah!' Now this report will get back to the king; so come, let us confer together."

⁸I sent him this reply: "Nothing like what you are saying is happening; you are just making it up out of your head."

⁹They were all trying to frighten us, thinking, "Their hands will get too weak for the work, and it will not be completed."

⌐But I prayed,⌐ "Now strengthen my hands."

ᵃ2 Or *in Kephirim*   ᵇ6 Hebrew *Gashmu*, a variant of *Geshem*

6:1 . . . the rest of our enemies . . .

The reference is to the Ammonites and Ashdodites, mentioned earlier (4:1). The entire entourage of those who wanted to see Jerusalem unfortified and undefended had tried first veiled then open threats without success. Now they attempted treachery. Nehemiah reports that they were moved to action when they heard **that I had rebuilt the wall.** Clearly he was not boasting about doing the work single-handed. But he knew that they recognized that he was the primary person driving the project, and if they could eradicate him, the work would stop. The wall was complete, but the doors had not been set in the gates. Each gate required two doors, swinging on upright beams set in upper and lower sockets. Each door was made of heavy planks. Raising them to the perpendicular and fitting them into their sockets was a major undertaking requiring strong men and coordinated effort. So the final touches on the fortifications were several days away, because there were approximately ten gates requiring the installation of doors.

6:2-4 Sanballat and Geshem . . .

Why Tobiah is not mentioned here is puzzling but requires no explanation. As two who controlled the northern and southern territories adjacent to Yehud, these two were sufficient to arrange the entrapment of Nehemiah. Apparently this was an oral message carried by a young man (*na'ar*) who was in the service of Sanballat (v. 5). The invitation was for Nehemiah to meet with them **in one of the villages on the plain of Ono**. The plain was perhaps twenty miles slightly northwest of Jerusalem in the region between Gezer and Lod (Ezra 2:33; Neh 11:35). Apparently it was within Yehud but on the border with Ashdod and Samaria. At that distance from Jerusalem, Nehemiah would have been at the mercy of the conspirators. The NEB translates הַכְּפִירִים (*hakkᵉphîrîm*, **villages**), as a place name, "Hakkephirim." This is an alternative, although no other mention of it occurs, and it cannot be related to Kephirah in Ezra 2:25.

The invitation contained no meeting agenda, and Nehemiah was suspicious of their intent. He concluded that they wanted to eliminate him. Rather than sending a reply by Sanballat's servant, he sent some of his own men as messengers to carry his verbal reply to their invitation. **And cannot go down** refers not to coming down off the wall but to descending from the mountains of Jerusalem to the coastal plain where they wanted to meet. Nehemiah's "excuse" was that he could not afford the travel time to meet with them because of the importance of the project on which he was working. If he were to leave it, the work would slow to a stop. They were persistent but he was resistant. Nehemiah probably regretted the time lost from the project by his messengers' four trips to carry his response to Sanballat and Geshem.

6:5 The fifth effort by the confederates included the oral invitation combined with **an unsealed letter**. It would most likely have been written on a sheet of papyrus, although it could have been inscribed on a potsherd or a wooden tablet. An open letter is a blatant invitation for any and all who had the opportunity to read it, including leaders of the Jews in Jerusalem.

6:6-7 The intent of the letter was to bring Nehemiah's motives for completing the wall under suspicion. In light of what had happened a few years earlier (Ezra 4:11-23) when construction efforts in Jerusalem had been suspended, this letter was certain to alarm the Jewish community with the hoped-for result that the work would grind to a halt.

It is reported among the nations, that is, among the neighboring people.

—and Geshem says it is true—

The NIV footnote draws attention to the alternate spelling of the Arab leader's name that appears here, "Gashmu." This is not unique in the OT. Moses' father-in-law is called Jethro in Exodus 3:1 and Jether in Exodus 4:18.

According to Sanballat, the rumors circulating are (1) a revolt of the Jews led by Nehemiah is brewing; that is why the wall is being built; (2) Nehemiah will soon be proclaimed king and has enlisted prophets to proclaim the same. The slick tactics of Sanballat are clear. He no doubt recalled that the king had stopped earlier construction in Jerusalem on the hint that a rebellion might ensue if it continued, as would any of the Jews who might have had the opportunity to read the letter. The rumor that Nehemiah was about to become king with prophetic endorsement suggests that Nehemiah might have been a descendant of the Davidic line, but this is nowhere indicated in the OT. Fensham suggests that Sanballat "wanted to stress that in Jerusalem, according to his information, a messianic movement was started to make Nehemiah king . . . [and] . . . it could be true. In such circumstances the Persian king must be informed . . . ."[136] Sanballat cunningly suggests that they confer on this matter. On the surface it sounds as if they will give him a chance to clear himself of the accusation which was circulating freely among the surrounding people.

---

[136]Ibid., p. 201.

With this open letter, Sanballat provides a reason for the invitation to meet. This was lacking in the earlier oral communications. However, his calculating remarks failed to veil suspicion. Why would the governor of a neighboring province want to meet with a rumored revolutionary? By doing so he would also be under suspicion of involvement. And why would he invite Nehemiah to a secret meeting by sending him an open letter?

6:8 Having served in close association with Artaxerxes, Nehemiah was no doubt well-schooled in the matter of intrigue. Persian kings were always alert to palace plots. His response was sharp and to the point. Neither of the two rumors was true. (Nehemiah knew that he was doing exactly what Artaxerxes had authorized.) Whether Nehemiah sent a written or an oral reply, his closing remark was withering: **you are just making it up out of your head**. Word for word the original states, "but from your heart [mind] you are fabricating them." The word underlying "just making it up" appears only here and in 1 Kings 12:33, where Jeroboam devised his own religious calendar.

6:9 Nehemiah saw through this latest effort to halt the final phases of rebuilding the walls. His assessment of the situation, spelled out here, was the basis for his response to Sanballat. The ultimate effect of Sanballat's tactics was to increase Nehemiah's resolve. Sanballat had sought to weaken working hands; Nehemiah prayed, **"Now strengthen my hands."** The words, **But I prayed**, do not appear in the Hebrew text; however, they may be implied. The NRSV, following its heritage from the RSV back to the KJV, expands thus, "But now, O God, strengthen my hands." Some, however, because the usual formula for invoking God is missing, would translate, "I will strengthen my hands," or, "So I applied myself to it with greater energy" (NEB). Whether or not Nehemiah intended this as a prayer, which seems most reasonable, makes little difference. Time and again we have seen his recognition of the hand of God at work in this initiative to restore the walls of Jerusalem.

B. INTERNAL CONSPIRATORS (6:10-14)

[10]One day I went to the house of Shemaiah son of Delaiah, the

son of Mehetabel, who was shut in at his home. He said, "Let us meet in the house of God, inside the temple, and let us close the temple doors, because men are coming to kill you—by night they are coming to kill you."

[11]But I said, "Should a man like me run away? Or should one like me go into the temple to save his life? I will not go!" [12]I realized that God had not sent him, but that he had prophesied against me because Tobiah and Sanballat had hired him. [13]He had been hired to intimidate me so that I would commit a sin by doing this, and then they would give me a bad name to discredit me.

[14]Remember Tobiah and Sanballat, O my God, because of what they have done; remember also the prophetess Noadiah and the rest of the prophets who have been trying to intimidate me.

6:10 One day . . .

The Hebrew has no time indicator, literally, "And I entered the house of Shemaiah . . . ." (His name means, "Hear, O Yah[weh].") It is implicit in the narrative, however, that this occurred a short time after the preceding incidents. Although not stated, Nehemiah must have been invited by **Shemaiah** to meet in his home. While Shemaiah is identified by name and lineage, he is not otherwise known. If his father was the **Delaiah** named in 1 Chronicles 24:18, then he was a priest. That he was a priest is likely, otherwise he would not have suggested meeting **inside the temple**. Only priests were allowed within the temple proper, and that is where he is asking Nehemiah to meet him, because he wants them to **close the temple doors**. Men other than priests were allowed in certain courtyards within the temple complex.

The expression **who was shut in at his home** is as much an interpretation as a translation of the two Hebrew words upon which it is built: עָצוּר אֱהוּא (wehû' 'āṣûr, "and he was shut up"). The word in Jeremiah 36:5 is translated "restricted," of the prophet's house arrest. But that category of restriction does not fit this situation. Williamson, after reviewing various proposals others have offered, tentatively translates, "who was looking extremely worried."[137] He suggests that Shemaiah sent a message to Nehemiah indicating that

---

[137]Williamson, *Ezra, Nehemiah*, pp. 247, 249.

he had a word from the Lord for him. And when Nehemiah came, he played his deceitful role well, with a worried demeanor. Slotki notes that the expression is usually taken to mean that he was prevented from mingling with the people or approaching the temple because he was ritually impure.[138] Under those circumstances, however, it is unlikely that he would have suggested meeting Nehemiah there because he would be violating the religious taboo. We do not know why he was restricted, and Nehemiah, recalling the incident many years later as he penned this remembrance, simply did not include some details we would like to know.

It is worth noting that the (false) prophetic word from Shemaiah is given in poetic form, similar to true prophetic oracles. The meter is that of *a lament, 3 + 2, 3 + 2, 3*. Fensham sets it off in appropriate form and translates:

> "Let us meet at the temple of God,
>   in the inside of the sanctuary;
> let us lock the doors of the sanctuary;
>   for they are coming to kill you,
> they are coming to kill you tonight."[139]

Let us meet . . . and let us close the temple doors, because men are coming to kill you . . . .

The word "men" does not occur in the Hebrew text. An indeterminate subject is understood, but Shemaiah either named Tobiah and Sanballat (v. 12), or Nehemiah assumed they were the culprits.

6:11-13 Nehemiah's response was based in part on his clear sense of self. Could a man in his position, responsible to both God and the king, think of his personal safety in the face of a threat to his life? To follow such a course would have weakened his public image and destroyed his ability to lead.

His response was also based on his religious convictions. The Hebrew behind **Or should one like me go into the temple to save his life?** is more pointed. Nehemiah says literally, "Could one like me enter the temple and live?" Someone like Nehemiah, from a non-

---

[138]Slotki, *Daniel, Ezra, and Nehemiah*, p. 217.
[139]Fensham, *The Books of Ezra and Nehemiah*, p. 204.

priestly family, could go into the temple courts and gain sanctuary by grasping the horns of the altar under certain circumstances (Exod 21:13-14; 1 Kgs 1:50-53; 2:28 ff.). But seeking asylum to escape a foreign enemy was not one of them. Nehemiah was more fearful of unlawfully entering the holy place restricted to priests than he was of any mortal enemies. For him to enter was forbidden on penalty of death (Num 3:10; 18:7). But more than the legal stipulations, as Williamson observes, he must have believed "that direct contact with the divine sphere when in an unprepared state would lead to death (see, e.g., Exod 20:21; 33:20; Deut 5:25; Judg 13:22; 2 Chr 26:16-21; etc.). The verse thus sheds rare but welcome and revealing light on Nehemiah's respect and humility in relation to God."[140]

Shemaiah's words did not ring true. Nehemiah was quick to discern that his archenemies had hired him to speak these things. He was not God-sent. Shemaiah's proposal that he enter the temple and transgress God's law was enough for Nehemiah to see through the deception. It was not that his enemies were actually going to break into a hiding place within the temple to murder him, it was a ruse to get him to make a fool of himself before the entire community.

Tobiah and Sanballat had hired him

The change of order, naming Tobiah first, indicates that he was the primary person behind this effort to humiliate Nehemiah. It is apparent that Tobiah, was on good terms with the Jerusalem priests (cf. 13:4) and apparently had access to Shemaiah to hatch the plan.

6:14 Nehemiah here uses a recurring phrase, **Remember**. It appears with positive connotations in 5:19; 13:14,22,31 and with negative implications here and in 13:29. It recalls Nehemiah's earlier prayer against these same enemies in 4:4-5. Again, as in verse 12, **Tobiah** is listed before **Sanballat**. Nehemiah leaves their just recompense and reward for their evil deeds with God, rather than personally seeking revenge.

He also asks God to remember **the prophetess Noadiah**, along with other unnamed prophets. Surprisingly, Shemaiah is not mentioned. We know nothing more about Noadiah (whose name means "appointed of Yah[weh]") nor the incident Nehemiah had in mind.

---

[140]Williamson, *Ezra, Nehemiah*, p. 259.

Noadiah is a reminder that prophetesses were not uncommon in biblical times; some were good (Miriam, Deborah, Huldah) and some were bad (Ezek 13:17-23).

It is clear that Shemaiah, Noadiah, and **the rest of the prophets who have been trying to intimidate me** were among those within the Jewish community who opposed Nehemiah's program. As Fensham observes, "in the time of Nehemiah a group of visionaries was around, but their spiritual standards were indeed low."[141] It is apparent that the true prophetic spirit was waning. Jewish tradition holds that after Haggai, Zechariah, and Malachi prophecy ceased; the age of Ezra saw the end of the prophetic era.[142]

XXI. THE COMPLETION OF THE WALL (6:15–7:3)

A. THE WALL COMPLETED (6:15-16)

[15]**So the wall was completed on the twenty-fifth of Elul, in fifty-two days. [16]When all our enemies heard about this, all the surrounding nations were afraid and lost their self-confidence, because they realized that this work had been done with the help of our God.**

6:15 So the wall was completed . . . .

What an accomplishment! The month of Elul was the sixth month of their calendar, which had begun with Nisan. In that half year, Nehemiah had obtained the king's permission and authorization, had made his journey from Susa, had assessed the situation in Jerusalem, had whipped up the enthusiasm of the people of Jerusalem and Judah, had confronted external adversaries and internal dissensions lasting right up to the point the project was completed, and had rebuilt the wall in the amazing time of fifty-two days. In the account of Josephus, the construction period is given as two years and four months (*Ant.* Xi.5.8). However, scholars generally agree that textual corruption has likely crept into his text in the course of

---

[141]Fensham, *The Books of Ezra and Nehemiah*, p. 206.
[142]Samuel Sandmel, *Judaism and Christian Beginnings* (New York: Oxford University Press, 1978), p. 174.

transmission, so his length of time should be ignored, and the LXX and the Vulgate translations reflect the Hebrew text.

If it seems impossible to rebuild a wall some 2860 yards long, we should keep in mind that it was a restoration of the wall. Needed stones were largely at hand in the rubble, reducing the amount of quarrying needed. The only completely new section was a part of the eastern wall, and archaeological results provide evidence that it was made in haste. The people had a mind to work as well, and they worked not only rapidly but from dawn to dusk. The importance of the task and the passion of their leader drove them. We may note, also, that the Greek historian, Thucydides (i.93) reported that the wall around Athens was rebuilt in a month (we do not know the length of it).

The exact date of completion is open to argument, but many scholars now consider it to have been October 2.

6:16 When all our enemies . . .
is no doubt a reference to Sanballat, Tobiah, Geshem and the Arabs, and the leaders of the Ammonites, and the Ashkelonites – the adversaries.

all the surrounding nations were afraid . . .
The surrounding nations were simply the ordinary folk of Samaria, Transjordan, the Negev to the south, and the mixture of Canaanites, Philistines, and Phoenicians to the west. The NEB "[they] saw it" (also in the 1978 edition NIV) follows a suggested change in the text. What they saw would have been the completed wall. However, the Hebrew, followed by LXX and the Vulgate, reads "all the nations *feared*," that is, they were overawed that the wall had been rebuilt so quickly and completely. It was a blow to their own self-confidence and belittling attitude toward the Jews. And they were forced to acknowledge what Nehemiah knew all along, **that this work had been done with the help of our God**. For the Jews, on the other hand, the completion of the project removed their "disgrace" (1:3; 2:17) and annulled the "insults" (4:5) they had endured.

B. TOBIAH'S CONNIVING CORRESPONDENTS (6:17-19)

[17]Also, in those days the nobles of Judah were sending many letters to Tobiah, and replies from Tobiah kept coming to them. [18]For

many in Judah were under oath to him, since he was son-in-law to Shecaniah son of Arah, and his son Jehohanan had married the daughter of Meshullam son of Berekiah. ¹⁹Moreover, they kept reporting to me his good deeds and then telling him what I said. And Tobiah sent letters to intimidate me.

Normally, after the announcement that the wall had been completed, one would expect a celebration and dedication to follow. It is delayed in the account until 12:27-47. Looking back as he writes, Nehemiah recalls that throughout the period of his governorship, Tobiah's negative influence was at work against him.

6:17 Also, in those days . . .

This is a general indication of a span of time. Although Tobiah was not physically present in Jerusalem during the two-month period when the wall was under reconstruction, correspondence had continued to flow to and from him. His Jerusalem correspondents and confidants were **the nobles of Judah**. These remain largely unnamed but they were the leaders of the Jewish community. Williamson believes that the mutually friendly relationship between Tobiah and the elite of Judah began some years before Nehemiah's arrival in Jerusalem and continued during the latter's governorship. Although there is no textual evidence, he suggests that Tobiah was "some kind of official from Samaria; perhaps, therefore, after the forcible stopping of the building work in Jerusalem (Ezra 4:23), he was appointed to temporary authority in Judah under the jurisdiction of Samaria until the next full governor should be appointed."[143] If that were so, Tobiah would have resided for a period in Jerusalem prior to Nehemiah's arrival. He may have unexpectedly been displaced by this new arrival from Susa with letters of authority in hand. That would have been a considerable irritation, to say the least, contributing to his animosity.

6:18 For many in Judah were under oath to him, . . .

No doubt important economic relationships were established on oath between Tobiah and the nobles of Judah. It was in their mutual interests to continue these ties after Nehemiah's arrival. Further, he had cemented affiliations with the community by marriage. He

---

[143]Williamson, *Ezra, Nehemiah,* p. 184.

was apparently a Jew, since his name ends with a form of the name of God, but likely a member of a family that never experienced exile in Babylon. **His son, Jehohanan** ("Yahweh has shown mercy"), also bears a Jewish name.

Tobiah married into the Arah family who were among the first returnees (7:10; cf. Ezra 2:5). We know nothing more about **Shecaniah**. Jehohanan **had married the daughter of Meshullam**. He was a supporter of Nehemiah's efforts to rebuild the wall (3:4,30), but apparently he was also Tobiah's friend. As we will see in 13:4, Tobiah also had an intimate relationship with Eliashib the (high) priest.

6:19 Tobiah's "friends in high places" continued to tell Nehemiah about Tobiah's **good deeds** and were **telling him what I said**. דְּבָרִים (d⁰bārîm), "words," can also signify "deeds." With the latter meaning, Tobiah's friends would have been reporting to him Nehemiah's activities. The nobles may have intended to negotiate between Tobiah and Nehemiah, but letters Tobiah sent directly to Nehemiah were intended **to intimidate me**. His wily ways were also evident in the plot he had arranged with Shemaiah to discredit Nehemiah.

C. SECURITY MEASURES FOR JERUSALEM (7:1-3)

¹**After the wall had been rebuilt and I had set the doors in place, the gatekeepers and the singers and the Levites were appointed. ²I put in charge of Jerusalem my brother Hanani, along with**ᵃ **Hananiah the commander of the citadel, because he was a man of integrity and feared God more than most men do. ³I said to them, "The gates of Jerusalem are not to be opened until the sun is hot. While the gatekeepers are still on duty, have them shut the doors and bar them. Also appoint residents of Jerusalem as guards, some at their posts and some near their own houses."**

ᵃ2 Or *Hanani, that is,*

7:1-3 These verses connect to verse 15, continuing the narrative flow. The intervening materials are indirectly related in time to the restoration project. They were probably inserted by Nehemiah as they came to mind, particularly the continuing problems with Tobiah.

. . . were appointed.

Nehemiah did not directly assign the gatekeepers, singers, and Levites. He may have left those matters in the hands of **Hanani** and **Hananiah**. **The singers and the Levites** would not normally be assigned to responsibilities apart from the temple area. However, this was likely an emergency situation, and a wary Nehemiah wanted to make certain that the security of the city was tight. Nehemiah placed two men in whom he had complete trust in charge of the city's security. Hananiah was already **commander of the citadel**. Already in charge of the fortress at the northwest end of the temple compound, he brought both experience and integrity to the task of assuring the security of the entire city. Nehemiah 3:9 identifies Rephaiah as "ruler of the half-district of Jerusalem" and 3:12 notes Shallum as ruler of the other half-district. Hanani and Hananiah did not replace them, for they were in charge of the area outside the city rather than within it.

Nehemiah's instructions to Hanani and Hananiah are not as clear in the Hebrew as the NIV translation appears. The question is whether or not the construction עַד־חֹם הַשֶּׁמֶשׁ (*'ad-ḥōm haššemeš*) means **until the sun is hot** or "*during* the heat of the day" (NEB). The NIV calls for an opening of the gates late in the morning; normally, they would be opened at dawn. Ostensibly, this would prevent an early morning attack. The following related command, **While the gatekeepers are still on duty, have them shut the doors and bar them** is then taken to mean that the gates shall be closed before it grows dark in the evening. Williamson's arguments favor the alternative translation and he renders, "The gates of Jerusalem are not to be left open during the heat of the day, but while they are still on duty they must shut the doors and secure them."[144] Without pursuing the details, the line of argument is that the gates are to be closed during the siesta period. In the heat of the day lethargy sets in, and the danger of a surprise attack would be highest when the sun was at its zenith.

Another strategy the two men in charge of the city's security were to use was to establish a home guard. Some would have regular duty assignments **at their posts** and others (whose houses were

---

[144]Williamson, *Ezra, Nehemiah*, p. 263.

adjacent to the city walls) around their homes. In this instance once again Nehemiah shows a deep understanding of human nature. We tend to guard best that which is nearest and dearest to us. (It is interesting that such a home guard of residents in Jerusalem's suburbs is in use today, although not within city walls.)

NEHEMIAH 7:4-13:31 — PART TWO

RENEWAL AND REFORM

Whereas Part One of Ezra–Nehemiah focused on the return from Babylonia and the reconstruction of first the temple and ultimately the city walls, the narrative now turns to the expansion of the population and the reformation of its inhabitants in the direction of becoming the Holy City.

I. THE LIST OF THE EXILES WHO RETURNED (7:4-73a)

A. CONFIRMING GENEALOGIES (7:4-7a)

⁴Now the city was large and spacious, but there were few people in it, and the houses had not yet been rebuilt. ⁵So my God put it into my heart to assemble the nobles, the officials and the common people for registration by families. I found the genealogical record of those who had been the first to return. This is what I found written there:

⁶These are the people of the province who came up from the captivity of the exiles whom Nebuchadnezzar king of Babylon had taken captive (they returned to Jerusalem and Judah, each to his own town, ⁷in company with Zerubbabel, Jeshua, Nehemiah, Azariah, Raamiah, Nahamani, Mordecai, Bilshan, Mispereth, Bigvai, Nehum and Baanah):

7:4 . . . there were few people in it . . .

Having arranged for the basic security of the city, Nehemiah now recognized that with a relatively small population it was still vulnerable to attack. The problem is introduced into the narrative of events here, but its resolution will not be addressed until chapter 11. Recognition of the problem was the beginning of a related chain of events that will first be recounted. The population was meager because not enough houses had been rebuilt. The major reason, however, was that most of the returnees settled mainly in villages in rural areas.

7:5 So my God put it into my heart . . . .

Nehemiah was very sensitive to the leading of the Lord. He not only recognized that the ideas he had concerning the resolution of the problem were from God, he wants whoever may read this account he is writing to understand that truth. Further, he wanted all to know that this census was approved by the Lord and not Satan, as occurred with David (1 Chr 21:1).

The plan was to take a census by assembling the heads of the families of community leaders and common people alike. His intent was to draw some from each of the authentic families, those with an authentic Jewish genealogy, to populate Jerusalem. Two motivations are clear here: to increase the number of inhabitants and to ensure the ethnic purity and separateness of the enlarged community. In preparation for this, he discovered a very important genealogical list, quite likely in the temple archives.

The list Nehemiah discovered was virtually the same list as the one appearing in Ezra 2. Though the lists are very similar, its appearance twice in such a short book as Ezra–Nehemiah has resulted in many scholarly arguments, suppositions, and explanations. It is clear, however, that each serves a different function. In Ezra 2 it is an historical description; in Nehemiah 7, it is an instrument for identifying families from which can be drawn new inhabitants for Jerusalem. The differences between the Ezra 2 list and this one are in the main conflicting numbers, the order of some of the family names, the different spelling of several names, and a few omissions and additions. For most of these, reference should be made to the comments on Ezra 2.

Ibn Ezra, a renowned medieval Jewish commentator, attributed the differences in names and numbers between this list and that of Ezra 2 as the result of changes wrought by time. Some of the people had died, and others who were then too young to be included had by now grown up and secured a place in the list.[1] As simple and

---

[1]Slotki, *Daniel, Ezra and Nehemiah*, p. 221.

attractive as that explanation may seem, it does not do justice to the complicated literary development that can be discerned in the text.[2]

B. IDENTIFIED BY FAMILY (7:7b-25)

The list of the men of Israel:

[8]the descendants of Parosh	2,172
[9]of Shephatiah	372
[10]of Arah	652
[11]of Pahath-Moab (through the line of Jeshua and Joab)	2,818
[12]of Elam	1,254
[13]of Zattu	845
[14]of Zaccai	760
[15]of Binnui	648
[16]of Bebai	628
[17]of Azgad	2,322
[18]of Adonikam	667
[19]of Bigvai	2,067
[20]of Adin	655
[21]of Ater (through Hezekiah)	98
[22]of Hashum	328
[23]of Bezai	324
[24]of Hariph	112
[25]of Gibeon	95

Compare Ezra 2:3-19.

C. IDENTIFIED BY PLACE (7:26-38)

[26]the men of Bethlehem and Netophah	188
[27]of Anathoth	128
[28]of Beth Azmaveth	42

[2]For a careful analysis of the relationship of the two lists to the history of the composition of Ezra–Nehemiah, see Williamson, *Ezra, Nehemiah*, pp. xxxiii-xxxv.

[29]of Kiriath Jearim, Kephirah and Beeroth	743
[30]of Ramah and Geba	621
[31]of Micmash	122
[32]of Bethel and Ai	123
[33]of the other Nebo	52
[34]of the other Elam	1,254
[35]of Harim	320
[36]of Jericho	345
[37]of Lod, Hadid and Ono	721
[38]of Senaah	3,930

Compare Ezra 2:20-35.

D. IDENTIFIED AS PRIESTS (7:39-42)

[39]The priests:

the descendants of Jedaiah	
(through the family of Jeshua)	973
[40]of Immer	1,052
[41]of Pashhur	1,247
[42]of Harim	1,017

Compare Ezra 2:36-39.

E. IDENTIFIED AS LEVITES, SINGERS, AND GATEKEEPERS (7:43-45)

[43]The Levites:

the descendants of Jeshua (through Kadmiel	
through the line of Hodaviah)	74

[44]The singers:

the descendants of Asaph	148

[45]The gatekeepers:

the descendants of	
Shallum, Ater, Talmon, Akkub, Hatita and Shobai	138

Compare Ezra 2:40-42.

F. IDENTIFIED AS TEMPLE SERVANTS (7:46-56)

[46]The temple servants:

the descendants of
  Ziha, Hasupha, Tabbaoth,
  [47]Keros, Sia, Padon,
  [48]Lebana, Hagaba, Shalmai,
  [49]Hanan, Giddel, Gahar,
  [50]Reaiah, Rezin, Nekoda,
  [51]Gazzam, Uzza, Paseah,
  [52]Besai, Meunim, Nephussim,
  [53]Bakbuk, Hakupha, Harhur,
  [54]Bazluth, Mehida, Harsha,
  [55]Barkos, Sisera, Temah,
  [56]Neziah and Hatipha

Compare Ezra 2:43-54.

G. IDENTIFIED AS SERVANTS OF SOLOMON (7:57-60)

[57]The descendants of the servants of Solomon:

the descendants of
  Sotai, Sophereth, Perida,
  [58]Jaala, Darkon, Giddel,
  [59]Shephatiah, Hattil, Pokereth-Hazzebaim and Amon

[60]The temple servants and the
  descendants of the servants of Solomon   392

Compare Ezra 2:55-58.

H. THOSE UNABLE TO PROVE ISRAELITE
IDENTIFICATION (7:61-65)

[61]The following came up from the towns of Tel Melah, Tel Harsha, Kerub, Addon and Immer, but they could not show that their families were descended from Israel:

⁶²the descendants of

Delaiah, Tobiah and Nekoda					642

⁶³And from among the priests:

the descendants of

Hobaiah, Hakkoz and Barzillai (a man who had married a daughter of Barzillai the Gileadite and was called by that name).

⁶⁴These searched for their family records, but they could not find them and so were excluded from the priesthood as unclean. ⁶⁵The governor, therefore, ordered them not to eat any of the most sacred food until there should be a priest ministering with the Urim and Thummim.

Compare Ezra 2:59-63.

I. TOTALS AND RESULTS (7:66-73a)

⁶⁶The whole company numbered 42,360, ⁶⁷besides their 7,337 menservants and maidservants; and they also had 245 men and women singers. ⁶⁸There were 736 horses, 245 mules,^a ⁶⁹435 camels and 6,720 donkeys.

⁷⁰Some of the heads of the families contributed to the work. The governor gave to the treasury 1,000 drachmas^b of gold, 50 bowls and 530 garments for priests. ⁷¹Some of the heads of the families gave to the treasury for the work 20,000 drachmas^c of gold and 2,200 minas^d of silver. ⁷²The total given by the rest of the people was 20,000 drachmas of gold, 2,000 minas^e of silver and 67 garments for priests.

⁷³The priests, the Levites, the gatekeepers, the singers and the temple servants, along with certain of the people and the rest of the Israelites, settled in their own towns.

^a68 Some Hebrew manuscripts (see also Ezra 2:66); most Hebrew manuscripts do not have this verse. ^b70 That is, about 19 pounds (about 8.5 kilograms) ^c71 That is, about 375 pounds (about 170 kilograms); also in verse 72 ^d71 That is, about 1 1/3 tons (about 1.2 metric tons) ^e72 That is, about 1¼ tons (about 1.1 metric tons)

Compare Ezra 2:64-70.

7:68 The NIV note indicates that this verse does not appear in most Hebrew manuscripts. It was apparently a marginal reading, based on Ezra 2:66, that crept into some manuscripts in the course of scribal transmission.

7:70 The governor gave to the treasury . . .

This information does not appear in Ezra 2:68. The governor is not named, although it would have been either Sheshbazzar or Zerubbabel. Neither are the items nor amounts in the list in Ezra. Myers has suggested that the differences in the total values (61,000 drachmas in Ezra 2:69; 41,000 here) can be explained by allowing a value of 20,000 drachmas for the bowls and garments.[3] Also notable is that here the contributions are **to the work**; in Ezra 2:68 they are "toward the rebuilding of the house of God." This may be an editorial adaptation of the list to the two different situations.

II. EZRA READS THE LAW (7:73b–8:18)

A. PUBLIC READING OF THE LAW (7:73b–8:8)

[73]**When the seventh month came and the Israelites had settled in their towns, [1]all the people assembled as one man in the square before the Water Gate. They told Ezra the scribe to bring out the Book of the Law of Moses, which the LORD had commanded for Israel.**

[2]**So on the first day of the seventh month Ezra the priest brought the Law before the assembly, which was made up of men and women and all who were able to understand. [3]He read it aloud from daybreak till noon as he faced the square before the Water Gate in the presence of the men, women and others who could understand. And all the people listened attentively to the Book of the Law.**

[4]**Ezra the scribe stood on a high wooden platform built for the occasion. Beside him on his right stood Mattithiah, Shema, Anaiah, Uriah, Hilkiah and Maaseiah; and on his left were Pedaiah, Mishael, Malkijah, Hashum, Hashbaddanah, Zechariah and Meshullam.**

---

[3]Myers, *Ezra and Nehemiah*, p. 148.

⁵**Ezra opened the book. All the people could see him because he was standing above them; and as he opened it, the people all stood up.** ⁶**Ezra praised the LORD, the great God; and all the people lifted their hands and responded, "Amen! Amen!" Then they bowed down and worshiped the LORD with their faces to the ground.**

⁷**The Levites—Jeshua, Bani, Sherebiah, Jamin, Akkub, Shabbethai, Hodiah, Maaseiah, Kelita, Azariah, Jozabad, Hanan and Pelaiah—instructed the people in the Law while the people were standing there.** ⁸**They read from the Book of the Law of God, making it clear**ᵃ **and giving the meaning so that the people could understand what being read.**

ᵃ*8 Or God, translating it*

7:73b When the seventh month came

No year is indicated; we assume it was as noted in 6:15, in the twentieth year of Artaxerxes I, thus, in the fall of 445 B.C. Tishri (Sept/Oct) was a very significant month for religious activities in Judaism. According to Leviticus 23:24,26, and 34, events included the Feast of Trumpets on the first day (later identified as Rosh Hashanah, the New Year); the Day of Atonement (Yom Kippur) on the tenth; and the Feast of Tabernacles (Succoth, or Booths), beginning on the fifteenth day.

and the Israelites had settled in their towns,

Note that this is a repetition of the same statement at the end of the list of the initial returnees in 7:73a. Because Nehemiah 8–10 involves Ezra, some scholars propose that at least Nehemiah 8 originally followed the end of Ezra 8. It appears peculiar that no mention is made there of the settlement in Judah of those who returned with Ezra. A realistic suggestion, then, is that he has taken from the Ezra Memoir this account of Ezra's reading of the law and has inserted it here.[4] He has used the repetition of the clause we are noting to serve as a bridge between the list in Nehemiah 7 and the unrelated activities in chapter 8. His interest is in the religious reformation of the people rather than in a sequenced flow of events.

---

[4]Since this is a third person account, these are not Nehemiah's words. The first person account continues at 12:31.

The activities detailed in Nehemiah 8–10 testify to a spiritual awakening of the people. What is revealed is a recommitment on the part of the Jewish community in Yehud and Jerusalem to the covenant with the Lord. It began with the reading of the law. It is no coincidence that in that law provision was made every seventh year during the feast of Tabernacles for the law to be read (Deut 31:10-13). It was to be a public reading before the assembled people.

8:1 all the people assembled as one man

Breneman has pointed out that in the first twelve verses of this chapter the phrase "the people" occurs thirteen times, and "all the people" nine of those occurrences.[5] Clearly the editor has primarily the people in focus. Revivals are often mass movements sparked by a hunger for God's word and presence.

The place of assembly was **in the square before the Water Gate**. It was not in the courts of the temple, but outside the temple compound virtually in its shadow. The Water Gate was noted previously in 3:26 as giving access to the waters of the Gihon Spring. If this assembly was after the arrival of Ezra, the reference would be to the gate in the old, destroyed, city wall at the base of the eastern slope of the City of David. If it was after the reconstruction of the city wall, then it would have been in an open area before a new Water Gate built into the new line of wall on the crest of the hill, which seems the more likely.

. . . the Book of the Law of Moses, . . .

This was the scroll form of the book. The codex form, with the columns cut into pages and sewn along one side, was first developed and used by the Romans about the time of Christ.

The scroll that the people asked Ezra the scribe to bring out was very likely a Torah scroll, much like those still in use in Jewish synagogues. It contained the Pentateuch, the five books from Genesis through Deuteronomy. Since the five books require an extra long scroll, it may have been five smaller scrolls containing the Pentateuch. The place from which it was to be brought is not indicated, but one might surmise that it was kept in one of the storage rooms in the temple. As a priest as well as a scribe, Ezra had access to the areas around the temple forbidden to ordinary people.

---

[5]Breneman, *Ezra, Nehemiah, Esther*, p. 223.

The Book of the Law of Moses has been the center of intense scholarly study for well over the last two centuries. The result of this concentrated study has been the development of theories to explain how and when the biblical books were written. The dominant theory among scholars for at least the last century has been the Documentary Hypothesis.[6] This is the view favored by liberals. A conservative view is that "Although it is unlikely that Moses wrote the Pentateuch *as it exists in its final form,* the connectedness and uniformity of the evidence certainly affirms that he is the originator, instigator, and most important figure in the stream of literary activity that produced it."[7]

8:2 . . . men and women . . . .

The congregation included women and children old enough to understand. Had they assembled within the temple courts, the women and children would have been separated from the men into their respective courts.

8:3 He read it aloud . . . .

The root קָרָא (*qārā'*, "to read, call") is the basis for הַמִּקְרָא (*hammiqrā'*, v. 8), the Bible. The focus is upon reading aloud to an audience out of the one precious scroll which the community possessed. Before our modern era, few people had even a single book as a personal possession. The pattern of oral reading continues in syna-

---

[6]The explanation it offers is that the Pentateuch is a composite of four documentary strands labeled J, E, D, and P, each the work of unknown authors or schools, which reached its final form during the period of the exile. Thus, the completed Pentateuch would have been new in Ezra's time. This is in contrast to the traditional view that Moses wrote the entire Pentateuch in the fifteenth century B.C. Neither time nor space allows a review of the arguments for and against these two differing viewpoints. Brief treatments of the subject may be found in "Pentateuch," *ISBE,* 3:740-753; "Torah," *ABD,* 6:605-622; "Pentateuch," *NBD,* 957-964; Roland K. Harrison, *Introduction to the Old Testament* (Grand Rapids: Eerdmans, 1969).

[7]W.S. LaSor, D.A. Hubbard, and F.W. Bush, *Old Testament Survey* (Grand Rapids: Eerdmans, 1982), p. 63. The Dead Sea Scrolls, discovered since 1947, have provided glimpses into the manuscript traditions of the Pentateuch dating to the last two centuries before Christ and the first century of the Christian era. M. Abegg, Jr., P. Flint, & E. Ulrich, *The Dead Sea Scrolls Bible* (New York: HarperCollins, 1999) provides convenient access to the results.

gogues and in churches. Ezra read **from daybreak till noon**. He read selectively, "in/from it" (בֹּו, *bô*) rather than "it" (אֹתֹו, *'ōthô*); the oral reading of the entire scroll would have required more than six hours.

8:4 The general introduction to activities related to the reading of the Torah were given above. The specifics are given in verses 4-8.

As with a pulpit, the raised **platform** enabled Ezra's voice to be heard more clearly and for a greater distance. The prior preparation of this platform indicates that the assembly was more planned than spontaneous. With Ezra on the platform were the men named. These were community leaders, not priests. Priests and Levites are normally so designated in the text. Williamson suggests that the men may have been chosen by Ezra from the laity to assist in the reading of the Torah, "a task not restricted to priests or Levites in postexilic Judaism."[8] He may thereby have been clearly demonstrating that the Torah was for all the people, not just for religious personnel and the ruling elite.

8:5 Ezra opened the book. . . .

Ezra unrolled the scroll, and out of reverence for the sacred text **the people all stood up** (cf. 9:3). From this came the Rabbinic regulation that the congregation must stand in the presence of the Torah scroll. Many churches continue the tradition of standing when Scripture is read.

8:6 Before reading, **Ezra praised the LORD** by acknowledging Yahweh as **the great God**. God is great and worthy to be praised. The people responded with upraised hands and a chorus of "Amens," agreeing with Ezra. Then they bowed their heads and prostrated themselves, an act of submission and humility before the greatness of God. The practice of praying while kneeling with one's face to the ground or floor is still observed among some groups.

8:7-8 Thirteen Levites are named. Although no explanation is required, the same number of laymen are mentioned standing by Ezra in verse 4. These men **instructed the people in the Law**, a responsibility assigned to them (cf. Deut 33:10; 2 Chr 17:7-9). When they instructed is clear; how they instructed the people is unclear.

---

[8]Williamson, *Ezra, Nehemiah*, p. 289.

They may have broken the assembly into thirteen subgroups, with one Levite explaining to each group. With this scenario, Ezra would pause after he had read a portion, permitting the Levites to explain. They may also have assisted Ezra in the reading of **the Book of the Law of God**. It clearly is identical with "the Book of the Law of Moses" (v. 1). Every effort was being made to help the people understand what was read. The NIV footnote for **making it clear** provides an alternative meaning for מְפֹרָשׁ (*mᵉphōrāš*), "translating it." The KJV renders the word, "distinctly," but the NRSV has "with interpretation." Interpreters must choose from two possibilities: one emphasizes clarity of reading, the other suggests that the Levites were translating into Aramaic, the common language of the people, what was being read in Hebrew. The latter was the language in which the scroll was written.

Biblical literacy and understanding are at a low ebb in our modern culture, often even among believers. Understanding Scripture is paramount to living a life of faith, calling for prayerful time in the Word of God. Those mature in the faith ought always to help others to understand God's word and will. This account provides an instructive example for people in every generation.

B. A TIME FOR CELEBRATION (8:9-12)

⁹Then Nehemiah the governor, Ezra the priest and scribe, and the Levites who were instructing the people said to them all, "This day is sacred to the LORD your God. Do not mourn or weep." For all the people had been weeping as they listened to the words of the Law.

¹⁰Nehemiah said, "Go and enjoy choice food and sweet drinks, and send some to those who have nothing prepared. This day is sacred to our Lord. Do not grieve, for the joy of the LORD is your strength."

¹¹The Levites calmed all the people, saying, "Be still, for this is a sacred day. Do not grieve."

¹²Then all the people went away to eat and drink, to send portions of food and to celebrate with great joy, because they now understood the words that had been made known to them.

8:9 When the people heard the reading of the law and were instructed as to its meaning for them, they wept in remorse for failure to observe its demands. Ezra, Nehemiah, and the others instructing the people called for the people to stop weeping, for this was a holy day to the Lord (see v. 2).

8:10-12 Nehemiah said, . . .

The NIV has added Nehemiah. The Hebrew simply reads, "he said," as in the KJV, however, the RSV, NRSV, and NEB insert Nehemiah.

Rather than fasting and mourning, this was a day for joyous feasting. The people were encouraged to eat delicacies not a part of their normal diets. Special days call for special foods in all cultures. **Choice food** is literally "of the fat," as in the KJV and RSV, that is, the choicest portions. **Sweet drinks** may have been sweet wine; the Vulgate indicates wine mixed with honey. The instruction to **send some to those who have nothing prepared** is taken by a Jewish commentator to refer to the poor.[9] This day was holy to the Lord and all of the people should share in the joy of it. All are to receive renewed strength by rejoicing in the Lord. The Levites must have helped the people to understand the grace of God so that they could celebrate with great joy. Williamson points to the importance of Ezra's interpretation of the Torah to the people: "In this late period, when circumstances had changed so much from the time of the original law-giving, there had arisen the danger that the Law would slip into being a document of only antiquarian interest. It was Ezra's hermeneutic that brought it to life again for the community. Although in theory the text of Scripture alone was normative, in practice it could only be that text as it came to be interpreted that would shape the future mold of Judaism."[10] Every generation needs to be confronted afresh with the meaning of God's word and will for that generation.

---

[9]Slotki, *Daniel, Ezra and Nehemiah*, p. 231.
[10]Williamson, *Ezra, Nehemiah*, p. 293.

C. THE FEAST OF BOOTHS KEPT (8:13-18)

¹³On the second day of the month, the heads of all the families, along with the priests and the Levites, gathered around Ezra the scribe to give attention to the words of the Law. ¹⁴They found written in the Law, which the LORD had commanded through Moses, that the Israelites were to live in booths during the feast of the seventh month ¹⁵and that they should proclaim this word and spread it throughout their towns and in Jerusalem: "Go out into the hill country and bring back branches from olive and wild olive trees, and from myrtles, palms and shade trees, to make booths"—as it is written.^a

¹⁶So the people went out and brought back branches and built themselves booths on their own roofs, in their courtyards, in the courts of the house of God and in the square by the Water Gate and the one by the Gate of Ephraim. ¹⁷The whole company that had returned from exile built booths and lived in them. From the days of Joshua son of Nun until that day, the Israelites had not celebrated it like this. And their joy was very great.

¹⁸Day after day, from the first day to the last, Ezra read from the Book of the Law of God. They celebrated the feast for seven days, and on the eighth day, in accordance with the regulation, there was an assembly.

^a*15* See Lev. 23:37-40.

8:13 Ezra's reading of the Law of God had a powerful effect on the assembled congregation on the first day of the month Tishri. While most of the people returned to their homes for the joyous feasting and the return to the press of everyday activities, **the heads of all the families**, along with the religious personnel of the temple met with Ezra for further instruction in the Law. These were the leaders of extended families and responsible for religious instruction and practice in their households (Deut 6:4-9). By God's design, religious instruction is not to trickle down but to flow from one generation to another.

8:14-15 Gathered around Ezra, they listened and discussed the words of the Law. He drew their attention to one or all of the ref-

erences to the Feast of Booths (Exod 23:16; Lev 23:34-43; Num
29:12-28; Deut 16:13-17).[11] This was to be a pilgrimage feast, a גח
(ḥāg). It was to be celebrated according to Deuteronomy 16:15 "at
the place the LORD will choose." In the course of time this came to
be understood as at the temple in Jerusalem. Leviticus 23:40
instructs the people to observe this feast "before the LORD your
God," which also came to be understood as at the Jerusalem temple.
Jerusalem was the center of the festival, but it was to be observed in
homes throughout Yehud (v. 16).The fact that they **found** this information suggests that the keeping of this feast had not been regularly practiced, although its observance is mentioned in Ezra 3:4. Now
they would observe it **as it is written**, as inscribed and as explained
by Ezra.

8:16-17 . . . on their own roofs, . . .

Throughout history and to the present, village houses in the
lands of the Bible are built with flat roofs. Those built **in the courts
of the house of God** were likely for the priests and Levites who
served there.

The temporary shelters in which they were to live for seven days
were an authentic reminder of their forefathers' experience living in
the wilderness after escaping the exile in Egypt. It was a reminder,
too, of the presence of God, for the tabernacle in the wilderness was
a symbol of his presence among their ancestors. It was most appropriate for them to celebrate this feast with great joy, for they had
experienced a second exodus from exile in Babylon by God's grace.
He had been at work behind the scenes in the Persian court as he
had in Pharaoh's palace. He had brought them safely into the land
of their forefathers, the land of promise. The good hand of God had
made it possible to restore their homes, the temple, and Jerusalem
in the face of enemies, as he had fought for them in the days of
Joshua. Never had there been an occasion like this one for celebrat-
ing the Feast of Booths since **the days of Joshua son of Nun.**

An alternative form of the name Joshua appears in the original,
Jeshua. A high priest with the same name was among the first
returnees (Ezra 2:2), but the two are distinguished by the great

---

[11]This feast is also known as Succoth, Tabernacles, and Ingathering or
Harvest, the stimulus for our annual Thanksgiving Day each fall.

leader's ancestry, **son of Nun**. Jeshua became Jesus in Greek, which explains the confusing reference to Joshua in Hebrews 4:8.[12]

8:18 Along with the stipulated festivities and offerings in the temple, a portion of the Torah was read on each of the seven days of the festival. The reading of the Law during the Feast of Tabernacles (Booths) at the end of every seven years was legislated in Deuteronomy 31:10-13. This practice is followed annually in synagogues to the present by reading portions of the Law.

. . . on the eighth day . . . .

Each year, Jews observe *Simchat Torah, "the joy of the Torah,"* on the eighth day of the feast, that is the day following the end of the Feast of Booths. It marks the completion of the annual cycle of reading the Torah and the beginning of the next cycle. This practice may have begun in the time of Ezra. In time the Jews came to be known as "the people of the Book," due to the integral part the Torah has played in their lives and culture. In time, too, that attribution was passed on to their spiritual heirs in the church. Church leaders today ought to take seriously the charge Paul gave to the elders of Ephesus to keep watch over the flock and to feed the church of God (Acts 20:28). Likewise, all believers are to "not merely listen to the word, and so deceive yourselves. Do what it says" (Jas 1:22).

III. THE ISRAELITES CONFESS THEIR SINS (9:1-37)

A. A DAY OF FASTING AND PENITENCE (9:1-5a)

[1]On the twenty-fourth day of the same month, the Israelites gathered together, fasting and wearing sackcloth and having dust on their heads. [2]Those of Israelite descent had separated themselves from all foreigners. They stood in their places and confessed their sins and the wickedness of their fathers. [3]They stood where they were and read from the Book of the Law of the LORD their God for a quarter of the day, and spent another quarter in

---

[12]See James Girdwood and Peter Verkruyse, *Hebrews,* The College Press NIV Commentary Series (Joplin, MO: College Press, 1997), p. 137.

confession and in worshiping the LORD their God. ⁴Standing on the stairs were the Levites—Jeshua, Bani, Kadmiel, Shebaniah, Bunni, Sherebiah, Bani and Kenani—who called with loud voices to the LORD their God. ⁵And the Levites—Jeshua, Kadmiel, Bani, Hashabneiah, Sherebiah, Hodiah, Shebaniah and Pethahiah—said: "Stand up and praise the LORD your God, who is from everlasting to everlasting.ᵃ"

ᵃ5 Or *God for ever and ever*

9:1 On the twenty-fourth day of the same month, . . .

This occurred two days after the observance of Tabernacles in the month Tishri. Following the assembly the day after the feast, they had one day off before they were gathered together again. But this time, feasting turned to **fasting**.

This rather dramatic change has raised the suspicion that this chapter, in particular the long prayer (vv. 5b-37), originally occurred elsewhere and was incorporated into Nehemiah by the editor for his purposes. The majority of researchers think that it came from the Ezra Memoir and originally stood between Ezra 10:15 and 16 or following that chapter. The arguments presented are frequently intricate, but the basic reasoning is that the national day of mourning seems to be related to the incident of putting away foreign wives in Ezra, and it does not flow smoothly and directly from the events in Nehemiah 8. Others have considered the prayer of penitence in Nehemiah 9:5b-37 as a separate composition acquired and used by the editor from an otherwise unknown source, perhaps liturgical. That being so, only a part of verses 1-5 would have originally stood in the Ezra source.[13]

As interesting as these possibilities may be, we should attempt to understand the text as it has come down to us in its final form. That was the final editor/author's intent. The chapter makes good sense here. After the reading of the Law in 8:4-8, the people were mourning and weeping, under conviction that they had sinned against God by their failure to keep his commandments. They were temporarily diverted from their genuine sorrow and repentance by the urging of

[13]For a detailed discussion of the issues involved, see Williamson, *Ezra, Nehemiah*, pp. 305-310.

Nehemiah and the Levites (8:10-11) to go and keep the joyous Feast of Booths as God had ordained it. Once having kept God's commandments in reference to that feast, it was appropriate that they return to the unfinished business of confession and recommitment to their covenant relationship to the Lord.

Wearing sackcloth was a traditional symbol of mourning and repentance (cf. Dan 9:3; Jonah 3:5,8; and 1 Chr 21:16). It was an outward symbol of poverty of soul. Sackcloth was woven of rough, coarse fibers, in contrast to softer, finer woven clothing for normal wear. **Having dust on their heads** also indicated the depths of despair and sorrow (cf. 1 Sam 4:12; 2 Sam 1:2; and Job 2:12).

9:2 Those of Israelite descent had separated themselves from all foreigners. . . .

The exclusion of all foreigners from the assembly relates to Ezra 9:2, where the charge was that they had *not* separated themselves from their non-Israelite neighbors.

It stands to reason that foreigners living in Jerusalem and Yehud would have no reason to confess their sins and those of their forefathers in failing to obey the commandments of Yahweh. Israel was a covenant people; others were not. They had no historical or religious connection with the "seed" of Israel.

By confessing not only their own sins but also the **wickedness** of their (fore)fathers, they were identifying themselves with past generations. This is a repeated theme in Ezra–Nehemiah. The following psalm will expand on **their sins** (vv. 33-37) and **the wickedness of their fathers** (vv. 16-30).

9:3 This verse describes the procedure followed. It consisted of Scripture, followed by confession while standing, and worship while bowed down or prostrate on the ground. Rather than everyone reading from **the Book of the Law of the LORD their God**, it was read to them (as in the NEB), no doubt by the Levites (8:7-8).

It is useful to note that occasionally we need to read major sections of Scripture. Daily devotions with a few verses are worthwhile but not a substitute for reading widely in God's word. The combination of hearing God's word, confession, and worship are important for God's people in every time and season.

9:4-5a Standing on the stairs . . . .

We do not know where this assembly took place, but it was like-ly in the temple compound. There were steps leading up into the temple courts, because the temple complex was built on top of and down the slopes of a hill. According to Jewish tradition, in the refur-bished temple constructed by Herod, the Levites stood to sing on the fifteen steps between the court of the women and the court of Israel. By standing on the steps, the Levites could be more easily seen and heard. It was normal for the Levites to lead public worship (2 Chr 20:21).

Two groups of Levites are listed, or is it one group listed twice? It is unclear; however, even with the overlap of five names, each list has three of its own. On the name **Jeshua**, see 8:17 above. Some of the names also occur in 8:7. Kidner suggests that the two groups had separate functions, with the first group voicing the distress of God's people and the second group leading in corporate praise.[14]

Stand up and praise the Lord your God, . . .

The call to stand arises from the last activity in which those assembled were engaged, worship (v. 3, מִשְׁתַּחֲוִים, *mištaḥăwîm*), "pros-trating themselves." A textual difficulty, noted by the NIV footnote, makes the exact meaning of verse 5a difficult to determine. **Praise** is literally, "bless,"(בָּרַךְ, *brk*, rather than הלל, *hll*) similar to Psalm 103:1, "Bless the LORD, O my soul, and all that is within me, bless his holy name" (NRSV).

The phrase **from everlasting to everlasting** is an attribute of God, suggesting something has dropped out here. On the basis of a slight change of the Hebrew, Williamson translates:

> "Stand up and bless the Lord your God:
> May you be blessed, O Lord our God, from everlasting to everlasting, And may your glorious name be blessed, although it is exalted above all blessing and praise."[15]

This would attach the phrase to the following prayer.

---

[14]Kidner, *Ezra & Nehemiah*, p. 111.
[15]Williamson, *Ezra, Nehemiah*, p. 300.

B. THE PRAYER OF PRAISE TO GOD (9:5b-37)

This prayer appears only here in the Bible, yet it reflects ideas and patterns of thought such as we find in the psalms classified as historical (Ps 78; 105; 106; 135; and 136). Expressions that appear in this prayer can also be found throughout the OT. Myers has collected a multitude of examples, then comments, "The author of our prayer psalm drew upon a wide knowledge of the theology and traditions of his people, skillfully weaving into it elements of instruction, exhortation, and confession."[16] This clearly indicates that the author was intimately familiar with the Pentateuch essentially as we have it today as well as the other biblical writings from which he draws inspiration.

1. For Creating Heaven and Earth (9:5b-6)

"Blessed be your glorious name, and may it be exalted above all blessing and praise. ⁶You alone are the LORD. You made the heavens, even the highest heavens, and all their starry host, the earth and all that is on it, the seas and all that is in them. You give life to everything, and the multitudes of heaven worship you.

5b-6 Several versions insert "And Ezra said" at the beginning of this prayer, based on the LXX. However, the NIV rightly adheres to the MT; interestingly, Ezra is not mentioned in this chapter.

. . . above all blessing and praise. . . .

Here both Hebrew roots noted above are used. First, God is addressed by name, Yahweh, and his uniqueness is acknowledged. He only is God (cf. Deut 6:4; Isa 44:6; Ps 83:18). God is to be blessed and praised for every aspect of his creation, reflecting Genesis 1:1; 2:1. The **multitudes of heaven**, the heavenly court and host of angels (cf. 1 Kgs 22:19; Ps 103:21), bow down or prostrate themselves (the same word noted in v. 5a) before the Lord.

---

[16]Myers, *Ezra–Nehemiah*, pp. 167-170.

2. For the Covenant with Abraham (9:7-8)

7"You are the LORD God, who chose Abram and brought him out of Ur of the Chaldeans and named him Abraham. 8You found his heart faithful to you, and you made a covenant with him to give to his descendants the land of the Canaanites, Hittites, Amorites, Perizzites, Jebusites and Girgashites. You have kept your promise because you are righteous.

9:7-8 God is to be praised for choosing and calling **Abram** ("exalted father") out of southern Mesopotamia into the land of promise. For giving him the name **Abraham** ("father of many") he is also to be blessed (Gen 17:5). With that change came the promises of a special covenantal relationship with Abraham's descendants and the promised land. God is the subject here, not Abraham. God is **righteous**, that is, faithful to his word, proven by the fulfillment of his promises. By faith we become children of Abraham, so Israel's history becomes a part of our history.

The names of nations to be dispossessed here differs from that in Genesis 15:19-21: Kenites, Kenizzites, Kadmonites, Hittites, Perizzites, Rephaites, Amorites, Canaanites, Girgashites, and Jebusites. The author is not quoting. The shortened list is sufficient to remind his readers of the whole.

3. For the Exodus (9:9-11)

9"You saw the suffering of our forefathers in Egypt; you heard their cry at the Red Sea.ᵃ 10You sent miraculous signs and wonders against Pharaoh, against all his officials and all the people of his land, for you knew how arrogantly the Egyptians treated them. You made a name for yourself, which remains to this day. 11You divided the sea before them, so that they passed through it on dry ground, but you hurled their pursuers into the depths, like a stone into mighty waters.

ᵃ9 Hebrew *Yam Suph*; that is, Sea of Reeds

9:9-11 God is to be praised for saving their forefathers from Egyptian bondage by his mighty acts against Pharaoh in the exodus. The Lord God made a name for himself by all the mighty deeds related to that event, and the luster of it **remains to this day**. The memories of that awesome event are a composite of expressions from the Book of Exodus. Breneman observes that of some forty Hebrew words used to speak of miracles, appearing about 500 times in the OT, some 250 refer to the miracles of the exodus.[17]

4. For the Law and the Desert Experience (9:12-21)

[12]**By day you led them with a pillar of cloud, and by night with a pillar of fire to give them light on the way they were to take.**
[13]**"You came down on Mount Sinai; you spoke to them from heaven. You gave them regulations and laws that are just and right, and decrees and commands that are good.** [14]**You made known to them your holy Sabbath and gave them commands, decrees and laws through your servant Moses.** [15]**In their hunger you gave them bread from heaven and in their thirst you brought them water from the rock; you told them to go in and take possession of the land you had sworn with uplifted hand to give them.**
[16]**"But they, our forefathers, became arrogant and stiff-necked, and did not obey your commands.** [17]**They refused to listen and failed to remember the miracles you performed among them. They became stiff-necked and in their rebellion appointed a leader in order to return to their slavery. But you are a forgiving God, gracious and compassionate, slow to anger and abounding in love. Therefore you did not desert them,** [18]**even when they cast for themselves an image of a calf and said, 'This is your god, who brought you up out of Egypt,' or when they committed awful blasphemies.**
[19]**"Because of your great compassion you did not abandon them in the desert. By day the pillar of cloud did not cease to guide them on their path, nor the pillar of fire by night to shine on the way they were to take.** [20]**You gave your good**

---

[17]Breneman, *Ezra, Nehemiah, Esther*, p. 237.

Spirit to instruct them. You did not withhold your manna from their mouths, and you gave them water for their thirst. [21]For forty years you sustained them in the desert; they lacked nothing, their clothes did not wear out nor did their feet become swollen.

9:12-15 The **pillar of cloud** and the **pillar of fire** (Exod 13:21; Num 14:14) manifested God's protective care crossing the sea and on the wilderness journey. His gifts at Sinai and later included the Sabbath, the (Ten) commandments, and laws all described as **good**. All these were channeled through Moses, God's servant. Only Moses and Abraham are named in this prayer; the focus is upon God's blessings and faithfulness displayed in this history. God even provided the necessities of life, bread and water, in a dry and desolate wilderness. The **bread from heaven** refers to manna, but it is also an important theme in the NT (cf. John 6:22-40; Rev 2:17). God ultimately brought them to the border of **the land you had sworn with uplifted hand to give them**. All these mighty, beneficial acts of grace made God all the more worthy to be praised.

9:16-18 But, that incriminating contrastive conjunction, is implied in the text; it is literally, "And they." The forefathers **became stiff-necked**. The image is that of an animal which struggles against being yoked or harnessed. The expression is used twice, the second time referring specifically to the rebellion in the wilderness. **They . . . appointed a leader** (v. 17) is based on Numbers 14:4; however, there the action is merely suggested, but nothing came of it. Nevertheless, considering such an action is as much an offense against God as if it had been committed. The Sermon on the Mount testifies to the same principle in respect of adulterous looks (Matt 5:27-28).

A clear contrast is drawn between the inclination of his people to be stiff-necked and God's nature. He is acknowledged in this prayer as **forgiving**, **gracious**, **compassionate**, **slow to anger**, and **abounding in love**. This assessment of God's nature was proven in the case of the golden calf (Exod 32:4), Even in the face of that most dastardly deed, God **did not desert them**.

9:19-21 God did not abandon his undeserving people in the desert because of his **great compassion**. The word for "compassion" derives from a Hebrew word, רֶחֶם (*reḥem*), which is related to the womb. It speaks of the deep emotional bond a mother feels for her child. In addition to the pillars of cloud and fire, physical guides for the wilderness travelers, God gave his **good Spirit to instruct them**. The statement likely alludes to Numbers 11:17 (cf. Ps 143:10). God provided sustenance for their minds, for man shall not live by bread alone. He also provided the essentials of life for their bodies All this he did for them in the desert, not for a brief time, but for forty years.

5. For the Land of Canaan (9:22-25)

[22]**"You gave them kingdoms and nations, allotting to them even the remotest frontiers. They took over the country of Sihon[a] king of Heshbon and the country of Og king of Bashan.** [23]**You made their sons as numerous as the stars in the sky, and you brought them into the land that you told their fathers to enter and possess.** [24]**Their sons went in and took possession of the land. You subdued before them the Canaanites, who lived in the land; you handed the Canaanites over to them, along with their kings and the peoples of the land, to deal with them as they pleased.** [25]**They captured fortified cities and fertile land; they took possession of houses filled with all kinds of good things, wells already dug, vineyards, olive groves and fruit trees in abundance. They ate to the full and were well-nourished; they reveled in your great goodness.**

[a]**22 One Hebrew manuscript and Septuagint; most Hebrew manuscripts** *Sihon, that is, the country of the*

9:22-25 This section on how God gave them the land of promise picks up and expands on verse 8. The connection between the land of promise and God's people is a basic part of OT theology. An essential part of the reason for the return from Babylon and the reestablishment of a community of God's people in Jerusalem and Yehud was the powerful memory of that promise. This prayer is an expression of the faith of the renewed community that, just as God had cared for their forefathers, he would care for them.

. . . allotting to them even the remotest frontiers. . . .
is clearly a reference to the areas of Transjordan, which their
Israelite forefathers had occupied. This was an expansion beyond
the original promise of the land of Canaan, west of the Jordan River.
The sequence of the prayer follows generally the pattern of the conquest, beginning in Transjordan then spreading across the Jordan to
the west. This was possible and by God's design because he had
made their sons as numerous as the stars in the sky, an allusion to
the promise to Abraham (Gen 22:17). The conquest gave to the people of the promise **all kinds of good things** portrayed in this section
of the prayer, and it was all because of God's **great goodness**. Again,
God is worthy to be praised for this evidence of his grace and goodness. Acknowledging God's benevolence is a means of thanksgiving.
In the NT, we are urged in everything to give thanks, for that is the
will of God for his people in Christ Jesus (1 Thess 5:18).

6. For Grace and Mercy to Forefathers (9:26-31)

[26]"But they were disobedient and rebelled against you;
they put your law behind their backs. They killed your
prophets, who had admonished them in order to turn them
back to you; they committed awful blasphemies. [27]So you
handed them over to their enemies, who oppressed them.
But when they were oppressed they cried out to you. From
heaven you heard them, and in your great compassion you
gave them deliverers, who rescued them from the hand of
their enemies.

[28]"But as soon as they were at rest, they again did what was
evil in your sight. Then you abandoned them to the hand of
their enemies so that they ruled over them. And when they
cried out to you again, you heard from heaven, and in your
compassion you delivered them time after time.

[29]"You warned them to return to your law, but they became
arrogant and disobeyed your commands. They sinned
against your ordinances, by which a man will live if he obeys
them. Stubbornly they turned their backs on you, became
stiff-necked and refused to listen. [30]For many years you were
patient with them. By your Spirit you admonished them

**through your prophets. Yet they paid no attention, so you
handed them over to the neighboring peoples. [31]But in your
great mercy you did not put an end to them or abandon
them, for you are a gracious and merciful God.**

9:26-31 The prayer turns again to the contrast between God's
goodness to his people and their rebellious ways against him. In the
land of which they had taken possession, they **put your law behind
their backs**. The word for "law," Torah, signifies instruction as
much as law. The implication here is that they willfully ignored
God's guidance for their lives through his word. They were so defi-
ant that they **killed** some of God's messengers. Instances where this
happened are recorded in 1 Kings 19:10; Jeremiah 26:20ff.; and
2 Chronicles 24:20 ff.

The prayer does not follow a strict chronology in recalling the
untoward ways of the forefathers. The writer's mind reverts back to
the period of the Judges and the cycle of unfaithfulness and oppression followed by the appeals for help and God's compassionate
response. The emphasis again is on his continuing compassion.

The patience of God was sorely tried through the many years in
which they disobeyed his commands. The pattern of stiff-necked
refusal to return to his law continued for many years, even though
he tried to admonish them by his spirit through his prophets. When
they paid no attention, **you handed them over to the neighboring
peoples**. The historical recollection has come to the time of the
exile. The phrase "neighboring peoples" refers to the Assyrians and
the Babylonians. In all this, God did not **put an end to them or
abandon them**. This is again a proof of God's great mercy and compassion. To recount this is to praise the Lord God.

7. Petition for Present Grace and Mercy (9:32-37)

[32]**"Now therefore, O our God, the great, mighty and awesome God, who keeps his covenant of love, do not let all this
hardship seem trifling in your eyes—the hardship that has
come upon us, upon our kings and leaders, upon our priests
and prophets, upon our fathers and all your people, from the
days of the kings of Assyria until today. [33]In all that has hap-**

pened to us, you have been just; you have acted faithfully, while we did wrong. ³⁴Our kings, our leaders, our priests and our fathers did not follow your law; they did not pay attention to your commands or the warnings you gave them. ³⁵Even while they were in their kingdom, enjoying your great goodness to them in the spacious and fertile land you gave them, they did not serve you or turn from their evil ways.

³⁶"But see, we are slaves today, slaves in the land you gave our forefathers so they could eat its fruit and the other good things it produces. ³⁷Because of our sins, its abundant harvest goes to the kings you have placed over us. They rule over our bodies and our cattle as they please. We are in great distress.

9:32 Now therefore, . . .

In light of all the high and low points of God's relation to his people, the poet has reached the point where his ultimate concerns reside, with his people in their current situation. As he nears the end of his (and the people's) prayer, before uttering the petition, he recalls again the true nature of God. Besides being great, mighty, and awesome, above all else he **keeps his covenant of love**. This attitude reflects the great truth of 2 Chronicles 7:14: "If my people, who are called by my name, will humble themselves and pray and seek my face and turn from their wicked ways, then will I hear from heaven and will forgive their sins and will heal their land." It is the nature of God that gives hope for the future.

The first request is that God **not let all this hardship seem trifling**. The hardships have fallen on the entire spectrum of their society. The hardships of exile, loss of home, land, and freedom all began in **the days of the kings of Assyria** (cf. 2 Kgs 15:29; 17:24). They continue **until today**. The author uses **us**, thereby identifying with the kings and leaders, priests and prophets, the fathers and all the people. He can do this because the effects of God's righteous judgment upon their forefathers' failure to keep the covenant still has its effects upon the restored community.

9:33-37 The second and major request is that God in his great goodness recognize that their current hardship was not a trifling matter either. The forefathers, **even while they were in their kingdom** and were not serving God and were continuing in their evil ways, enjoyed the fruits of the land. By contrast, the author and his community, while living in the land of promise, were not free to enjoy the produce of that land. The abundance of the harvest went to **the kings you have placed over us**. The reference is to the unnamed rulers of Persia. Persian taxation policies left the people virtual slaves **in great distress**. To be a slave in the land of exile was one thing. Should they continue to be slaves in the land of promise?

The implied request is for the great, mighty, and awesome God who keeps his covenant of love to do something to ease their situation. Confession is a part of this petition; the current situation is **because of our sins**. The prayer ends this way because it is a statement of faith. They knew that their only hope was in what God would do for them, not in what the Persian kings would do.

IV. THE AGREEMENT OF THE PEOPLE (9:38–10:39)

Chapter 8 informed the people of the content of the Law. As a result and in retrospect, they came under conviction of their failures. Therefore, in Chapter 9 they confessed their sins. Their forefathers and they themselves had not kept the covenant. The result was that they were in dire circumstances. In Chapter 10 they commit themselves anew to obedience to the Law of God.

A. THE INTENT TO MAKE A BINDING AGREEMENT (9:38)[18]

38"In view of all this, we are making a binding agreement, putting it in writing, and our leaders, our Levites and our priests are affixing their seals to it."

9:38 The phrase **In view of all this** connects chapter 10 directly with the preceding chapter. It is likely the work of the editor/author. But scholars hold a variety of opinions on the origin of the list of names in this chapter.[19] Clearly the establishment of this agreement represents a climax in the restoration work of Ezra and Nehemiah.

---

[18]This verse is 10:1 in the Hebrew Bible.
[19]See Williamson, *Ezra, Nehemiah*, pp. 320, 325-331, for details.

In the expression **binding agreement**, אֲמָנָה (*'ămānāh*) replaces the usual word for "covenant," בְּרִית (*bᵉrîth*). They are covenanting together to obey the Torah, refrain from mixed marriages, observe the Sabbath, and pay their temple dues regularly. Since this was to be a written document stamped with the seals of the signatories, it was likely deposited in the temple archives.

B. SIGNERS OF THE AGREEMENT (10:1-27)

¹Those who sealed it were:
Nehemiah the governor, the son of Hacaliah.
Zedekiah, ²Seraiah, Azariah, Jeremiah,
³Pashhur, Amariah, Malkijah,
⁴Hattush, Shebaniah, Malluch,
⁵Harim, Meremoth, Obadiah,
⁶Daniel, Ginnethon, Baruch,
⁷Meshullam, Abijah, Mijamin,
⁸Maaziah, Bilgai and Shemaiah.
These were the priests.

⁹The Levites:

Jeshua son of Azaniah, Binnui of the sons of Henadad, Kadmiel,
¹⁰and their associates: Shebaniah,
Hodiah, Kelita, Pelaiah, Hanan,
¹¹Mica, Rehob, Hashabiah,
¹²Zaccur, Sherebiah, Shebaniah,
¹³Hodiah, Bani and Beninu.

¹⁴The leaders of the people:

Parosh, Pahath-Moab, Elam, Zattu, Bani,
¹⁵Bunni, Azgad, Bebai,
¹⁶Adonijah, Bigvai, Adin,
¹⁷Ater, Hezekiah, Azzur,
¹⁸Hodiah, Hashum, Bezai,
¹⁹Hariph, Anathoth, Nebai,
²⁰Magpiash, Meshullam, Hezir,
²¹Meshezabel, Zadok, Jaddua,

[22]Pelatiah, Hanan, Anaiah,
[23]Hoshea, Hananiah, Hasshub,
[24]Hallohesh, Pilha, Shobek,
[25]Rehum, Hashabnah, Maaseiah,
[26]Ahiah, Hanan, Anan,
[27]Malluch, Harim and Baanah.

10:1 Nehemiah as governor naturally signed first. The NIV joins **Zedekiah** with the following list of priests, but "and" joins the name with Nehemiah in the Hebrew text. He was apparently a lay person, but we know nothing more about him, although the Zadok of 13:13 — a secretary — may be the same individual.

10:3-8 The priests are listed by family rather than by personal names. Neither Ezra nor the high priest Eliashib are named, but both were members of the Seraiah family. First Chronicles 24:17-18 lists twenty-four divisions while only twenty-one appear here. Why this is so is a matter of conjecture.

10:9-13 The names of seventeen Levites or levitical households are listed. These may be compared with other levitical lists in Ezra 2:40; 8:18-19 and Nehemiah 7:43; 8:7: 9:5; and 12:8-9,24-25.

10:14-27 Under the heading **the leaders of the people** appear mostly family representatives. Fourteen of the first twenty-one names also appear in Ezra 2 and Nehemiah 7. The additional families can be accounted for as later returnees, as newer families developed from the older ones, and some who had never gone into exile but had joined the revived community.

C. VOCAL SEALERS OF THE AGREEMENT (10:28-29)

[28]"The rest of the people—priests, Levites, gatekeepers, singers, temple servants and all who separated themselves from the neighboring peoples for the sake of the Law of God, together with their wives and all their sons and daughters who are able to understand— [29]all these now join their brothers the nobles, and bind themselves with a curse and an oath to follow the Law of God given through Moses the servant of

God and to obey carefully all the commands, regulations and decrees of the LORD our Lord.

10:28 The rest of the people are those in the categories that follow. They had not signed and sealed the binding agreement, but were consenting parties to it. The community is identified particularly by their separation from the neighboring peoples **for the sake of the Law of God**. This included everyone, male and female, young and old, who was able to understand the Torah. It was impossible for outsiders to know and obey the Law of God. To fail to maintain separation from outsiders was to start down the slippery slope of disobedience. Disobedience had been the downfall of their forefathers and the cause of their current great distress.

10:29 They bound themselves with **a curse and an oath**. This was a binding agreement, the establishment of a solemn covenant between the community and God. The procedures for establishing covenants in the ancient Near East between kings and nations included blessings for keeping covenants and curses for breaking them. The same pattern appears earlier in the Bible (cf. the curses in Deut 27:15-26; 30:19). Under Joshua's leadership, blessings and curses are read to the nation assembled at Shechem (Joshua 24). The curse and the oath are directly related; breaking the oath automatically activates the curse.

D. SPECIFICS OF THE AGREEMENT (10:30-39)

Underlying the stipulations of this section are the laws of the Pentateuch, but now applied to this particular situation. In Clines's opinion, the levitical lawyers drew up this covenant agreement as a group of standards or norms to be followed. This practice of interpreting the older legislation to newer circumstances is similar to the "halakot" (requirements for one's walk through life) of later rabbis. He thinks that Nehemiah 10 represents the beginning of the process of scriptural exegesis and legal definition that developed later into the Mishna and Talmud.[20]

---

[20]D.J.A. Clines, "Nehemiah 10 as an Example of Early Jewish Biblical Exegesis," *JSOT* 21 (1981): 111-117.

[30]"We promise not to give our daughters in marriage to the peoples around us or take their daughters for our sons.

[31]"When the neighboring peoples bring merchandise or grain to sell on the Sabbath, we will not buy from them on the Sabbath or on any holy day. Every seventh year we will forgo working the land and will cancel all debts.

[32]"We assume the responsibility for carrying out the commands to give a third of a shekel[a] each year for the service of the house of our God: [33]for the bread set out on the table; for the regular grain offerings and burnt offerings; for the offerings on the Sabbaths, New Moon festivals and appointed feasts; for the holy offerings; for sin offerings to make atonement for Israel; and for all the duties of the house of our God.

[34]"We—the priests, the Levites and the people—have cast lots to determine when each of our families is to bring to the house of our God at set times each year a contribution of wood to burn on the altar of the LORD our God, as it is written in the Law.

[35]"We also assume responsibility for bringing to the house of the LORD each year the firstfruits of our crops and of every fruit tree.

[36]"As it is also written in the Law, we will bring the firstborn of our sons and of our cattle, of our herds and of our flocks to the house of our God, to the priests ministering there.

[37]"Moreover, we will bring to the storerooms of the house of our God, to the priests, the first of our ground meal, of our ⌞grain⌟ offerings, of the fruit of all our trees and of our new wine and oil. And we will bring a tithe of our crops to the Levites, for it is the Levites who collect the tithes in all the towns where we work. [38]A priest descended from Aaron is to accompany the Levites when they receive the tithes, and the Levites are to bring a tenth of the tithes up to the house of our God, to the storerooms of the treasury. [39]The people of Israel, including the Levites, are to bring their contributions of grain, new wine and oil to the storerooms where the arti-

cles for the sanctuary are kept and where the ministering priests, the gatekeepers and the singers stay.
"We will not neglect the house of our God."

ᵃ*32 That is, about ⅛ ounce (about 4 grams)*

10:30 The first promise is negative; they will refrain from intermarriage, perhaps because it was such a persistent and pernicious problem in the community (cf. Ezra 9–10).

10:31 The remainder of the promises are positive. In the first of these, they promise to keep the Sabbath. The observance of the Sabbath is the first of the positive commandments among the Ten Commandments (Exod 20:8-11; Deut 5:12-15). It rightly takes precedence here. This stipulation likely grew out of the practices to be noted in Nehemiah 13. Sabbath restrictions are now extended to **any holy day**. Apparently they came to comprehend that they had not understood the full implications of the law's requirements until now, following the instructions given by Ezra and the Levites. They also vow to observe the sabbatical year (Exod 23:10-11; Lev 25:2-7). That included allowing fields, orchards, and vineyards to grow unattended, with any produce to be harvested by the poor. (In order to survive the sabbatical year, they needed to store grain, wine, and dried fruits during the other six years.)

The cancellation of all debts is rooted in Deuteronomy 15:1-3, rather than in the laws on the sabbatical year in Exodus 23, but here they are joined. It may have grown out of the problems noted in Nehemiah 5. Hebrew slaves (enslaved because of debts) were also to be released from servitude in the seventh year (Exod 21:2-6).

10:32-33 There is no direct legislation in the Pentateuch requiring payment of a temple tax. Exodus 30:11-16 and 38:25-26 provide an example of a one-time contribution. With an increasingly monetary economy in the Persian empire, annual dues were required in addition to the usual sacrificial offerings. Again, this is another example of the application and expansion of earlier laws to a new situation. Jesus paid a temple tax of one-half shekel (Matt 17:24-27).

The bread set out on the table refers to twelve loaves arranged on the golden table in two rows of six each at the beginning of each Sabbath. In Exodus 25:30 it is called the "bread of the Presence."

The **New Moon** offering is legislated in Numbers 28:11-15 and
marked the beginning of each month.

10:34 The wood offering is not mentioned in the Pentateuch,
but the fire on the altar was to be kept burning at all times (Lev 6:12-
13). The last clause of verse 34 relates to that passage. The arrangement here described was shared across all segments of the community. Josephus (*War* II. Xvii. 6) notes the observation of the festival
of wood-bringing, when everyone was to bring wood for the altar.
The Mishnah indicates that this was scheduled nine times in a year.[21]

10:35-36 The stipulations concerning firstfruits are given in
Exodus 23:19; 34:26; Numbers 18:13; Deuteronomy 26:2ff. Apparently this requirement was being ignored (cf. Mal 3:8-12).

The firstborn son was to be redeemed and the money given to
the priests (Exod 13:13; Num 18:15f.) As an infant, Jesus was
brought to the temple to be redeemed (Luke 2:22-24), indicating
continuing obedience by God-fearing parents.

10:37-39 Tithes represent firstfruits. No matter what a person
contributes, there are no "offerings" as long as the tithe remains in
the hands of the worshiper, for the tithe is the LORD's (Lev 27:30).
Tithes were brought to the temple in the past, but Nehemiah apparently instituted the practice of having the Levites go out to **all the
towns** to collect the tithes. He may have been following tax-collecting practices learned from the Persian court.

Verses 38-39a specify in greater detail the procedures for collecting and handling tithes and offerings. There is a change from the
first person "we" to the third person, perhaps indicating editorial
activity. The final statement is a reaffirmation (using "we") to all the
commitments made in verses 32-39.

The central focus of this chapter has been on the temple. The
institution was vital to the life of the renewed community. That community had now established an agreement that would bind them all
together in support of the restored house of God in the refortified
Jerusalem. The narrative can now return to where it was suspended
in 7:4-5, to the concern for the sparse population of Jerusalem.

---

[21]Slotki, *Daniel, Ezra, Nehemiah*, p. 246.

V. THE NEW RESIDENTS OF JERUSALEM (11:1-36)

A. THE PLAN FOR REPOPULATION (11:1-4a)

¹Now the leaders of the people settled in Jerusalem, and the rest of the people cast lots to bring one out of every ten to live in Jerusalem, the holy city, while the remaining nine were to stay in their own towns. ²The people commended all the men who volunteered to live in Jerusalem.

³These are the provincial leaders who settled in Jerusalem (now some Israelites, priests, Levites, temple servants and descendants of Solomon's servants lived in the towns of Judah, each on his own property in the various towns, ⁴while other people from both Judah and Benjamin lived in Jerusalem):

11:1 The **leaders of the people** were already living in Jerusalem, as we would expect because it was the administrative center of the province. Nehemiah had recognized the need for increasing the population of the city (7:4-5). Under his leadership, the leaders understood the importance of enlarging the population for security purposes. They must have communicated those concerns throughout Yehud. The concern of a few soon involved **the rest of the people**. They cast lots to determine who would move from their own towns into the city. Casting lots was a sacred activity by which to reveal God's will in the matter. It was based on ancient precedents (Num 26:55; Josh 7:14,16-18; 14:2; 18:6,8; 1 Sam 10:20-21; 14:41-42; Prov 16:33). It may have taken place within the temple compound.

The description of Jerusalem as **the holy city** is rare in the OT (Isa 48:2; 53:1; Dan 9:24), but occurs in Tobit 13:9; Matthew 4:5; 27:53 and Revelation 11:2. The Arabic name for the city, *el quds* (the holy), retains the connotation. Its holy attributes included the "Holy of Holies," the inner sanctum with the presence of Yahweh, then holy temple itself, with the sanctity spreading to the entire city.

11:2 The people commended those who **volunteered** to move into **Jerusalem**. Apparently it was considered a sacrifice to do so, suggesting that life in the villages and towns was preferable. The larger the number of volunteers, the fewer needed to be selected by casting lots.

11:3-4a A comparison of verses 3-19 with 1 Chronicles 9:2-17 shows considerable similarity. There are enough differences between the two lists to indicate that one was not copied from the other, but a common source in the temple archives was likely drawn upon by both authors. The author of Chronicles (writing later than our author) associates the list with the first returnees after the exile. The compiler of Ezra–Nehemiah connects the list to the need to repopulate Jerusalem after Nehemiah's reconstruction of the city's defenses. In fact, Nehemiah is not mentioned again until 12:26, and we do not return to Nehemiah's first-person account until 12:31.

The NIV has set off a part of these verses in parentheses. The biblical writer wants the reader to know that, while the following list is of the **provincial leaders** who dwelt **in Jerusalem** after the casting of lots, others dwelt throughout the province in their own towns. Note that the professional religious workers were not all clustered in Jerusalem. They dwelt among all the people. This practice continued in NT times; Zachariah was in Jerusalem only to serve with his division (Luke 1:8), but he lived in a town in the hill country of Jerusalem (Luke 1:39).

B. SPECIFIC INHABITANTS AND LOCALES (11:4b-20)

From the descendants of Judah:

> Athaiah son of Uzziah, the son of Zechariah, the son of Amariah, the son of Shephatiah, the son of Mahalalel, a descendant of Perez; ⁵and Maaseiah son of Baruch, the son of Col-Hozeh, the son of Hazaiah, the son of Adaiah, the son of Joiarib, the son of Zechariah, a descendant of Shelah. ⁶The descendants of Perez who lived in Jerusalem totaled 468 able men.

⁷**From the descendants of Benjamin:**

> Sallu son of Meshullam, the son of Joed, the son of Pedaiah, the son of Kolaiah, the son of Maaseiah, the son of Ithiel, the son of Jeshaiah, ⁸and his followers, Gabbai and Sallai—928 men. ⁹Joel son of Zicri was their chief officer, and Judah son of Hassenuah was over the Second District of the city.

¹⁰**From the priests:**

> Jedaiah; the son of Joiarib; Jakin; ¹¹Seraiah son of Hilkiah, the son of Meshullam, the son of Zadok, the son of Meraioth, the son of Ahitub, supervisor in the house of God, ¹²and their associates, who carried on work for the temple—822 men; Adaiah son of Jeroham, the son of Pelaliah, the son of Amzi, the son of Zechariah, the son of Pashhur, the son of Malkijah, ¹³and his associates, who were heads of families—242 men; Amashsai son of Azarel, the son of Ahzai, the son of Meshillemoth, the son of Immer, ¹⁴and hisª associates, who were able men—128. Their chief officer was Zabdiel son of Haggedolim.

¹⁵**From the Levites:**

> Shemaiah son of Hasshub, the son of Azrikam, the son of Hashabiah, the son of Bunni; ¹⁶Shabbethai and Jozabad, two of the heads of the Levites, who had charge of the out-side work of the house of God; ¹⁷Mattaniah son of Mica, the son of Zabdi, the son of Asaph, the director who led in thanksgiving and prayer; Bakbukiah, second among his associates; and Abda son of Shammua, the son of Galal, the son of Jeduthun. ¹⁸The Levites in the holy city totaled 284.

¹⁹**The gatekeepers:**

> Akkub, Talmon and their associates, who kept watch at the gates—172 men.

²⁰The rest of the Israelites, with the priests and Levites, were in all the towns of Judah, each on his ancestral property.

ª*14* Most Septuagint manuscripts; Hebrew *their*

11:4b-6 The tribe of **Judah**, the major portion of the population, takes precedence over Benjamin. **Perez** is first mentioned in Genesis 38:29. Other descendants of Perez, not mentioned here, also lived in Jerusalem at this time, according to 1 Chronicles 9:4. Apparently **Athaiah** moved from elsewhere into the city in Nehemiah's time. **Maaseiah** is the only other head of a family from Judah listed. His ancient forefather was Shelah (Num 26:20). No total for the

Shilonites is given, but the reference to **able men** of the Perezites indicates the qualities desired in the new inhabitants.

11:7-9 Only one leader from the tribe of Benjamin is mentioned by name as settling in the city, **Sallu**. He heads the similar list in 1 Chronicles 9:7-9, but his lineage in the two lists is not identical. Also, in Chronicles Elah and Meshullam are added as heads of Benjamite families. Such discrepancies are the result of editorial selectivity and likely copyist errors. The observation that **Joel** was the **chief officer** suggests that each clan comprised a unit under the charge of an officer. The men who moved into Jerusalem were to function as military defensive units.

11:10-14 There are problems in attempting to correlate this list of priestly names with other lists (1 Chr 9:10-13; Ezra 2:36-39). Detailed discussions of the problems are presented in more comprehensive commentaries[22] Despite the textual problems, the purpose of the list is to identify by name priestly leaders who agreed to move into Jerusalem from outlying settlements and to confirm their Jewish lineage.

Supervisor in the house of God designates the chief priest (cf. 2 Chr 31:10 and 13), although some commentators hold that the function was to act as the custodian of the physical temple. The reference is to the ancestor, Ahitub, rather than to Seraiah son of Hilkiah.

It was important that priests as well as laymen be **able men**, should the city come under attack. **Haggedolim,** "the great ones," is taken as a family name. Nowhere else in the OT does the word serve that purpose, so it remains puzzling.

11:15-18 Here singers are listed with Levites. This is counter to the practice in Nehemiah and Ezra (cf. 7:7), where they are listed separately. Williamson notes: "At the time of the return, none of the singers, gatekeepers, and others were regarded as Levites. Later, they all were; cf. 1 Chr 23-26. In our list, we find that this development has started, but has not yet been completed, since the singers are now clearly accepted as Levites (v. 17), but the gatekeepers are not (v. 19)."[23]

[22]Fensham, *The Books of Ezra and Nehemiah*, pp. 243-246; Myers, *Ezra–Nehemiah*, p. 187; Williamson, *Ezra, Nehemiah*, pp. 344-350.
[23]Williamson, *Ezra, Nehemiah*, pp. 347.

The outside work of the house of God may refer to building maintenance. The same expression occurs in 1 Chronicles 26:29, however, with the added explanation, "as officials and judges over Israel." It is possible that the collection of tithes is intended here (cf. 10:37-39).

Mattaniah is identified as a descendant of **Asaph**, who was a musician in the Solomonic temple (2 Chr 5:12), as was also **Jeduthun**. Rather than **director who led in thanksgiving and prayer**, Fensham follows two ancient versions and translates "the leader of the praise songs."[24] **Bakbukiah** was apparently the associate director.

11:19-20 First Chronicles 9:17-27 lists the duties of gatekeepers to include not only the security at the gates of the temple but also charge of the rooms and treasuries in the house of God. They regularly inventoried the articles used in the temple service, including flour, wine, oil, incense, and spices. These gatekeepers are not to be confused with the gatekeepers at the city gates (Neh 7:3).

The rest of the Israelites . . . .

Having identified those who were chosen or who volunteered to live in Jerusalem, this restates that the remaining nine out of ten stayed in their own towns (v. 1).

C. INDIVIDUALS BEARING OFFICIAL RESPONSIBILITIES (11:21-24)

[21]**The temple servants lived on the hill of Ophel, and Ziha and Gishpa were in charge of them.**

[22]**The chief officer of the Levites in Jerusalem was Uzzi son of Bani, the son of Hashabiah, the son of Mattaniah, the son of Mica. Uzzi was one of Asaph's descendants, who were the singers responsible for the service of the house of God.** [23]**The singers were under the king's orders, which regulated their daily activity.**

[24]**Pethahiah son of Meshezabel, one of the descendants of Zerah son of Judah, was the king's agent in all affairs relating to the people.**

---

[24]Fensham, *The Books of Ezra and Nehemiah*, pp. 246-247.

Williamson argues and Myers allows that these verses are a later addition, interrupting the continuing description of where the people outside Jerusalem lived.[25] That subject will be resumed in verse 25.

11:21 The **temple servants** (נְתִינִים, *n°thînîm*, "given [to God]") are described in Ezra 8:20 as given by David and the princes to assist the Levites. Two hundred and twenty had returned with Ezra. Ophel was located between the City of David and the Temple Mount.

11:22-24 The singers **were under the king's orders**. King David had instituted the singers, but the reference here must be to the Persian monarch. The Achaemenid rulers had a continuing concern in the cultic matters of their subject peoples. Uzzi, the chief officer of the Levites, was likely charged with the specific administration of the general orders of the king in respect of cultic matters. Petha-hiah, on the other hand, was a representative of Judean affairs at the king's court because he was, literally, "at the king's hand."

D. THE VILLAGES OF JUDAH AND BENJAMIN (11:25-36)

[25]As for the villages with their fields, some of the people of Judah lived in Kiriath Arba and its surrounding settlements, in Dibon and its settlements, in Jekabzeel and its villages, [26]in Jeshua, in Moladah, in Beth Pelet, [27]in Hazar Shual, in Beersheba and its settlements, [28]in Ziklag, in Meconah and its settlements, [29]in En Rimmon, in Zorah, in Jarmuth, [30]Zanoah, Adullam and their villages, in Lachish and its fields, and in Azekah and its settlements. So they were living all the way from Beersheba to the Valley of Hinnom.

[31]The descendants of the Benjamites from Geba lived in Micmash, Aija, Bethel and its settlements, [32]in Anathoth, Nob and Ananiah, [33]in Hazor, Ramah and Gittaim, [34]in Hadid, Zeboim and Neballat, [35]in Lod and Ono, and in the Valley of the Craftsmen.

[36]Some of the divisions of the Levites of Judah settled in Benjamin.

---

[25]Williamson, *Ezra, Nehemiah*, pp. 349, 352; Myers, *Ezra–Nehemiah*, p. 188.

This list is a later expansion on verse 20. Some of these places are mentioned elsewhere in Ezra (2 and its parallel in Neh 7) and Nehemiah (3, 12). It follows closely Joshua 15, except Dibon, Jeshua, and Meconah are listed here but not in Joshua 15. The list thus gives the impression that the Jews lived in a much larger area than the Persian province of Yehud. While some scholars see this as the writer's effort to idealize the borders of Judah as they were after the conquest, a more attractive explanation is that some of the Jews lived outside the province in areas largely controlled by others. They were free under Persian policy to move about the empire and settle where they wished. A comparison with the lists of levitical cities in Joshua 21:8ff. and 1 Chronicles 4:54ff. also suggests that the compiler of the list had an interest in the Levites.

11:25 Kiriath Arba is another name for Hebron (Gen 23:2; Judg 1:10). It was under Edomite control in the Persian era, as was the area to the south in the Negeb. The Edomites were closely associated with the Arab tribes of the region. Geshem seems to have had general authority over the lands to the south of Yehud. The **surrounding settlements** are literally "her daughters," that is, villages dependent upon the larger walled city nearby.

Dibon is not to be confused with the place of the same name in Moab. It may be identified either with Debir (Josh 15:49) or Dimonah (Josh 15:22). **Jekabzeel** is an alternate spelling for Kabzeel (Josh 15:21).

11:26 Jeshua is not listed elsewhere as the name of a town, but it may be the Shema of Joshua 15:26.

11:28 Meconah is not otherwise known.

11:30 From Beersheba to the Valley of Hinnom were the southern and northern limits of the territory of Judah after the conquest of Joshua. Hinnom is the valley on the western and southern sides of Jerusalem.

11:31-35 The list of places in the territory of Benjamin lie to the northwest, north, and northeast of Jerusalem. However, Jericho is not mentioned although Jews who had worked on the walls came from that city. **Hazor,** so far unidentified, should not be confused with the major walled city of Galilee. Several Hazors occur in the

Bible. The **Valley of the Craftsmen** was west of Jerusalem near Jaffa, the off-loading port for Lebanese lumber. The craftsmen may have been connected with that industry.

11:36 Finally, the writer notes that some Levites originally from Judah settled in towns in Benjamin. They may have been collectors of tithes for that region.

VI. PRIESTS AND LEVITES (12:1-26)

This compilation of priests and Levites has caused more controversies and differing proposals to resolve problems than any other section of Ezra–Nehemiah. The NIV notes hint at this. Neither space nor time allows the pursuit of the historical and compositional questions that have been raised. They may be followed in critical commentaries and learned journals.[26]

These lists continue the intrusion of materials not directly related to the dedication of the rebuilt walls of Jerusalem. The final compiler of Ezra–Nehemiah was obviously interested in names and genealogies. Their use allowed him to show the unified character of the work of Ezra and Nehemiah and the importance of their accomplishments for the benefit of his readers long after Ezra and Nehemiah had completed their work. The maintenance of authentic traditions established by God's grace was important to him. Breneman has observed, "It may seem tedious to us to find so many lists of genealogies and place names in Ezra and Nehemiah. But it reminds us again that God's work is done by individuals."[27]

A. RETURNEES WITH ZERUBBABEL (12:1-9)

¹These were the priests and Levites who returned with Zerubbabel son of Shealtiel and with Jeshua:
Seraiah, Jeremiah, Ezra,
²Amariah, Malluch, Hattush,

---

[26]Cf. the bibliography and Williamson, *Ezra, Nehemiah*, pp. 355-362.
[27]Breneman, *Ezra, Nehemiah, Esther*, p. 260.

³Shecaniah, Rehum, Meremoth,
⁴Iddo, Ginnethon,ª Abijah,
⁵Mijamin,ᵇ Moadiah, Bilgah,
⁶Shemaiah, Joiarib, Jedaiah,
⁷Sallu, Amok, Hilkiah and Jedaiah.
These were the leaders of the priests and their associates in the days of Jeshua.
⁸The Levites were Jeshua, Binnui, Kadmiel, Sherebiah, Judah, and also Mattaniah, who, together with his associates, was in charge of the songs of thanksgiving. ⁹Bakbukiah and Unni, their associates, stood opposite them in the services.

ª4 Many Hebrew manuscripts and Vulgate (see also Neh. 12:16); most Hebrew manuscripts *Ginnethoi*   ᵇ5 A variant of *Miniamin*

This list has a parallel in verses 12-21 and 10:3-9. The similarities and differences are striking and are the result in part of retrieving information from archives, in part due to spelling variants, and in part due to copyist errors. The names in the first list are clearly family names.

12:1-7 Jeremiah and **Ezra** clearly are not references to the prophet and the scribe. **Hattush** must have been accidentally lost out of verse 14. There are twenty-two names listed here. Later, twenty-four priestly courses were established (1 Chr 24:7-18), and that number continued until the destruction of the temple in A.D. 70.

Names with alternate spellings due to the transposition of consonants include: **Shecaniah** (v. 3) and **Shebaniah** (v. 14, NIV note); **Rehum** (v. 3) and **Harim** (v. 15); **Meremoth** (v. 3) and **Meraioth** (v. 15, NIV note); **Mijamin** (v. 5) and **Miniamin** (v. 17); and **Maadiah** (v. 5, Hebrew; NIV has *Moadiah*) and **Moadiah** (v. 17). Most commentators agree that the "and" (not in NIV) before **Joiarib** (cf. also v. 19) signals that the names following are later additions to the list. Pashur from Ezra 2:38 is also missing, although it appeared in the list of Nehemiah 10:3.

12:8-9 A levitical list also occurs in 10:9-13 as well as below in verses 24-25. Only **Jeshua** and **Kadmiel** are included in all of them. The **Mattaniah** (v. 8) here was the grandfather of Uzzi, chief officer of the Levites in Nehemiah's time (11:22). The word "and" (not in

NIV) before **Bakbukiah and Unni** indicates that they are later additions to the list. Antiphonal singing is indicated by **stood opposite them in the services** (cf. Ezra 3:11; 2 Chr 7:6).

B. THE HIGH PRIESTS (12:10-11)

[10]**Jeshua was the father of Joiakim, Joiakim the father of Eliashib, Eliashib the father of Joiada,** [11]**Joiada the father of Jonathan, and Jonathan the father of Jaddua.**

12:10-11 Jeshua refers back to the end of verse 7, rather than verse 8. From Jeshua to **Jaddua** covers the period from 538 B.C. to at least 332 B.C., the end of the Persian period. According to Josephus (*Ant.* 11.viii), Jaddua was high priest when Alexander the Great passed through the region. That would indicate a late addition to this list.

In such a long span of time, it is also possible that some names have dropped out of the list. **Eliashib** was high priest when Nehemiah arrived and was involved in the rebuilding of the walls (3:1). **Joiada** is mentioned again only in 13:28, where it is noted that one of his sons had married a daughter of Sanballat. **Jonathan** is to be identified with the **Johanan** of verses 22-23 and Ezra 10:6. He is also mentioned in the Elephantine Papyri (ca. 410 B.C.)

C. HEADS OF PRIESTLY FAMILIES (12:12-21)

[12]**In the days of Joiakim, these were the heads of the priestly families:**
of Seraiah's family, Meraiah;
of Jeremiah's, Hananiah;
[13]**of Ezra's, Meshullam;**
of Amariah's, Jehohanan;
[14]**of Malluch's, Jonathan;**
of Shecaniah's,[a] **Joseph;**
[15]**of Harim's, Adna;**
of Meremoth's,[b] **Helkai;**
[16]**of Iddo's, Zechariah;**

of Ginnethon's, Meshullam;
[17]of Abijah's, Zicri;
of Miniamin's and of Moadiah's, Piltai;
[18]of Bilgah's, Shammua;
of Shemaiah's, Jehonathan;
[19]of Joiarib's, Mattenai;
of Jedaiah's, Uzzi;
[20]of Sallu's, Kallai;
of Amok's, Eber;
[21]of Hilkiah's, Hashabiah;
of Jedaiah's, Nethanel.

[a]*14* Very many Hebrew manuscripts, some Septuagint manuscripts and Syriac (see also Neh. 12:3); most Hebrew manuscripts *Shebaniah's*   [b]*15* Some Septuagint manuscripts (see also Neh. 12:3); Hebrew *Meraioth's*

12:12-21 Except as noted above, the priestly family names are now repeated and the particular head of each family is noted by name. These were priests serving under the high priest **Joiakim**. In the Bible, he is only mentioned in this chapter.

D. HEADS OF LEVITICAL FAMILIES (12:22-26)

[22]The family heads of the Levites in the days of Eliashib, Joiada, Johanan and Jaddua, as well as those of the priests, were recorded in the reign of Darius the Persian. [23]The family heads among the descendants of Levi up to the time of Johanan son of Eliashib were recorded in the book of the annals. [24]And the leaders of the Levites were Hashabiah, Sherebiah, Jeshua son of Kadmiel, and their associates, who stood opposite them to give praise and thanksgiving, one section responding to the other, as prescribed by David the man of God.

[25]Mattaniah, Bakbukiah, Obadiah, Meshullam, Talmon and Akkub were gatekeepers who guarded the storerooms at the gates. [26]They served in the days of Joiakim son of Jeshua, the son of Jozadak, and in the days of Nehemiah the governor and of Ezra the priest and scribe.

12:22-23 Before providing the names of the heads of levitical families, the writer explains his sources. A register of family heads of both priests and Levites was kept in the temple archives. **Darius the Persian** is to be identified with Darius I, rather than Darius Nothus (424–404 B.C.) or Darius Codomannus (336–331 B.C.). The **book of the annals** is not to be equated with our Book of Chronicles, although the annals were likely one of the sources for that author. **Johanan son of Eliashib**, when compared with the list of high priests in verse 11, is evidently an alternate name for Jonathan.

12:24 . . . one section responding to the other, . . .
repeats the concept of antiphonal singing and chanting noted in verse 9. Here reference is made to **David** as the person responsible for prescribing what must have been an innovation in worship practices when it was begun (cf. 1 Chr 14:4; 23:27-31). The expression **man of God** usually signifies a prophet, which does not seem to apply here. It is repeated of David in verse 36 and 2 Chronicles 8:14, and he is called "the servant of the Lord" in the heading of Psalm 18. Here the expression is related to his work in organizing worship.

12:25 Mattaniah, Bakbukiah, Obadiah are listed as singers in 11:17 (Abda there is a shortened form of Obadiah), Fensham clarifies this by inserting "(were singers)" after Obadiah.[28]

12:26 . . . in the days of Nehemiah the governor and of Ezra the priest and scribe.
This chronological marker indicates the time period in which both these Levites (and the priests?) were active, from ca. 460–445 B.C. From the order of names here, one should not conclude that Nehemiah historically preceded Ezra, although some scholars do. The sequence is based on their official order of importance. Nehemiah was a governor by appointment of the royal court; Ezra fulfilled a one-time function with the support of the monarch.

It is useful to keep in mind that the compiler of Ezra–Nehemiah was composing this work with a theological, rather than strictly historical, purpose in mind. He was presenting the spectrum from the time of the return to Jerusalem through the periods of Ezra and Nehemiah as a unified movement. He tended to compress history

---

[28]Fensham, *The Books of Ezra and Nehemiah*, p. 253.

and to integrate later additions in the lists. His purpose was not to give a careful chronology but to show the continuity of the community in reestablishing the worship of Yahweh, the restoration of temple and city, and the reformations of Ezra and Nehemiah. All of this was through people working under the hand of God. Surely his readers, or those who heard it read, would benefit from these examples of leadership under and obedience to the will of God.

VII. DEDICATION OF THE WALL OF JERUSALEM (12:27-43)

A. PREPARATIONS (12:27-30)

²⁷At the dedication of the wall of Jerusalem, the Levites were sought out from where they lived and were brought to Jerusalem to celebrate joyfully the dedication with songs of thanksgiving and with the music of cymbals, harps and lyres. ²⁸The singers also were brought together from the region around Jerusalem—from the villages of the Netophathites, ²⁹from Beth Gilgal, and from the area of Geba and Azmaveth, for the singers had built villages for themselves around Jerusalem. ³⁰When the priests and Levites had purified themselves ceremonially, they purified the people, the gates and the wall.

12:27 The account now returns to events connected with the completion of the wall. The completion was noted in 6:15; however, the seeking out of the Levites **where they lived** connects also to 11:36. We may assume that the Levites, as with the priests who lived outside Jerusalem were assigned a normal rotation of duties in the temple. This was a special occasion, however, and special occasions call for special arrangements. More Levites were required for the **songs of thanksgiving** as an integral part of the dedication. The emphasis is upon joy and thanksgiving. **Cymbals, harps and lyres** are modern English approximations for the ancient instruments, particularly for the latter two. Both were handheld, stringed instruments that could be played while walking.

12:28-29 Mention of levitical songs of thanksgiving above and of **singers** here suggests the developing loss of distinction between the two groups. On **Netophah** see Ezra 2:22; **Geba**, Ezra 2:26; and **Asmaveth**, Ezra 2:24. **Beth Gilgal** is likely to have been ancient Gilgal near Jericho, perhaps Khirbet Mefjir, about two miles northeast of Jericho.

12:30 The preparation for the dedication of the walls around the holy city required ritual purification as a part of the preparations. The participants would end up within the sacred precincts of the temple. Drawing on texts related to ritual purification, Myers suggests that the religious personnel fasted, abstained from sexual intercourse, and offered a sin offering. The other participants washed their garments and bathed.[29] Ritual sprinkling of **the people, the gates and the wall** preceded the dedicatory procession; for the latter two a procedure similar to that of purifying a house may have been followed (cf. Lev 14:49-53). "Holiness is one of the central themes of the Bible and something that God calls us to (Lev 11:44; 20:7; 20:26; Rom 7:12; 12:1; 2 Tim 1:9; 1 Pet 1:15-16; 2 Pet 3:11)."[30]

B. ORDER OF MARCH (12:31-39)

[31]**I had the leaders of Judah go up on top**[a] **of the wall. I also assigned two large choirs to give thanks. One was to proceed on top**[b] **of the wall to the right, toward the Dung Gate.** [32]**Hoshaiah and half the leaders of Judah followed them,** [33]**along with Azariah, Ezra, Meshullam,** [34]**Judah, Benjamin, Shemaiah, Jeremiah,** [35]**as well as some priests with trumpets, and also Zechariah son of Jonathan, the son of Shemaiah, the son of Mattaniah, the son of Micaiah, the son of Zaccur, the son of Asaph,** [36]**and his associates—Shemaiah, Azarel, Milalai, Gilalai, Maai, Nethanel, Judah and Hanani—with musical instruments ⌐prescribed by⌐ David the man of God. Ezra the scribe led the procession.** [37]**At the Fountain Gate they continued directly up the steps of the City of David on the ascent to the wall and passed above the house of David to the Water Gate on the east.**

[38]**The second choir proceeded in the opposite direction. I followed them on top**[c] **of the wall, together with half the people—past**

---

[29]Myers, *Ezra–Nehemiah*, pp. 202-203.
[30]Breneman, *Ezra, Nehemiah, Esther*, p. 265.

the Tower of the Ovens to the Broad Wall, ³⁹over the Gate of
Ephraim, the Jeshanah Gate, the Fish Gate, the Tower of Hananel
and the Tower of the Hundred, as far as the Sheep Gate. At the
Gate of the Guard they stopped.

^a*31 Or go alongside*   ^b*31 Or proceed alongside*   ^c*38 Or them alongside*   ^d*39
Or Old*

12:31a Although in the preceding verses the author apparently
drew upon Nehemiah's memoirs, here the narrative returns to the
first person. The NIV footnote draws attention to a textual problem;
the parading parties may have walked along the base of the wall. The
problem centers on the interpretation of מֵעַל (*mēʿal*), which may
mean either "beside" or "upon." In association with the verb עָלָה
(*ʿālāh*), however, "upon" is to be favored. The walls were wide
enough for walking on them; a fragment of Nehemiah's wall uncovered by Kathleen Kenyon measured nine feet wide.

Apart from holiness, mention of **choirs to give thanks** points to
another emphasis. It is noted again in verse 40.

12:31b-39 The starting point is not stated but the Valley Gate is likely the place. Two groups were formed, one led by Ezra (v. 36) marching counterclockwise (south and east) and the other by Nehemiah
going in the opposite direction, both following choirs. Williamson
notes that "neither procession encircled the whole city, and that the
section between the Water Gate and the Sheep Gate was not covered by either. The processions were rather a celebration of the
completed work and as such a stimulus to thanksgiving and a means
of commitment, dedication, of the whole to God. The chanting of
such Psalms as 48 (cf. especially vv. 13-14 [12-13]) and 147 would
have provided an appropriate accompaniment."[31]

Although the musicians consisted of Levites and singers, there
were **some priests with trumpets**. (These were not shofars, ram's
horns, but metal instruments.) Apparently this was an activity limited to the priests (cf. Num 10:8; 31:6; 1 Chr 15:24; 16:6).

Mention of the **house of David** (v. 37) is unexpected. The royal
palaces must have been destroyed by the Chaldeans. Some of the
ruins were perhaps still visible and so identified.

---

[31]Williamson, *Ezra, Nehemiah*, p. 374.

They stopped **at the Gate of the Guard**, a location otherwise unattested. It was possibly at the south entrance to the temple compound, associated by some with the Inspection Gate (3:31).

C. THANKSGIVING IN THE HOUSE OF GOD (12:40-43)

[40]**The two choirs that gave thanks then took their places in the house of God; so did I, together with half the officials,** [41]**as well as the priests—Eliakim, Maaseiah, Miniamin, Micaiah, Elioenai, Zechariah and Hananiah with their trumpets—** [42]**and also Maaseiah, Shemaiah, Eleazar, Uzzi, Jehohanan, Malkijah, Elam and Ezer. The choirs sang under the direction of Jezrahiah.** [43]**And on that day they offered great sacrifices, rejoicing because God had given them great joy. The women and children also rejoiced. The sound of rejoicing in Jerusalem could be heard far away.**

12:40-41 In the house of God is the equivalent of "within the courts of the temple." Nehemiah does not mention the other **half of the officials** with Ezra's procession. No doubt he assumed that the reader would understand that they entered the temple as well.

12:42 The choirs sang songs of thanksgiving within the temple as well as during the procession. Psalm 100:4 advises, "Enter his gates with thanksgiving and his courts with praise; give thanks to him and praise his name."

12:43 The focus on **joy** is evident. The term "joy" occurs five times in this verse. While the processions were apparently all male, it is noteworthy that **the women and children also rejoiced.** The Herodian phase of the Second Temple had a Court of Women, but there is no evidence that it was a part of the temple of Zerubbabel. We must assume that the women and children were outside the temple courts listening to the choirs sing and smelling the smoke of the sacrifices wafting from the altar. As with the laying of the temple foundations (Ezra 3:13), the joyful sounds **could be heard far away**.

This event marked the culmination of Nehemiah's primary reason for returning to Jerusalem. There was great joy on the part of the people in completing a community project and in protecting the city from hostile attackers as well as intruders not part of the restored community. And their joy was multiplied by the realization that God had made it possible. In the final analysis, they had the Lord to thank for their success.

VIII. THE USE AND ABUSE OF
THE TEMPLE CHAMBERS (12:44–13:14)

A. PROPER AND PUBLIC SUPPORT OF THE TEMPLE
(12:44–13:3)

⁴⁴At that time men were appointed to be in charge of the storerooms for the contributions, firstfruits and tithes. From the fields around the towns they were to bring into the storerooms the portions required by the Law for the priests and the Levites, for Judah was pleased with the ministering priests and Levites. ⁴⁵They performed the service of their God and the service of purification, as did also the singers and gatekeepers, according to the commands of David and his son Solomon. ⁴⁶For long ago, in the days of David and Asaph, there had been directors for the singers and for the songs of praise and thanksgiving to God. ⁴⁷So in the days of Zerubbabel and of Nehemiah, all Israel contributed the daily portions for the singers and gatekeepers. They also set aside the portion for the other Levites, and the Levites set aside the portion for the descendants of Aaron.

¹On that day the Book of Moses was read aloud in the hearing of the people and there it was found written that no Ammonite or Moabite should ever be admitted into the assembly of God, ²because they had not met the Israelites with food and water but had hired Balaam to call a curse down on them. (Our God, however, turned the curse into a blessing.) ³When the people heard this law, they excluded from Israel all who were of foreign descent.

12:44 At that time . . .

"On that day," as the RSV and NEB literally render it, is an indeterminate chronological marker. It does not specify the day on which the joyous dedication of the walls occurred. Nor is this section written in the first person, so we should recognize the hand of the compiler here rather than that of Nehemiah.

The **contributions** (תְּרוּמֹת, *t⁾rûmôth*) are dedicated gifts, sacred donations. They, the firstfruit offerings, and tithes were to be brought in as **required by the Law** (cf. 10:37-38).

The passage testifies to a fully-staffed and efficiently functioning system which provided for the religious personnel and practices according to the Mosaic legislation. The people had agreed to do this and were happy to do so, **for Judah was pleased with the ministering priests and Levites**.

12:45-46 The priests and Levites are cited for faithfully performing **the service of their God**, the daily offerings and related activities in the Holy Place. They were also loyal in performing the **service of purification**, defined in 1 Chronicles 23:28 as the purifying of all holy things (cf. Lev 11–15). As the priests and Levites were faithful in obeying the Law, so the **singers and gatekeepers** fulfilled their responsibilities as established by **David** and **Solomon** (1 Chr 23–26; 2 Chr 8:14).

12:47 According to the writer, this ideal situation continued **in the days of Zerubbabel and of Nehemiah**. Part of his motivation may have been to contrast the deviations that he would soon record.

During the time indicated, conditions were not always ideal. This is evident in the difficulties both Ezra and Nehemiah addressed and in the words of Haggai and Malachi. As Williamson has commented,

> We see here the start of . . . [the] periodizing of post-exilic history . . . . Though separated sometimes by many decades, the steps in the process of restoration are gradually isolated from their contexts and merged into a continuous "history of salvation."
>
> Periods of regression (cf. Mal 3:7-12; Neh 13:10!) are steadily foreshortened, if not completely forgotten, so that the picture of an ideal emerges which may reflect to the glory of God and act as a stimulus to later generations.[32]

The writer must have desired to stimulate his own generation so that it, too, might bring glory to God.

13:1-2 On that day is a general time indicator, similar to that noted in 12:44. No specific date nor occasion (such as a feast day) is

---

[32]Williamson, *Ezra, Nehemiah*, pp. 384-385.

given. The reading from the **Book of Moses** (the Pentateuch) was likely following a regular liturgical schedule. The relevant passage was Deuteronomy 23:3-6. By drawing attention to this detail, the writer prepares the reader for Nehemiah's action against Tobiah in the following section, since he has previously been identified as **the Ammonite** (2:10).

The prohibition against the Moabites involved Balak, king of Moab, who hired **Balaam** to bring a **curse** on Israel (Num 22:4-6). That King David had Moabite blood in his veins was ignored by this postexilic audience (Ruth 4:13-22).

Ammonites and Moabites were to be excluded from **the assembly of God**, the קְהַל הָאֱלֹהִים (qᵉhal hā'ĕlōhîm), the cultic congregation of God allowed into the temple courts.

13:3 Israel is equivalent to the assembly of God noted above. The exclusion of foreigners was one with the emphasis in Ezra–Nehemiah on the ethnic purity of the restored community.

B. HIGH PRIESTLY ABUSE OF THE TEMPLE CHAMBERS (13:4-5)

⁴**Before this, Eliashib the priest had been put in charge of the storerooms of the house of our God. He was closely associated with Tobiah, ⁵and he had provided him with a large room formerly used to store the grain offerings and incense and temple articles, and also the tithes of grain, new wine and oil prescribed for the Levites, singers and gatekeepers, as well as the contributions for the priests.**

Although a return to the first-person narrative begins in verse 6, the majority of scholars accept that this section through to the end of the chapter is drawn from Nehemiah's Memoirs. Since it is an explanation of events during Nehemiah's absence, a third-person account seems appropriate.

13:4-5 Before this either refers to the time prior to the separation of foreigners from the assembly of God or, more likely, before the events that unfold after Nehemiah's return to Jerusalem. Nehemiah was gone from Jerusalem for an indeterminate time (v. 6).

The identity of **Eliashib the priest** is unclear. Was he the high priest, mentioned in verse 28 or another priest with the same name? That he was not designated high priest weighs on the side that he did not hold the high priestly office. This is further supported by the fact that he **had been put in charge . . .** , indicating a higher authority had assigned him the responsibility. Some time must have elapsed between Eliashib's assignment and the ordering of temple affairs noted in 12:44.

Eliashib was **closely associated** (קָרוֹב לְ, *qārôb + lᵉ*) **with Tobiah**. The phrase is ambiguous. It may signify "connected by marriage" (NEB), "related to" (NRSV), "connected with" (RSV), or "a relative of."[33] The association could also have been commercial. Tobiah took advantage of this close association to wangle space in the temple compound.

. . . provided him with a large room formerly used . . .

Either Tobiah displaced the usual offerings stored in the great room, or the contributions had fallen off to the point that it was little used (v. 10), thus making his acquisition of it for his own use possible.

C. NEHEMIAH'S RIGHTEOUS INDIGNATION AND ACTION (13:6-14)

⁶**But while all this was going on, I was not in Jerusalem, for in the thirty-second year of Artaxerxes king of Babylon I had returned to the king. Some time later I asked his permission ⁷and came back to Jerusalem. Here I learned about the evil thing Eliashib had done in providing Tobiah a room in the courts of the house of God. ⁸I was greatly displeased and threw all Tobiah's household goods out of the room. ⁹I gave orders to purify the rooms, and then I put back into them the equipment of the house of God, with the grain offerings and the incense.**

¹⁰**I also learned that the portions assigned to the Levites had not been given to them, and that all the Levites and singers responsible for the service had gone back to their own fields. ¹¹So I rebuked the officials and asked them, "Why is the house of God**

---

[33]Ibid., p. 378.

neglected?" Then I called them together and stationed them at their posts.

¹²All Judah brought the tithes of grain, new wine and oil into the storerooms. ¹³I put Shelemiah the priest, Zadok the scribe, and a Levite named Pedaiah in charge of the storerooms and made Hanan son of Zaccur, the son of Mattaniah, their assistant, because these men were considered trustworthy. They were made responsible for distributing the supplies to their brothers.

¹⁴Remember me for this, O my God, and do not blot out what I have so faithfully done for the house of my God and its services.

13:6-7 A major reason Eliashib and Tobiah could work out this arrangement was the absence of Nehemiah. He gives no explanation why he had returned to the royal court nor how long he was there. The **thirty-second year of Artaxerxes**[34] was 433 B.C. Nehemiah had been governor in Jerusalem since 445 B.C. The audacity of **Eliashib** and **Tobiah** suggest that they expected Nehemiah to be gone for a long period, or perhaps never to return.

A number of commentators believe that he returned for a second term as governor. The text, however, nowhere indicates that appointment. Even without political authority, Nehemiah still possessed the moral authority to act decisively, as he did.

13:8-9 The thing Eliashib had done was evil on two counts. First, he had allowed an Ammonite extended access to the temple compound. Second, his presence had ritually polluted the large room that he had taken over, a room that had previously held the sanctified offerings for the house of God. A purification ritual was required to make the room again acceptable for its intended use. Not only was the great room purified, adjacent **rooms** were also polluted and required purification.

13:10-11 Religious leadership in Jerusalem weakened after the departure of Nehemiah, and Ezra may have died; we have no further mention of him in the narrative. This allowed the people to begin to treat lightly the covenant responsibilities they had sworn to fulfill in

---

[34]He is called "king of Babylon," which is peculiar; however, his forefather, Cyrus, had used that title. He also may have been residing in Babylon at this time.

10:37-39. The offerings that supported the religious personnel diminished so that many of them returned to their properties in Yehud to raise their own food. The result was that the house of God was **neglected**, even though the people had promised to "not neglect the house of our God" (10:39). The unnamed **officials** whom Nehemiah rebuked were clearly the religious leaders rather than those who had civil authority over the sections of Jerusalem (3:9,12). Acting decisively, Nehemiah called the laboring Levites back to Jerusalem and their duties, even before the flow of contributions returned.

13:12-13 All Judah, the lay members of the Jewish community in Yehud, responded under the dynamic leadership of Nehemiah. The selection of trustworthy men to oversee the storerooms and the distribution of supplies to the religious personnel would restore confidence on the part of the priests and Levites called back to serve. On **Shelemiah**, see 3:30; **Zadok**, 3:29; **Pedaiah**, 8:4; and **Mattaniah**, 11:17; 12:8,25. With swift and appropriate action, Nehemiah had resolved the problem so that the house of God was no longer neglected.

13:14 Another of Nehemiah's **"Remember me"** prayers (noted above at 5:19) is recorded here. He asks God to remember him for what he has done on behalf of the temple service because of his faith. He does not want that record to be blotted out. To **blot out** is to "completely [erase] the memory . . . from under heaven" (Exod 17:14). In the golden calf incident, Moses asked God to forgive the sin of the people, "but if not, then blot me out of the book you have written" (Exod 32:32). The idea continues into the NT (Luke 10:20; Rev 20:12; 21:27; and 22:29).

IX. NEHEMIAH'S FINAL REFORMS (13:15-31)

A. RESTORING RESPECT FOR THE SABBATH (13:15-22)

[15]In those days I saw men in Judah treading winepresses on the Sabbath and bringing in grain and loading it on donkeys, together with wine, grapes, figs and all other kinds of loads. And they were bringing all this into Jerusalem on the Sabbath. Therefore I warned them against selling food on that day. [16]Men from Tyre who lived in Jerusalem were bringing in fish and all kinds of mer-

chandise and selling them in Jerusalem on the Sabbath to the people of Judah. [17]I rebuked the nobles of Judah and said to them, "What is this wicked thing you are doing—desecrating the Sabbath day? [18]Didn't your forefathers do the same things, so that our God brought all this calamity upon us and upon this city? Now you are stirring up more wrath against Israel by desecrating the Sabbath."

[19]When evening shadows fell on the gates of Jerusalem before the Sabbath, I ordered the doors to be shut and not opened until the Sabbath was over. I stationed some of my own men at the gates so that no load could be brought in on the Sabbath day. [20]Once or twice the merchants and sellers of all kinds of goods spent the night outside Jerusalem. [21]But I warned them and said, "Why do you spend the night by the wall? If you do this again, I will lay hands on you." From that time on they no longer came on the Sabbath. [22]Then I commanded the Levites to purify themselves and go and guard the gates in order to keep the Sabbath day holy.

Remember me for this also, O my God, and show mercy to me according to your great love.

13:15 In those days again marks a general, unspecified period of time, no doubt referring back to the days after Nehemiah's return from Mesopotamia.

Apparently Nehemiah had traveled out into the countryside on several occasions when he had observed the commercial activities in which the Jewish population engaged on the Sabbath. Keeping the Sabbath is a major theme in the OT (Gen 2:2; Exod 16:23-29; 31:14-16; 35:2-3; Num 15:32-36). Grape harvest and winemaking were in September–October, which indicates the time of the year when he was on his inspection tour. **Grain** would have been harvested April into June; early **figs** in June, late figs in August–September; and olives ripen in September. **Wine**, olive oil, and dried figs and raisins could be stored and transported throughout the year. The inhabitants of Jerusalem depended upon outside sources for their food. Nehemiah's objection was to commercial activity on the Sabbath. He warned them **against selling food on that day**.

13:16 Not only were Jews marketing goods **on the Sabbath**, enterprising Phoenicians **from Tyre who lived in Jerusalem** were engaged in selling **fish** and a variety of other **merchandise**. The

Phoenicians were well known for their extensive commercial activities around the Mediterranean coast (cf. Ezek 27:12-36; 28:16). They were selling **in** the city, rather than outside the gates. The fish could have been both salted and fresh. Fresh fish from the port at Jaffa could have been brought to Jerusalem without spoilage.

Despite the fact that Jewish religious laws were not applicable to the Tyrians, Nehemiah recognized that the problem of selling on the Sabbath would continue unless action was taken against them as well as against the Jewish merchants. At this point, however, he refrained from action until he first confronted the community leaders.

13:17-18 The **nobles of Judah** are not the same as the temple officials in verse 11. They, as community leaders, were responsible for the city. They may not have regarded buying on the Sabbath as a breech of the rules since the merchants alone might be considered working. Nehemiah's charge is direct; they are **desecrating the Sabbath day**. The leaders of the people (10:14-27) had signed a binding agreement that they would not do this very thing (10:31).

A main theme in the OT is the observance of the Sabbath (Gen 2:2; Exod 16:23-29; 31:14-16; 35:2-3; Num 15:32-36). The prophets warned their people against desecrating it (Amos 8:5; Isa 58:13-14; Jer 17:19-27). Nehemiah pointed to their historic past to remind them of what had happened when their **forefathers** ignored the Sabbath — exile and foreign domination. He warns of more **wrath** to come, the wrath of God, because of their lax Sabbath practices.

13:19-21 The Sabbath began at sundown on Friday and lasted until sundown on Saturday. Nehemiah rescued the sanctity of the day of rest by closing the city gates and posting guards to assure that they remained closed until the end of the Sabbath. Temporarily he used his **own men** as guards.

The **merchants and sellers** were persistent, waiting outside the gates once or twice, apparently assuming that the people would come out of the city to buy merchandise. Nehemiah confronted them directly, threatening to forcibly remove them. They no doubt knew that he was not bluffing, in light of the recent expulsion of Tobiah from his quarters in the temple area. As he recalled this encounter, he must have chuckled in satisfaction as he wrote, "From that time on they no longer came on the Sabbath."

13:22 The Levites normally were not the guards at the city gates. However, because the **Sabbath** is to be kept **holy**, Nehemiah commanded them to **purify themselves** to carry out the sacred task of maintaining the sanctity of the holy day in the holy city. This appears to have been a permanent procedure. During the other days of the week the regular guards would be on duty.

Again Nehemiah inserts a brief "**Remember me**" prayer to close out his memory of that event. Nehemiah wants to be remembered for what he had done because he had acted out of his religious convictions. Above all, he wanted to be recognized as a faithful servant and to experience the merciful love of God.

B. CONDEMNATION OF MIXED MARRIAGES (13:23-29)

²³Moreover, in those days I saw men of Judah who had married women from Ashdod, Ammon and Moab. ²⁴Half of their children spoke the language of Ashdod or the language of one of the other peoples, and did not know how to speak the language of Judah. ²⁵I rebuked them and called curses down on them. I beat some of the men and pulled out their hair. I made them take an oath in God's name and said: "You are not to give your daughters in marriage to their sons, nor are you to take their daughters in marriage for your sons or for yourselves. ²⁶Was it not because of marriages like these that Solomon king of Israel sinned? Among the many nations there was no king like him. He was loved by his God, and God made him king over all Israel, but even he was led into sin by foreign women. ²⁷Must we hear now that you too are doing all this terrible wickedness and are being unfaithful to our God by marrying foreign women?"

²⁸One of the sons of Joiada son of Eliashib the high priest was son-in-law to Sanballat the Horonite. And I drove him away from me.

²⁹Remember them, O my God, because they defiled the priestly office and the covenant of the priesthood and of the Levites.

13:23 . . . **in those days** introduces another incident that Nehemiah confronted sometime after his return to Jerusalem. He **saw men of Judah** who **had married** non-Jewish women. Implicit is the understanding that these were but a few such men. This situation differs from the widespread situation reported in Ezra 9–10. Nevertheless, it was not a situation to be ignored. Intermarriage posed a threat to the unity and future of the renewed community in Jerusalem and Yehud. That community had made a solemn covenant to live under the law of God. Children raised in mixed-marriage homes would have weaker ties to the religious community. Nehemiah knew that one generation's weakened faith and practice would have a residual effect on subsequent generations.

Only women from **Ashdod** (cf. 4:7), **Ammon, and Moab** were involved. (But note v. 28 below, in a related incident.) These areas were either immediately to the east or west of Yehud; however, the context suggests that the families were residing in Jerusalem.

13:24 What apparently drew Nehemiah's attention to the situation was overhearing some of the children speaking in unusual dialects. The descendants of the Philistines had assimilated to Canaanite culture long before, including the language. Moabite and Ammonite were similar to Hebrew, **the language of Judah** (cf. 2 Kgs 18:26,28). But regional dialectic variations must have been noticeable so that **half of their children** did not know how to speak Hebrew. The dominant influence of mothers is thereby indicated.

The surprise exhibited by Nehemiah at this state of affairs suggests that his time away from Jerusalem had been extended. It was of sufficient duration for the marriages and resulting offspring old enough to be heard speaking in the streets.

13:25 Typically, Nehemiah's reaction was swift and decisive. **I rebuked them**, better, "I contended (רִיב, *rîb*, RSV) with them," that is, he argued with them before the Lord, no doubt quoting Scripture against such marriages. He **called curses down on them**. He likely invoked the curse that they had bound themselves by in 10:29, and had now broken. He even struck some of them and pulled some hair. Apparently there was some resistance to his arguing, even though he had not demanded from them, as Ezra had, putting away their foreign wives. Finally, he made them swear in the name of God not to be a party to any further mixed marriages in their families.

13:26-27 Finally Nehemiah gave them a pointed lesson from history, the sorry story of **Solomon** and his foreign wives (1 Kgs 11:1-13).

If foreign wives could wreak such havoc with a king whom God loved and to whom he gave great dominion, what **terrible wickedness** in our time may result from your unfaithfulness to God **by marrying foreign women**? Neglect of the religious tongue, Hebrew, and undermining the purity of their religion could bring dire consequences.

13:28 One of the sons of Joiada . . .

Earlier, the entire community had entered a binding agreement, for the sake of the Law of God, not to intermarry with the people around them. They had bound themselves with a curse and an oath (10:1-30). The weakening of that covenant began at the top of their society, in the family of the high priest. Leviticus 21:13-15 prohibits the high priest from marrying a Gentile. Ezekiel 44:21-22 extends that prohibition, as a word from the Lord, to all priests. Any member of the high priestly family could become high priest. This marriage was a direct threat to the purity of the priestly line and an erosion of the sanctity of the Law of God.

Likely the marriage of the grandson of **Eliashib the high priest** to a daughter of **Sanballat the Horonite** encouraged the other men to marry foreign women, noted above. It showed, too, the wily cunning of Sanballat, Nehemiah's persistent enemy (cf. 2:10; 4:1-2,7-8; 6:1-14). All marriages in that culture were arranged marriages. By negotiating this marriage, Sanballat had reestablished his presence in the highest levels of Jerusalem's society. He had outdone his crafty companion Tobiah the Ammonite, who had only arranged for his personal quarters within the temple compound.

Josephus (*Ant.* xi. 7. 2) records a similar incident in which a Sanballat of Samaria married his daughter Nicaso to Manasseh, a brother of the high priest Jaddua. The time is a century after Nehemiah, because Sanballat was an official of Darius III. It was the latter Darius whom Alexander the Great conquered. As the story goes, the elders of Jerusalem expelled Manasseh from Jerusalem. By way of revenge, he then built a rival temple on Mt. Gerizim, founded the Samaritan sect, and was the high priest. The discovery of the papyri from Samaria in the Wadi Daliyeh cave has shown that two or three governors of Samaria bore the name Sanballat. There also may have been more than one Jaddua in the high-priestly family in

Jerusalem. Nevertheless, Josephus seems to have garbled the incident recorded here in Nehemiah, so it should be ignored. The building of the Samaritan temple in the period after Alexander's conquest seems warranted, however, with its destruction by John Hyrcanus, the Hasmonean, ca. 128 B.C.

Nehemiah apparently did not offer the offending priest the option of divorcing the woman, as Ezra had in the earlier situation. He **drove him away**, that is, he was banished from Jerusalem and probably Yehud. We may assume that he and his wife found refuge in her father's house.

13:29 This incident is closed and set off from what follows by a familiar **Remember** prayer. This prayer is in the negative, however, as was the one against Sanballat and Tobiah in 6:14. Nehemiah is asking God to remember them for the evil they did rather than for good. The **covenant of the priesthood and the Levites** is not specifically identifiable in the Pentateuch; however, it is mentioned in Malachi 2:4-8. Among other things, it called for reverence toward God and faithfulness in the instruction of the people. The high priestly family of Eliashib had failed on both these counts.

C. NEHEMIAH'S CONCLUDING SELF-ASSESSMENT (13:30-31)

30So I purified the priests and the Levites of everything foreign, and assigned them duties, each to his own task. 31I also made provision for contributions of wood at designated times, and for the firstfruits.

Remember me with favor, O my God.

13:30 So I purified the priests and Levites . . . .

The NEB, RSV, and NRSV follow the Hebrew, which does not specify "the priests and Levites," but employs a pronominal element: "I purified them." The pronoun may refer to the entire people of Jerusalem and Yehud. He also **assigned them duties**. Here the pronoun "them" replaces "for the priests and for the Levites" in the original text.

13:31 Nehemiah also recalls arranging for a schedule of **wood** offerings and **firstfruits**, referring back to 10:34-36. Surprisingly, he makes no mention of his major accomplishment, the rebuilding of the walls of the city. Apparently the summary focuses primarily on the religious reforms he accomplished after his return to Jerusalem.

Devoted to the service of God as he was, it is fitting that he closed his memoirs with another brief **Remember me** prayer. The literal translation is, "Remember me, O my God, for good." It is a model prayer, fitting for anyone who has loved God wholeheartedly and lived a life dedicated to doing that which is good in his sight.

Reflecting on Ezra–Nehemiah overall, we can recognize the commitment of both Ezra and Nehemiah to the calling which they received from God. We know nothing of their final days, when or where they died and were buried. Providentially, both were wise enough to leave personal accounts of the passionate pursuit of each of them toward the reestablishment of a community of God's people in the Promised Land. We have called those accounts the Ezra Memoirs and the Nehemiah Memoirs.

Using the memoirs and other available resources, an anonymous third person compiled the work much as we presently have it. He assembled the book(s) for an audience years after Ezra and Nehemiah had gone to their eternal reward. He wrote for his own community of faith, as others in other generations would address theirs. They faced problems similar in nature to those confronted by Ezra and Nehemiah. His work was a challenge to act decisively in the face of danger and opposition. It was also a guide to help them overcome the threat of enemies of the faith, of the dangers posed by intermarriage with the foreign and faithless, and of the potential for disaster inherent in ignoring the Law of the God.

Thanks in part to these combined efforts, the Jewish community survived the turmoil of centuries. In the fullness of time, there were devout Jews like Simeon who were looking for the consolation of Israel (Luke 2:25-32). The way had been prepared for the gospel of Christ. "It was only with the coming of Christ and the interpretation of his coming by Paul that another new era was commenced in which the legal burden was removed from the shoulders of mankind and the center of religion placed in his vicarious suffering on the cross. It is the new era of faith and love in Jesus Christ."[35]

---

[35]Fensham, *The Books of Ezra and Nehemiah*, p. 268.